SENTENCE
SKILLS

A WORKBOOK FOR WRITERS
FORM C

Sentence Skills is also available in alternate editions known as Form A and Form B. The explanatory text is the same in each book, but the activities, tests, and writing assignments are different. An instructor can therefore use alternate versions of the book from one semester to the next.

Three learning aids are available with this book:

1 A set of *twenty-five ditto masters,* free to instructors adopting the text, provides extra activities and tests for many skills.
2 A *software disk* will help students review and practice many of the skills.
3 An *Instructor's Manual and Test Bank* contains a full answer key, additional tests, and a guide to the computer disk.

SENTENCE SKILLS

A Workbook for Writers

FOURTH EDITION

FORM C

JOHN LANGAN

Atlantic Community College

McGRAW-HILL, INC.

New York   St. Louis   San Francisco   Auckland   Bogotá   Caracas
Hamburg   Lisbon   London   Madrid   Mexico   Milan   Montreal
New Delhi   Paris   San Juan   São Paulo   Singapore
Sydney   Tokyo   Toronto

SENTENCE SKILLS:
A WORKBOOK FOR WRITERS, FORM C

2 3 4 5 6 7 8 9 0   DOC DOC   9 5 4 3 2 1

ISBN 0-07-036377-3

This book was set in Times Roman by Monotype Composition Company.
The editors were Lesley Denton and Susan Gamer;
the production supervisor was Leroy A. Young.
The cover was designed by Rafael Hernandez.
R. R. Donnelley & Sons Company was printer and binder.

Library of Congress Cataloging-in-Publication Data

Langan, John, (date).
    Sentence skills: a workbook for writers: form C / John Langan.—4th ed.
      p.   cm.
    Includes index.
    ISBN 0-07-036377-3
    1. English language—Rhetoric—Problems, exercises, etc.   2. English
language—Sentences—Problems, exercises, etc.   3. English language—
Grammar—1950—Problems, exercises, etc.   I. Title.
PE1441.L354   1991
808'.042—dc20   90-6498

Contents

PART THREE
SENTENCE VARIETY THROUGH COMBINING ACTIVITIES   377

PART FOUR
WRITING ASSIGNMENTS   423

APPENDIXES   443

To the Instructor

Sentence Skills will help students master the essential rules of grammar, mechanics, punctuation, and usage needed for clear writing. The book contains a number of features to aid teachers and their students.

- **Coverage of basic writing skills is exceptionally thorough.** The book pays special attention to fragments, run-ons, verbs, and other areas where students have serious problems. At the same time, a glance at the table of contents shows that the book treats skills (such as dictionary use and spelling improvement) not found in other texts. In addition, entire sections of the book are devoted to editing, proofreading, and sentence variety.

- **The book has a clear and flexible format.** Part One presents and gives practice in all the essential basic writing skills. Part Two then reinforces those skills through mastery, editing, and proofreading tests. Part Three uses sentence-combining exercises to help students achieve variety in their writing. Part Four presents writing assignments that enable students to transfer the skills they have learned to realistic writing situations. Since parts, sections, and chapters are self-contained, teachers can move easily from, for instance, a rule in Part One to a mastery test in Part Two to a combining activity in Part Three or a writing assignment in Part Four.

- **Practice materials are numerous.** Most skills are reinforced by activities, review tests, and mastery tests, as well as ditto masters and tests in the Instructor's Manual. For most of the skills in the book, there are over one hundred practice exercises.

● *Practice materials are varied and lively.* In many basic writing texts, exercises are monotonous and dry, causing students to lose interest in the skills presented. In *Sentence Skills*, exercises involve students in various ways. An inductive opening project allows students to see what they already know about a given skill. Within chapters, students may be asked to underline answers, add words, generate their own sentences, or edit passages. And the lively and engaging practice materials in the book both maintain interest and help students appreciate the value of vigorous details in writing.

● *Terminology is kept to a minimum.* In general, rules are explained using words students already know. A clause is a *word group;* a coordinating conjunction is a *joining word;* a nonrestrictive element is an *interrupter.* At the same time, traditional grammatical terms are mentioned briefly for those students who learned them at an earlier point in school and are comfortable seeing them again.

● *Self-teaching is encouraged.* Students may check their answers to the introductory projects and the practice activities in Part One by referring to the answers in Appendix B. In this way, they are given the responsibility for teaching themselves. At the same time, to ensure that the answer key is used as a learning tool only, answers are *not* given for the review tests in Part One or for any of the reinforcement tests in Part Two. These answers appear only in the Instructor's Manual; they can be copied and handed out to students at the discretion of the instructor.

● *Diagnostic and achievement tests are provided.* These tests appear in Appendix A of the book. Each test may be given in two parts, the second of which gives teachers a particularly detailed picture of a student's skill level.

● *Three valuable learning aids accompany the book.* A set of *twenty-five ditto masters,* ready to run, enables teachers to check students' progress on most of the skills in the book. A *software disk* will help students review and practice many of the skills in the text. And the comprehensive *Instructor's Manual* includes (1) a complete set of additional mastery tests, (2) a model syllabus along with suggestions for both teaching the course and using the software, and (3) an easily-copied answer key. The manual is 8½ by 11 inches in size, so that both the answer pages and the added mastery tests can be conveniently reproduced on copying machines.

    The ditto masters, software disk, and Instructor's Manual are available by contacting the local McGraw-Hill representative or by writing to the College English Editor, College Division, McGraw-Hill, Inc.,1221 Avenue of the Americas, New York, New York 10020.

CHANGES IN THE FOURTH EDITION

The helpful comments of writing instructors who have used *Sentence Skills* have prompted some changes in the book. Here they are.

1   The chapter on run-ons has been expanded. Students are given more explanation of the common types of run-ons (fused sentences and comma splices) and more practice in correcting each type. And another set of passages on run-ons has been added to the Editing and Proofreading Tests in Part Two.

2   Also added to the Editing and Proofreading Tests are passages that give students practice in correcting misplaced and dangling modifiers.

3   An explanation of relative pronouns is now included in the chapter ''Pronoun Types'' in Part One.

4   Many minor changes have been made. For example, there is now a separate practice on linking verbs in the chapter ''Subjects and Verbs.'' Added review tests are now provided for subject-verb agreement and consistent verb tense. More examples of wordy expressions have been added to the chapter ''Effective Word Choice.''

5   Last, a revised computer disk accompanies the other supplements for the book. Richard D. Hathaway, Professor of English at the State University of New York in New Paltz, has done the computer programming; the result is that the previous version of a disk for *Sentence Skills* has been much improved. He has also written a new lesson to go with the existing activities. The disk runs very quickly, and other ''user-friendly'' features include an opening menu of the lessons on the disk, explanations of all answers, automatic scorekeeping, and frequent use of the student's first name. A guide in the Instructor's Manual provides further information and a partial printout of the material on the disk.

A NOTE ON THE THREE FORMS OF THE BOOK

Sentence Skills is also available in alternate editions known as Form A and Form B. Teachers can therefore use a different form of the book from one semester to the next. The explanatory text is the same in all three books, but the activities, tests, and writing assignments are different.

ACKNOWLEDGMENTS

Reviewers who have provided assistance include Anna Y. Bradley, C. S. Mott Community College; Elizabeth Buckmaster, Pennsylvania State University at D.C.; Denise Campos, Hartnett College; James Creel, Alvin Community College; Joseph F. Dunne, St. Louis Community College; Rachel Erlanger, Queens College; Mary Faggan, Kellogg Community College; Martha French, Fairmont State College; Eric Hoem, Mount Hood Community College; Ruth Koenig, Danville Area Community College; Susan Lagunoff, Florissant Community College; Stacey A. Lovin-Boyd, Purdue University at Calumet; Cecilia Macheski, City University of New York at LaGuardia; Elaine Newman, Queens College; Janet McReynolds, Southern Illinois University; Mary Sue Ply, Pan American University; Betty Quinn, Craven Community College; Heloise Ruskin, Bergen Community College; Ed Sams, Gavilan College; Charles Smires, Florida Community College at Jacksonville; Arlette Miller Smith, El Centro College; Nancy Souza, Monterey Peninsula College; Wanda Van Goor, Prince George Community College; Susan Warrington, Phillips County Community College; and Arleda Watson, Leeward Community College. I am also grateful for help provided by Janet M. Goldstein and Carole Mohr.

John Langan

PART ONE

SENTENCE SKILLS

INTRODUCTION

Part One explains the basic skills needed to write clear, error-free sentences. Before you begin working with these skills, however, you will want to read the chapter titled "Why Learn Sentence Skills?" which explains how you will benefit personally from writing standard English. While the skills are presented within four traditional categories (grammar, mechanics, punctuation, and word use), each section is self-contained so that you can go directly to the skills you need to work on. Note, however, that you may find it helpful to cover "Subjects and Verbs" before turning to other skills. Typically, the main features of a skill are presented on the first pages of a section; secondary points are developed later. Numerous activities are provided so that you can practice skills enough to make them habits. The activities are varied and range from underlining answers to writing complete sentences involving the skill in question. One or more review tests at the end of each section offer additional practice activities.

Why Learn Sentence Skills?

THE IMPORTANCE OF SENTENCE SKILLS

Why should someone planning a career as a nurse have to learn sentence skills? Why should an accounting major have to pass a competency test in grammar as part of a college education? Why should a potential physical therapist or graphic artist or computer programmer have to spend hours on the rules of English? Perhaps you have asked questions like these after finding yourself in a class with this book. On the other hand, perhaps you *know* you need to strengthen basic writing skills, even though you may be unclear about the specific ways the skills will be of use to you. Whatever your views, you should understand why sentence skills—all the rules that make up standard English—are so important.

Clear Communication

Standard English, or "language by the book," is needed to communicate your thoughts to others with a minimal amount of distortion and misinterpretation. Knowing the traditional rules of grammar, punctuation, and usage will help you write clear sentences when communicating with others. You may have heard of the party game in which one person whispers a message to the next person; the message is passed, in turn, along a line of several other people. By the time the last person in line is asked to give the message aloud, it is usually so garbled and inaccurate that it barely resembles the original. Written communication in some form of English other than standard English carries the same potential for disaster.

To see how important standard English is to written communication, examine the pairs of sentences below and answer the questions in each case.

1. Which sentence indicates that there might be a plot against Ted?
    a. We should leave Ted. These fumes might be poisonous.
    b. We should leave, Ted. These fumes might be poisonous.
2. Which sentence encourages self-mutilation?
    a. Leave your paper and hand in the dissecting kit.
    b. Leave your paper, and hand in the dissecting kit.
3. Which sentence indicates that the writer has a weak grasp of geography?
    a. As a child, I lived in Lake Worth, which is close to Palm Beach and Alaska.
    b. As a child, I lived in Lake Worth, which is close to Palm Beach, and Alaska.
4. In which sentence does the dog warden seem dangerous?
    a. Foaming at the mouth, the dog warden picked up the stray.
    b. Foaming at the mouth, the stray was picked up by the dog warden.
5. Which announcer was probably fired from the job?
    a. Outside the Academy Awards theater, the announcer called the guests names as they arrived.
    b. Outside the Academy Awards theater, the announcer called the guests' names as they arrived.
6. On the basis of the opening lines below of two student exam essays, which student seems likely to earn a higher grade?
    a. Defense mechanisms is the way people hides their inner feelings and deals with stress. There is several types that we use to be protecting our true feelings.
    b. Defense mechanisms are the methods people use to cope with stress. Using a defense mechanism allows a person to hide his or her real desires and goals.
7. On the basis of the following lines taken from two English papers, which student seems likely to earn a higher grade?
    a. A big problem on this campus is apathy, students don't participate in college activities. Such as clubs, student government, and plays.
    b. The most pressing problem on campus is the disgraceful state of the student lounge area. The floor is dirty, the chairs are torn, and the ceiling leaks.

8. On the basis of the following sentences taken from two employee reports, which worker is more likely to be promoted?
   a. The spring line failed by 20 percent in the meeting of projected profit expectations. Which were issued in January of this year.
   b. Profits from our spring line were disappointing. They fell 20 percent short of January's predictions.

9. On the basis of the following paragraphs taken from two job application letters, which job prospect would you favor?
   a. Let me say in closing that their are an array of personal qualities I have presented in this letter, together, these make me hopeful of being interviewed for this attraktive position.

   sincerly yours'

   Brian Davis

   b. I feel I have the qualifications needed to do an excellent job as assistant manager of the jewelry department at Horton's. I look forward to discussing the position further at a personal interview.

   Sincerely yours,

   Richard O'Keeney

The first choice following each of the nine questions contains sentence-skills mistakes—from missing or misplaced commas to misspellings to wordy or pretentious language. As a result of these mistakes, clear communication cannot occur—and misunderstandings, lower grades, and missed job opportunities are probable results. The point, then, is that all the rules that make up standard written English should be a priority if you want your writing to be clear and effective.

Success in College

Standard English is essential if you want to succeed in college. Any report, paper, review, essay exam, or assignment you are responsible for should be written in the best standard English you can produce. If not, it won't matter how fine your ideas are or how hard you worked—most likely, you will receive a lower grade than you would otherwise deserve. In addition, because standard English requires you to express your thoughts in precise, clear sentences, training yourself to follow the rules can help you think more logically. And the basic logic you learn to practice at the sentence level will help as you work to produce well-reasoned papers in all your subjects.

Success at Work

Knowing standard English will also help you achieve job success. Studies have shown repeatedly that skillful communication, more than any other factor, is the key to job satisfaction and steady career progress. A solid understanding of standard English is a basic part of this vital communication ability. Moreover, most experts agree that we are now living in an ''age of information''—a time when people who use language skillfully have a great advantage over those who do not. Fewer of us will be working in factories or at other types of manual labor. Many more of us will be working with information in various forms— accumulating it, processing it, analyzing it. No matter what kind of job you are preparing yourself for, technical or not, you will need to know standard English to keep pace with this new age. Otherwise, you are likely to be left behind, limited to low-paying jobs that offer few challenges or financial rewards.

HOW THIS BOOK IS ORGANIZED

- A good way to get a quick sense of any book is to turn to the table of contents. By referring to pages *v–viii*, you will see that the book is organized into four basic parts. What are they?

  _____

  _____

  _____

  _____

- Part One deals with the sentence skills themselves. How many skills areas are covered in all (count them)? _____

- Part Two reinforces the skills presented in Part One. What are the four kinds of reinforcement activities in Part Two?

  _____

  _____

  _____

  _____

- Turn to the introduction to Part Three to learn the purpose of that part of the book and write the purpose here: _____

  _____

- Turn to the introduction to Part Four to find the purpose of that part of the book and write the purpose here: _____

  _____

● Helpful charts in the book include the (*fill in the missing words*) _____

on the inside front cover, the _____ charts in Appendix C,

and the _____ of sentence skills on the inside back cover.

● Finally, three appendixes at the end of the book contain:

_____ _____

_____

_____

HOW TO USE THIS BOOK

The first step in getting the most out of *Sentence Skills* is to take the diagnostic test on pages 445–450. By analyzing which sections of the test gave you trouble, you will discover which skills you need to concentrate on. When you turn to an individual skill, begin by reading and thinking about the introductory project. Often, you will be pleasantly surprised to find that you know more about this area of English than you thought you did. After all, you have probably been speaking English with fluency and ease for many years; you have an instinctive knowledge of how the language works. This knowledge gives you a solid base for refining your skills.

Your next step is to work on the skill by reading the explanations and completing the practices. You can check your answers to each practice activity by turning to the answer key at the back of the book. Try to figure out *why* you got some answers wrong—you want to uncover any weak spots in your understanding.

Finally, use the review tests at the end of a chapter to evaluate your understanding of the skill in its entirety. Your teacher may also ask you to take the mastery tests or other reinforcement tests in Part Two of the book. The answers to these tests are *not* in the answer key in order to help ensure that you take the time needed to learn each skill thoroughly.

While you are working through individual skills, you should also take time for the sentence-combining activities in Part Three and the writing assignments in Part Four. The writing assignments in Part Four are a brief but important part of the book. To make standard English an everyday part of your writing, you must write not just single sentences but paragraphs and essays. The writing assignments will prove to you that clear, logical writing hinges on error-free sentences. You will see how the sentence skills you are practicing ''fit in'' and contribute to the construction of a sustained piece of writing. In the world of sports, athletes spend many days refining the small moves—serves, backhands, pitches, lay-ups—so that they can reach their larger objective of winning the game. In the same way, you must work intently on writing clear sentences in order to produce effective papers.

The emphasis in this book is, nevertheless, on writing clear, error-free sentences, not on composition. And the heart of the book is the practice material that helps reinforce the sentence skills you learn. A great deal of effort has been taken to make the practices lively and engaging and to avoid the dull, repetitive skills work that has given grammar books such a bad reputation. This text will help you stay interested as you work on the rules you need to learn. The rest is a matter of your personal determination and hard work. If you decide—and only you can decide—that effective writing is important to your school and career goals and that you want to learn the basic skills needed to write clearly and effectively, this book will help you reach those goals.

Section 1: Grammar

Subjects and Verbs

INTRODUCTORY PROJECT

Understanding subjects and verbs is a big step toward mastering many sentence skills. As a speaker of English, you already have an instinctive feel for these basic building blocks of English sentences. See if you can put a suitable word into each space below. The answer will be a subject.

1. The _____ will soon be over.

2. _____ cannot be trusted.

3. A strange _____ appeared in my backyard.

4. _____ is one of my favorite activities.

Now insert a suitable word into the following spaces. Each answer will be a verb.

5. The prisoner _____ at the judge.

6. My sister _____ much harder than I do.

7. The players _____ in the locker room.

8. Rob and Marilyn _____ with the teacher.

Finally, add words that fit into the following spaces. In each sentence, the first word will be a subject, and the second word will be a verb.

9. The _____ almost _____ out of the tree.

10. Many _____ today _____ sex and violence.

11. The _____ carefully _____ the patient.

12. A _____ quickly _____ the ball.

The basic building blocks of English sentences are subjects and verbs. Understanding them is an important first step toward mastering a number of sentence skills.

Every sentence has a subject and a verb. Who or what the sentence speaks about is called the *subject;* what the sentence says about the subject is called the *verb.* In the following sentences, the subject is underlined once and the verb twice:

People gossip.
The truck stalled.
He waved at me.
That woman is a millionaire.
Alaska contains the largest wilderness area in America.

A SIMPLE WAY TO FIND A SUBJECT

To find a subject, ask *who* or *what* the sentence is about. As shown below, your answer is the subject.

Who is the first sentence about? People
What is the second sentence about? The truck
Who is the third sentence about? He
Who is the fourth sentence about? That woman
What is the fifth sentence about? Alaska

It helps to remember that the subject of a sentence is always a *noun* (any person, place, or thing) or a pronoun. A *pronoun* is simply a word like *he, she, it, you,* or *they* used in place of a noun. In the preceding sentences, the subjects include persons (*People, He, woman*), a place (*Alaska*), and a thing (*truck*). And note that one pronoun (*He*) is used as a subject.

A SIMPLE WAY TO FIND A VERB

To find a verb, ask what the sentence *says about* the subject. As shown below, your answer is the verb.

What does the first sentence *say about* people? They <u>gossip</u>.
What does the second sentence *say about* the truck? It <u>stalled</u>.
What does the third sentence *say about* him? He <u>waved</u>.
What does the fourth sentence *say about* that woman? She <u>is</u> (a millionaire).
What does the fifth sentence *say about* Alaska? It <u>contains</u> (the largest wilderness area).

A second way to find the verb is to put *I, you, he, she, it,* or *they* in front of the word you think is a verb. If the result makes sense, you have a verb. For example, you could put *they* in front of *gossip* in the first sentence above, with the result, *they gossip,* making sense. Therefore, you know that *gossip* is a verb. You could use the same test with the other verbs as well.

Finally, it helps to remember that most verbs show action. In the examples above, the action verbs are *gossip, stalled, waved,* and *contains.* Certain other verbs, known as *linking verbs,* do not show action. They do, however, give information about the subject. In ''That woman is a millionaire,'' the linking verb *is* tells us that the woman is a millionaire. Other common linking verbs include *am, are, was, were, feel, appear, look, become,* and *seem.*

Practice 1

In each of the following sentences, draw one line under the subject and two lines under the verb.

Ask *who* or *what* the sentence is about to find the subject. Then ask what the sentence *says about* the subject to find the verb.

1. Carl spilled cocoa on the pale carpet.
2. A ladybug landed on my shoulder.
3. Gary eats cold pizza for breakfast.
4. The waitress brought someone else's meal by mistake.
5. I found a blue egg under a tree in my backyard.
6. Diane stapled her papers together.
7. The audience applauded before the song was finished.
8. My boss has a lot of patience.
9. I tasted poached eggs today for the first time.
10. The new paperboy threw our newspaper under the car.

Practice 2

Follow the directions given for Practice 1. Note that all the verbs here are linking verbs.

1. I am always nervous on the first day of classes.
2. My parents were engaged for nine years.
3. Tri Lee was the first person to finish the exam.
4. Our dog becomes friendly after a few minutes of growling.
5. Estelle seems ready for a nervous breakdown.
6. That plastic hot dog looks good enough to eat.
7. Overweight people appear slimmer in clothes with vertical stripes.
8. Many students felt exhausted after finishing the placement exam.
9. A cheeseburger has more than seven times the sodium of French fries.
10. Yesterday, my telephone seemed to be ringing constantly.

Practice 3

Follow the directions given for Practice 1.

1. The rabbits ate more than their share of my garden.
2. My father prefers his well-worn jeans to new ones.
3. A local restaurant donated food for the homeless.
4. Stanley always looks ready for a fight.
5. An elderly couple relaxed on a bench in the shopping mall.
6. Lightning brightened the dark sky for a few seconds.
7. Our town council voted for a curfew on Halloween.
8. Lola's sore throat kept her from work today.
9. Surprisingly, Sally's little sister decided not to go to the circus.
10. As usual, I chose the slowest checkout line in the supermarket.

MORE ABOUT
SUBJECTS AND VERBS

Distinguishing Subjects
from Prepositional Phrases

The subject of a sentence never appears within a prepositional phrase. A *prepositional phrase* is simply a group of words beginning with a preposition and ending with the answer to a question such as *what, where,* or *when.* Here is a list of common prepositions.

about	before	by	inside	over
above	behind	during	into	through
across	below	except	of	to
among	beneath	for	off	toward
around	beside	from	on	under
at	between	in	onto	with

Cross out prepositional phrases when looking for the subject of a sentence.

In the middle of the night, we heard footsteps on the roof.
The magazines on the table belong in the garage.
Before the opening kickoff, a brass band marched onto the field.
The hardware store across the street went out of business.
In spite of our advice, Sally quit her job at Burger King.

Practice

Cross out prepositional phrases. Then draw a single line under subjects and a double line under verbs.

1. By accident, Fran dropped her folder in the mailbox.
2. Before the test, I glanced over my notes.
3. My car stalled on the bridge at rush hour.
4. I hung a photo of Whitney Houston above my bed.
5. On weekends, we visit my grandmother at a nursing home.

6. During the movie, some teenagers giggled at the love scenes.

7. A pedestrian tunnel runs beneath the street to the train station.

8. The parents hid their daughter's Christmas gifts in the garage.

9. All the teachers, except Mr. Blake, wear ties to school.

10. The strawberry jam in my brother's sandwich dripped onto his lap.

Verbs of More Than One Word

Many verbs consist of more than one word. Here, for example, are some of the many forms of the verb *help:*

helps	should have been helping	will have helped
helping	can help	would have been helped
is helping	would have been helping	has been helped
was helping	will be helping	had been helped
may help	had been helping	must have helped
should help	helped	having helped
will help	have helped	should have been helped
does help	has helped	had helped

Below are sentences that contain verbs of more than one word:

Diane is not working overtime this week.

Another book has been written about the Kennedy family.

We should have stopped for gas at the last station.

The game has just been canceled.

Notes

1 Words like *not, just, never, only*, and *always* are not part of the verb although they may appear within the verb.

Diane is not working overtime this week.
The boys should just not have stayed out so late.
The game has always been played regardless of the weather.

2 No verb preceded by *to* is ever the verb of a sentence.

Sue wants to go with us.
The newly married couple decided to rent a house for a year.
The store needs extra people to help out at Christmas.

3 No *-ing* word by itself is ever the verb of a sentence. (It may be part of the verb, but it must have a helping verb in front of it.)

We planning the trip for months. (This is not a sentence, because the verb is not complete.)
We were planning the trip for months. (a sentence)

Practice

Draw a single line under subjects and a double line under verbs. Be sure to include all parts of the verb.

1. Ellen has chosen blue dresses for her bridesmaids.
2. You should plan your weekly budget more carefully.
3. Felix has been waiting in line for tickets all morning.
4. We should have invited Terri to the party.
5. I would have preferred a movie with a happy ending.
6. Classes were interrupted three times today by a faulty fire alarm.
7. Sam can touch his nose with his tongue.
8. I have been encouraging my mother to quit smoking.
9. Tony has just agreed to feed his neighbor's fish over the holiday.
10. Many students have not been giving much thought to selecting a major.

A sentence may have more than one verb:

The dancer stumbled and fell.
Lola washed her hair, blew it dry, and parted it in the middle.

A sentence may have more than one subject:

Cats and dogs are sometimes the best of friends.
The striking workers and their bosses could not come to an agreement.

A sentence may have several subjects and several verbs:

Holly and I read the book and reported on it to the class.
Pete, Nick, and Fran caught the fish in the morning, cleaned them in the afternoon, and ate them that night.

Practice

Draw a single line under subjects and a double line under verbs. Be sure to mark *all* the subjects and verbs.

1. Boards and bricks make a nice bookcase.
2. We bought a big bag of peanuts and finished it by the movie's end.
3. A fly and a bee hung lifelessly in the spider's web.
4. The twins look alike but think, act, and dress quite differently.
5. Canned salmon and tuna contain significant amounts of calcium.
6. I waited for the bubble bath to foam and then slipped into the warm tub.
7. The little girl in the next car waved and smiled at me.
8. The bird actually dived under the water and reappeared with a fish.
9. Singers, dancers, and actors performed for the heart-association benefit.
10. The magician and his assistant bowed and disappeared in a cloud of smoke.

Review Test 1

Draw one line under the subjects and two lines under the verbs. Cross out prepositional phrases where needed to help find subjects. Underline all the parts of a verb. You may find more than one subject and verb in a sentence.

1. Most breakfast cereals contain sugar.

2. The drawer of the bureau sticks on rainy days.

3. Our local bus company offers special rates for senior citizens.

4. Drunk drivers in Norway must spend three weeks in jail at hard labor.

5. On weekends, the campus bookstore closes at five o'clock.

6. We wrapped and labeled all the Christmas gifts over the weekend.

7. Motorcycles have been banned from the expressway.

8. Episodes of this old television series are in black and white.

9. The computer sorted, counted, and recorded the ballots within minutes after the closing of the polls.

10. Eddie stepped to the foul line and calmly sank both free throws to win the basketball game.

◌ Review Test 2

Follow the directions given for Review Test 1.

1. Gasoline from the broken fuel line dripped onto the floor of the garage.

2. All the carrot tops in the garden had been eaten by rabbits.

3. An old man with a plastic trash bag collected aluminum cans along the road.

4. The majority of people wait until April 15 to file their income tax.

5. My mother became a college freshman at the age of forty-two.

6. At the delicatessen, Linda and Paul ate corned beef sandwiches and drank root beer.

7. The window fan made a clanking sound during the night and kept us from sleeping.

8. An umbrella tumbled across the street in the gusty wind and landed between two cars.

9. Telephones in the mayor's office rang continuously with calls on the city tax increase from angry citzens.

10. A teenager pushed a woman, grabbed her purse, and ran off through the crowd.

◌ Review Test 3

Write ten sentences of your own, with each containing two words: a subject and a verb.

Example   Greg shouted.

Sentence Fragments

INTRODUCTORY PROJECT

Every sentence must have a subject and a verb and must express a complete thought. A word group that lacks a subject or a verb and that does not express a complete thought is a *fragment*.

Listed below are a number of fragments and sentences. See if you can complete the statement that explains each fragment.

1. Children. *Fragment*
    Children cry. *Sentence*

    "Children" is a fragment because, while it has a subject (*Children*), it lacks a _____ (*cry*) and so does not express a complete thought.

2. Dances. *Fragment*
    Lola dances. *Sentence*

    "Dances" is a fragment because, while it has a verb (*Dances*), it lacks a _____ (*Lola*) and so does not express a complete thought.

3. Staring through the window. *Fragment*
    Bigfoot was staring through the window. *Sentence*

    "Staring through the window" is a fragment because it lacks a _____ (*Bigfoot*) and also part of the _____ (*was*) and because it does not express a complete thought.

4. When the dentist began drilling. *Fragment*
    When the dentist began drilling, I closed my eyes. *Sentence*

    "When the dentist began drilling" is a fragment because we want to know *what happened when* the dentist began drilling. The word group does not follow through and _____.

Answers are on page 458.

WHAT SENTENCE FRAGMENTS ARE

Every sentence must have a subject and a verb and must express a complete thought. A word group that lacks a subject or a verb and that does not express a complete thought is a *fragment*. Following are the most common types of fragments that people write:

1 Dependent-word fragments

2 *-ing* and *to* fragments

3 Added-detail fragments

4 Missing-subject fragments

Once you understand the specific kind or kinds of fragments that you may write, you should be able to eliminate them from your writing. The following pages explain all four fragment types.

1 DEPENDENT-WORD FRAGMENTS

Some word groups that begin with a dependent word are fragments. Here is a list of common dependent words:

after	if, even if	when, whenever
although, though	in order that	where, wherever
as	since	whether
because	that, so that	which, whichever
before	unless	while
even though	until	who
how	what, whatever	whose

Whenever you start a sentence with one of these words, you must be careful that a fragment does not result. The word group beginning with the dependent word *After* in the selection below is a fragment.

After I stopped drinking coffee. I began sleeping better at night.

A *dependent statement*—one starting with a dependent word like *After*—cannot stand alone. It depends on another statement to complete the thought. "After I stopped drinking coffee" is a dependent statement. It leaves us hanging. We expect in the same sentence to find out *what happened after* the writer stopped drinking coffee. When a writer does not follow through and complete a thought, a fragment results.

To correct the fragment, simply follow through and complete the thought:

After I stopped drinking coffee, I began sleeping better at night.

Remember, then, that *dependent statements by themselves* are fragments. They must be attached to a statement that makes sense standing alone.*

Here are two other selections with dependent-word fragments.

Brian sat nervously in the dental clinic. While waiting to have his wisdom tooth pulled.
Maria decided to throw away the boxes. That had accumulated for years in the basement.

"While waiting to have his wisdom tooth pulled" is a fragment; it does not make sense standing by itself. We want to know in the same statement *what Brian did* while waiting to have his tooth pulled. The writer must complete the thought. Likewise, "That had accumulated for years in the basement" is not in itself a complete thought. We want to know in the same statement what *that* refers to.

How to Correct
Dependent-Word Fragments

In most cases, you can correct a dependent-word fragment by attaching it to the sentence that comes after it or the sentence that comes before it:

After I stopped drinking coffee, I began sleeping better at night.
(The fragment has been attached to the sentence that comes after it.)

---

* Some instructors refer to a dependent-word fragment as a *dependent clause*. A *clause* is simply a group of words having a subject and a verb. A clause may be *independent* (expressing a complete thought and able to stand alone) or *dependent* (not expressing a complete thought and not able to stand alone). A dependent clause by itself is a fragment. It can be corrected simply by adding an independent clause.

Brian sat nervously in the dental clinic while waiting to have his wisdom tooth pulled.

(The fragment has been attached to the sentence that comes before it.)

Maria decided to throw away the boxes that had accumulated for years in the basement.

(The fragment has been attached to the sentence that comes before it.)

Another way of correcting a dependent-word fragment is to eliminate the dependent word and make a new sentence:

I stopped drinking coffee.
He was waiting to have his wisdom tooth pulled.
They had accumulated for years in the basement.

Do not use this second method of correction too frequently, however, for it may cut down on interest and variety in your writing style.

Notes

1   Use a comma if a dependent-word group comes at the *beginning* of a sentence (see also page 180):

After I stopped drinking coffee, I began sleeping better at night.

However, do not generally use a comma if the dependent-word group comes at the end of a sentence:

Brian sat nervously in the dental clinic while waiting to have his wisdom tooth pulled.

Maria decided to throw away the boxes that had accumulated for years in the basement.

2   Sometimes the dependent words *who, that, which,* or *where* appear not at the very start but *near* the start of a word group. A fragment often results.

Today I visited Hilda Cooper. A friend who is in the hospital. I was frightened by her loss of weight.

''A friend who is in the hospital'' is not in itself a complete thought. We want to know in the same statement *who* the friend is. The fragment can be corrected by attaching it to the sentence that comes before it.

Today I visited Hilda Cooper, a friend who is in the hospital.

Practice 1

Turn each of the dependent-word groups into a sentence by adding a complete thought. Put a comma after the dependent-word group if a dependent word starts the sentence.

Examples   After I got out of high school
          After I got out of high school, I spent a year traveling.

          The watch which I got fixed
          The watch which I got fixed has just stopped working again.

1. Before I eat breakfast

   _____

   _____

2. Because I have to work tonight

   _____

   _____

3. Since it was such a hot day

   _____

   _____

4. The dentist I go to

   _____

   _____

5. When my sister got married

   _____

   _____

Practice 2

Underline the dependent-word fragment (or fragments) in each selection. Then correct each fragment by attaching it to the sentence that comes before or the sentence that comes after—whichever sounds more natural. Put a comma after the dependent-word group if it starts the sentence.

1. When the waitress coughed in his food. Frank lost his appetite. He didn't even take home a doggy bag.

   _____

   _____

   _____

2. My little brother had chicken pox this summer. He was very upset. Because he didn't get to miss any school.

   _____

   _____

   _____

3. Tony doesn't like going to the ballpark. If he misses an exciting play. There's no instant replay.

   _____

   _____

   _____

4. After the mail carrier comes. I run to our mailbox. I love to get mail. Even if it is only junk mail.

   _____

   _____

   _____

5. Even though she can't read. My little daughter likes to go to the library. She chooses books with pretty covers. While I look at the latest magazines.

   _____

   _____

   _____

2 *-ING* AND *TO* FRAGMENTS

When an *-ing* word appears at or near the start of a word group, a fragment may result. Such fragments often lack a subject and part of the verb. Underline the word groups in the selections below that contain *-ing* words. Each is a fragment.

Selection 1

I spent all day in the employment office. Trying to find a job that suited me. The prospects looked bleak.

Selection 2

Lola surprised Tony on the nature hike. Picking blobs of resin off pine trees. Then she chewed them like bubble gum.

Selection 3

Mel took an aisle seat on the bus. His reason being that he had more legroom.

People sometimes write *-ing* fragments because they think the subject in one sentence will work for the next word group as well. In the first selection above, they might think the subject *I* in the opening sentence will also serve as the subject for ''Trying to find a job that suited me.'' But the subject must actually be *in* the sentence.

How to Correct *-ing* Fragments

1   Attach the fragment to the sentence that comes before or the sentence that comes after it, whichever makes sense. Selection 1 above could read, ''I spent all day in the employment office, trying to find a job that suited me.''

2   Add a subject and change the *-ing* verb part to the correct form of the verb. Selection 2 could read, ''She picked blobs of resin off pine trees.''

3   Change *being* to the correct form of the verb *be* (*am, are, is, was, were*). Selection 3 could read, ''His reason was that he had more legroom.''

How to Correct *to* Fragments

When *to* appears at or near the start of a word group, a fragment sometimes results.

> To remind people of their selfishness. Otis leaves handwritten notes on cars that take up two parking spaces.

The first word group in the selection above is a fragment. It can be corrected by adding it to the sentence that comes after it:

> To remind people of their selfishness, Otis leaves handwritten notes on cars that take up two parking spaces.

Practice 1

Underline the *-ing* fragment in each of the following selections. Then make the fragment a sentence by rewriting it, using the method described in parentheses.

Example   The dog eyed me with suspicion. <u>Not knowing whether its master was at home.</u> I hesitated to open the gate.
(Add the fragment to the sentence that comes after it.)

> *Not knowing whether its master was at home, I hesitated to*
> *open the gate.*

1. Vince sat nervously in the dentist's chair. Waiting for his x-rays to be developed. He prayed there would be no cavities.
   (Add the fragment to the preceding sentence.)

   _____

   _____

2. Looking through the movie ads for twenty minutes. Lew and Marian tried to find a film they both wanted to see.
   (Add the fragment to the sentence that comes after it.)

   _____

   _____

3. The jeep went too fast around the sharp curve. As a result, tipping over.
   (Add the subject *it* and change the verb *tipping* to the correct form, *tipped.*)

   _____

   _____

Practice 2

Underline the *-ing* or *to* fragment in each selection. Then rewrite each selection correctly, using one of the methods of correction described on pages 24–25.

1. Some workers dug up the street near our house. Causing frequent vibrations inside. By evening, all the pictures on our walls were crooked.

    _____

    _____

    _____

2. I had heard about the surprise party for me. I therefore walked slowly into the darkened living room. Preparing to look shocked.

    _____

    _____

    _____

3. Jen's stomach grumbled all morning. The reason being that she skipped breakfast to get to the bus on time.

    _____

    _____

    _____

4. As I was dreaming of a sunny day at the beach, the alarm clock rang. Wanting to finish the dream. I pushed the snooze button.

    _____

    _____

    _____

5. To get back my term paper. I went to see my English teacher from last semester. I also wanted some career advice.

    _____

    _____

    _____

3 ADDED-DETAIL FRAGMENTS

Added-detail fragments lack a subject and a verb. They often begin with one of the following words.

also	except	including
especially	for example	such as

See if you can locate and underline the one added-detail fragment in each of the following selections:

Selection 1

Tony has trouble accepting criticism. Except from Lola. She has a knack for tact.

Selection 2

My apartment has its drawbacks. For example, no hot water in the morning.

Selection 3

I've worked at many jobs while in school. Among them, busboy, painter, and security guard.

People often write added-detail fragments for much the same reason they write *-ing* fragments. They think the subject and verb in one sentence will serve for the next word group as well. But the subject and verb must be in *each* word group.

How to Correct Added-Detail Fragments

1 Attach the fragment to the complete thought that precedes it. Selection 1 could read: "Tony has trouble accepting criticism, except from Lola."

2 Add a subject and a verb to the fragment to make it a complete sentence. Selection 2 could read: "My apartment has its drawbacks. For example, there is no hot water in the morning."

3 Change words as necessary to make the fragment part of the preceding sentence. Selection 3 could read: "Among the many jobs I've worked at while in school have been busboy, painter, and security guard."

Practice 1

Underline the fragment in each selection below. Then make it a sentence by rewriting it, using the method described in parentheses.

Example   My husband and I share the household chores. <u>Including meals.</u>
I do the cooking and he does the eating.
(Add the fragment to the preceding sentence.)
My husband and I share the household chores, including meals.

1. Al can be pretty absentminded. For example, taking a bus home from work on a day he drove his car there.
(Correct the fragment by adding the subject *he* and changing *taking* to the proper form of the verb, *took.*)

   _____

   _____

2. My eleventh-grade English teacher picked on everybody. Except the athletes. They could do no wrong.
(Add the fragment to the preceding sentence.)

   _____

   _____

3. Bernardo always buys things out of season. For example, an air conditioner in December. He saves a lot of money this way.
(Correct the fragment by adding the subject and verb *he bought.*)

   _____

   _____

Practice 2

Underline the added-detail fragment in each selection. Then rewrite that part of the selection needed to correct the fragment. Use one of the three methods of correction described on page 27.

1. I find all sorts of things in my little boy's pockets. Including crayons, stones, and melted chocolate. Luckily, I haven't found anything alive there yet.

   _____

   _____

2. There are certain chores I hate to do. Especially cleaning windows. So I clean only the windows I look out of.

_____

_____

3. Harvey woke up grumpy as a bear. Also, weak as a kitten. His wife decided to take him to the veterinarian.

_____

_____

4. Some people on television really annoy me. For example, game show hosts. Their smiles look as if they were pasted on their faces.

_____

_____

5. By midnight, the party looked like the scene of an accident. With popcorn and crumpled napkins all over and people stretched out on the floor.

_____

_____

4 MISSING-SUBJECT FRAGMENTS

Underline the word group in which the subject is missing in each selection below.

Selection 1

One example of my father's generosity is that he visits sick friends in the hospital. And takes along get-well cards with a few dollars folded in them.

Selection 2

The weight lifter grunted as he heaved the barbells into the air. Then, with a loud groan, dropped them.

People write missing-subject fragments because they think the subject in one sentence will apply to the next word group as well. But the subject, as well as the verb, must be in each word group to make it a sentence.

How to Correct
Missing-Subject Fragments

1 Attach the fragment to the preceding sentence. Selection 1 could read: "One example of my father's generosity is that he visits sick friends in the hospital and takes along get-well cards with a few dollars folded in them."

2 Add a subject (which can often be a pronoun standing for the subject in the preceding sentence). Selection 2 could read: "Then, with a loud groan, he dropped them."

Practice

Underline the missing-subject fragment in each selection. Then rewrite that part of the selection needed to correct the fragment. Use one of the two methods of correction described above.

1. Artie tripped on his shoelace. Then looked around to see if anyone had noticed.

   _____

   _____

2. I started the car. And quickly turned down the blaring radio.

   _____

   _____

3. Rita manages to exercise at work. She does toe touches while sitting at her desk. Also, does deep-knee bends when she files.

   _____

   _____

4. An obnoxious driver tailgated me for five blocks. Then passed me on the right. Unfortunately, he didn't get a ticket.

   _____

   _____

5. My elderly aunt never stands on bus rides for long. She places herself in front of a seated young man. And stands on his feet until he gets up.

   _____

   _____

A REVIEW: HOW TO CHECK FOR SENTENCE FRAGMENTS

1 Read your paper aloud from the *last* sentence to the *first*. You will be better able to see and hear whether each word group you read is a complete thought.

2 Ask yourself of any word group you think is a fragment: Does this contain a subject and a verb and express a complete thought?

3 More specifically, be on the lookout for the most common fragments:

- Dependent-word fragments (starting with words like *after, because, since, when,* and *before*)

- *-ing* and *to* fragments (*-ing* or *to* at or near the start of a word group)

- Added-detail fragments (starting with words like *for example, such as, also,* and *especially*)

- Missing-subject fragments (a verb is present but not the subject)

Review Test 1

Turn each of the following word groups into a complete sentence. Use the space provided.

Examples   Feeling very confident
Feeling very confident, I began my speech.

Until the rain started
We played softball until the rain started.

1. After we ate dinner

_____

2. Whenever the teacher is late

_____

3. Under the bed

_____

4. If the weather is bad

_____

5. Dave, who is not very organized

_____

6. To get to know each other better

_____

7. Which was inconvenient

_____

8. Will meet me later

_____

9. Waiting for the stoplight to change

_____

10. While you park the car

_____

Review Test 2

Underline the fragment in each selection. Then correct the fragment in the space provided.

Example   Sam received all kinds of junk mail. Then complained to the post office. Eventually, some of the mail stopped coming.
Then he complained to the post office.

1. Fascinated, Nina stared at the stranger. Who was standing in the doorway. She wondered if she could convince him they had met before.

_____

_____

2. Trees can survive on a steep mountain slope if they obey two rules. They must grow low to the ground. And bend with the wind.

_____

_____

3. While waiting in line at the supermarket. I look in people's baskets. Their food choices give hints about their personalities.

_____

_____

4. I saw spectacular twin rainbows through the kitchen window. So I rushed to get my camera. To take a picture before they vanished.

_____

_____

5. Whenever you buy cotton clothes, get them one size too large. By allowing for shrinkage. You will get a longer life out of them.

_____

_____

6. My nutty cousin cuts the address labels off his magazines. Then pastes them on envelopes. This way, he doesn't have to write his return address.

_____

_____

_____

7. Marian never has to buy catsup or mustard. Because she saves the extra packets that come with fast-food orders.

_____

_____

8. Many maple tree seeds drifted to the ground. Spinning like tiny propellers. With help from the wind, some landed far from the tree.

_____

_____

9. My husband climbed his first mountain yesterday. Now he's calling all our friends. To tell them about his peak experience.

_____

_____

10. The trivia book listed some interesting facts about Babe Ruth. For instance, he spoke German fluently. Also, kept cool on hot days by putting wet cabbage leaves under his cap.

_____

_____

_____

Review Test 3

In the space provided, write *C* if a word group is a complete sentence; write *frag* if it is a fragment. The first two are done for you.

frag   1. When the bus drivers went on strike.

C   2. I saw many people giving rides to strangers.

_____   3. Some even drove out of their way for others.

_____   4. Especially when the weather was bad.

_____   5. One rainy day, I saw an elderly woman pull her car over to the curb.

_____   6. Yelling and waving for five shivering students to get into her car.

_____   7. Until the strike finally ended.

_____   8. Scenes like that were not uncommon.

_____   9. It seems that community problems bring people together.

_____   10. By weakening the feeling that we live very separate lives.

Now correct the fragments you have found. Attach each fragment to the sentence that comes before or after it, or make whatever other change is needed to turn the fragment into a sentence. Use the space provided. The first one is corrected for you.

1. *When the bus drivers went on strike, I saw many people giving rides to strangers.*

2. _____

_____

3. _____

_____

4. _____

_____

5. _____

_____

Review Test 4

Write quickly for five minutes about the house or apartment where you live. Don't worry about spelling, punctuation, finding exact words, or organizing your thoughts. Just focus on writing as many words as you can without stopping.

After you have finished, go back and make whatever changes are needed to correct any fragments in your writing.

Run-Ons

INTRODUCTORY PROJECT

A run-on occurs when two sentences are run together with no adequate sign given to mark the break between them. Shown below are four run-on sentences and four correctly marked sentences. See if you can complete the statement that explains how each run-on is corrected.

1. A man coughed in the movie theater the result was a chain reaction of copycat coughing. *Run-on*

    A man coughed in the movie theater. The result was a chain reaction of copycat coughing. *Correct*

    The run-on has been corrected by using a _____ and a capital letter to separate the two complete thoughts.

2. I heard laughter inside the house, no one answered the bell. *Run-on*

    I heard laughter inside the house, but no one answered the bell. *Correct*

    The run-on has been corrected by using a joining word, _____, to connect the two complete thoughts.

3. A car sped around the corner, it sprayed slush all over the pedestrians. *Run-on*

    A car sped around the corner; it sprayed slush all over the pedestrians. *Correct*

    The run-on has been corrected by using a _____ to connect the two closely related thoughts.

4. I had a campus map, I still could not find my classroom building. *Run-on*

    Although I had a campus map, I still could not find my classroom building. *Correct*

    The run-on has been corrected by using the subordinating word _____ to connect the two closely related thoughts.

Answers are on page 459.

WHAT ARE RUN-ONS?

A *run-on* is two complete thoughts that are run together with no adequate sign given to mark the break between them.* Some run-ons have no punctuation at all to mark the break between the thoughts. Such run-ons are known as *fused sentences*: they are fused or joined together as if they were only one thought.

Fused Sentence

Rita decided to stop smoking she didn't want to die of lung cancer.

Fused Sentence

The exam was postponed the class was canceled as well.

In other run-ons, known as *comma splices,* a comma is used to connect or "splice" together the two complete thoughts. However, a comma alone is *not enough* to connect two complete thoughts. Some stronger connection than a comma alone is needed.

Comma Splice

Rita decided to stop smoking, she didn't want to die of lung cancer.

Comma Splice

The exam was postponed, the class was canceled as well.

Comma splices are the most common kind of run-on mistake. Students sense that some kind of connection is needed between thoughts, and so they put a comma at the dividing point. But the comma alone is *not sufficient,* and a stronger, clearer mark between the two thoughts is needed.

---

* Some instructors refer to each complete thought in a run-on sentence as an *independent clause.* A *clause* is simply a group of words having a subject and a verb. A clause may be *independent* (expressing a complete thought and able to stand alone) or *dependent* (not expressing a complete thought and not able to stand alone). A run-on sentence is two independent clauses that are run together with no adequate sign given to mark the break between them.

A Warning:
Words That Can Lead to Run-Ons

People often write run-ons when the second complete thought begins with one of the following words:

I	we	there	now
you	they	this	then
he, she, it		that	next

Remember to be on the alert for run-ons whenever you use one of these words in your writing.

CORRECTING RUN-ONS

Here are three common methods of correcting a run-on:

1   Use a period and a capital letter to separate the two complete thoughts. (In other words, make two separate sentences of the two complete thoughts.)

Rita decided to stop smoking. She didn't want to die of lung cancer.
The exam was postponed. The class was canceled as well.

2   Use a comma plus a joining word (*and, but, for, or, nor, so, yet*) to connect the two complete thoughts.

Rita decided to stop smoking, for she didn't want to die of lung cancer.
The exam was postponed, and the class was canceled as well.

3   Use a semicolon to connect the two complete thoughts.

Rita decided to stop smoking; she didn't want to die of lung cancer.
The exam was postponed; the class was canceled as well.

A fourth method of correcting a run-on is to use *subordination*. The following pages will give you practice in the first three methods. The use of subordination will be described on page 46, and again on page 387, in a section of the book that deals with sentence variety.

METHOD 1:
PERIOD AND A CAPITAL LETTER

One way of correcting a run-on is to use a period and a capital letter at the break between the two complete thoughts. Use this method especially if the thoughts are not closely related or if another method would make the sentence too long.

Practice 1

Locate the split in each of the following run-ons. Each is a *fused sentence*—that is, each consists of two sentences that are fused or joined together with no punctuation at all between them. Reading each sentence aloud will help you "hear" where a major break or split in the thought occurs. At such a point, your voice will probably drop and pause.

Correct the run-on by putting a period at the end of the first thought and a capital letter at the start of the second thought.

Example   Gary was not a success at his job. His mouth moved faster than his hands.

1. The fern hadn't been watered in a month its leaves looked like frayed brown shoelaces.
2. The cats are scratching at the door I think they want their supper.
3. Joyce's recipe for chocolate fudge is very easy to make it is also very expensive.
4. Watching television gave the old man something to do he didn't have many visitors anymore.
5. Jon accidentally dyed his underwear gray a black sock fell in his load of white clothes.
6. The first Olympic Games were held in 776 B.C. the only event was a footrace.
7. Gloria decorated her apartment creatively and cheaply she papered her bedroom walls with magazine covers.
8. There were papers scattered all over Lena's desk she spent twenty minutes looking for a missing receipt.
9. Spring rain dripped into the fireplace the room smelled like last winter's fires.
10. The car swerved dangerously through traffic its rear bumper sticker read, "School's Out—Drive Carefully."

Practice 2

Locate the split in each of the following run-ons. Some of the run-ons are fused sentences, and some of them are *comma splices*—run-ons spliced or joined together only with a comma. Correct each run-on by putting a period at the end of the first thought and a capital letter at the start of the next thought.

1. My father is a very sentimental man he still has my kindergarten drawings.
2. Sue dropped the letter in the mailbox, then she regretted mailing it.
3. Certain street names are very common the most common is ''Park.''
4. Bacteria are incredibly tiny, a drop of liquid may contain fifty million of them.
5. The fastest dog in the world is the greyhound it can run over forty-one miles an hour.
6. Miners have dug deeply for gold some have gone down as far as two and a half miles.
7. The thunderstorm was a severe one, the power was out in our neighborhood for two days.
8. A shadow on the kitchen wall was lovely it had the shape of a plant on the windowsill.
9. The little girl hated seeing her father drink, one day, she poured all his liquor down the kitchen drain.
10. Children have been born at odd times for instance, one child was born during his mother's funeral.

Practice 3

Write a second sentence to go with each sentence below. Start the second sentence with the word given at the left.

Example   *He*   My dog's ears snapped up. *He had heard a wolf howling on television.*

He   1. Billy actually enjoys housecleaning. _____

_____

They   2. Ants marched across our kitchen floor. _____

_____

Now   3. Our TV is in the repair shop. _____

_____

There   4. Raccoons knocked over our garbage cans. _____

_____

Then   5. First I stopped at the bakery. _____

_____

METHOD 2:
COMMA AND A JOINING WORD

Another way of correcting a run-on is to use a comma plus a joining word to connect the two complete thoughts. Joining words (also called *coordinating conjunctions*) include *and, but, for, or, nor, so,* and *yet.* Here is what the four most common joining words mean:

and   in addition, along with

Lola was watching Monday night football, and she was doing her homework as well.

(*And* means *in addition:* Lola was watching Monday night football; *in addition,* she was doing her homework as well.)

but   however, except, on the other hand, just the opposite

I voted for the president two years ago, but I would not vote for him today.

(*But* means *however:* I voted for the president two years ago; *however,* I would not vote for him today.)

for   because, the reason why, the cause for something

Saturday is the worst day to shop, for people jam the stores.

(*For* means *because:* Saturday is the worst day to shop *because* people jam the stores.) If you are not comfortable using *for,* you may want to use *because* instead of *for* in the activities that follow. If you do use *because,* omit the comma before it.

so   as a result, therefore

Our son misbehaved again, so he was sent upstairs without dessert.

(*So* means *as a result:* Our son misbehaved again; *as a result,* he was sent upstairs without dessert.)

Practice 1

Insert the comma and the joining word (*and, but, for, so*) that logically connect the two thoughts in each sentence.

for

Example   A trip to the zoo always depresses me I hate to see animals in cages.

1. I want to stop smoking I don't want to gain weight.
2. Packages are flown to distant cities during the night vans deliver them the next morning.
3. The weathered door of the cabin sagged on its hinges the boards were splintered and dry.
4. Jim wanted to buy his girlfriend a ring he began saving ten dollars a week.
5. I frequently enjoy watching television I still feel guilty about spending so much time in front of the tube.
6. It was too hot indoors to study I decided to go down to the shopping center for ice cream.
7. Lola's favorite female singer is Madonna her favorite male singer is Phil Collins.
8. The repairman couldn't find anything wrong with my washing machine I still had to pay for a service call.
9. I don't like to go to the doctor's office I'm afraid one of the other patients will make me really sick.
10. We knew there had been a power failure all the clocks were forty-five minutes slow.

Practice 2

Add a complete and closely related thought to go with each of the following statements. Use a comma plus the italicized joining word when you write the second thought.

> **Example** *but* I was sick with the flu, <u>*but I still had to study for the test.*</u>

but   1. We have the same taste in clothes _____

_____

so   2. Alex needed a little break from studying _____

_____

and   3. I hammered two nails in the wall _____

_____

for   4. The house was unusually quiet _____

_____

but   5. Lori meant to stick to her diet _____

_____

METHOD 3: SEMICOLON

A third method of correcting a run-on is to use a semicolon to mark the break between two thoughts. A *semicolon* (;) is made up of a period and a comma and is sometimes called a *strong comma*. The semicolon signals more of a pause than a comma alone but not quite the full pause of a period.

Semicolon Alone

Here are some earlier sentences that were connected with a comma plus a joining word. Notice that a semicolon, unlike the comma, can be used alone to connect the two complete thoughts in each sentence:

> Lola was watching Monday night football; she was doing her homework as well.
> I voted for the president two years ago; I would not vote for him today.
> Saturday is the worst day to shop; people jam the stores.

The occasional use of the semicolon can add variety to sentences. For some people, however, the semicolon is a confusing mark of punctuation. Keep in mind that if you are not comfortable using it, you can and should use one of the first two methods of correcting a run-on sentence.

Practice

Insert a semicolon where the break occurs between the two complete thoughts in each of the following sentences.

Example   She had a wig on; it looked more like a hat than a wig.

1. The problem with pound cake is obvious I gain a pound every time I eat a piece.
2. Fido quickly ate the baby watched with interest.
3. A huge green insect flopped against the screen it looked like a spaceship trying to land.
4. Lyle decided to let his Mohawk haircut grow out brown fuzz covered both sides of his head.
5. The first birthday parties in history were for kings and queens birth records were not yet kept for common people.

Semicolon with a Transition

A semicolon is sometimes used with a transitional word and a comma to join two complete thoughts:

I figured the ball game would cost me about five dollars; however, I didn't consider the high price of food and drinks.

Fred and Martha have a low-interest mortgage on their house; otherwise, they would move to another neighborhood.

Sharon didn't understand the teacher's point; therefore, she asked him to repeat it.

Note: Sometimes transitional words do not join complete thoughts but are merely interrupters in a sentence (see page 181):

My parents, moreover, plan to go on the trip.
I believe, however, that they'll change their minds.

Here is a list of common transitional words (also known as *adverbial conjunctions*). Brief meanings are given for the words.

Word	*Meaning*
however	but
nevertheless	however
on the other hand	however
instead	as a substitute
meanwhile	in the intervening time
otherwise	under other conditions
indeed	in fact
in addition	also, and
also	in addition
moreover	in addition
furthermore	in addition
as a result	thus, therefore
thus	as a result
consequently	as a result
therefore	as a result

Practice

Choose a logical transitional word from the box above and write it in the space provided. In addition, put a semicolon *before* the transition and a comma *after* it.

Example   It was raining harder than ever ___*; however,*___ Bobby was determined to go to the amusement park.

1. A new car is always fun to drive _____ the payments are never fun to make.
2. The fork that fell into our disposal looks like a piece of modern art _____ it is useless.
3. Auto races no longer use gasoline _____ spectators have nothing to fear from exhaust fumes.
4. We got to the stadium two hours before game time _____ all the parking spaces were already taken.
5. Mice use their sensitive whiskers as feelers _____ they scurry along close to walls.

A NOTE ON SUBORDINATION

A fourth method of joining together related thoughts is to use subordination. *Subordination* is a way of showing that one thought in a sentence is not as important as another thought. Here are three earlier sentences that have been recast so that one idea is subordinated to (made less emphatic than) the other idea:

Because Rita didn't want to die of lung cancer, she decided to stop smoking.

My dog's ears snapped up when he heard a wolf howling on television.

Although I voted for the president two years ago, I would not vote for him today.

Subordination is explained in full on page 387.

A REVIEW: HOW TO CHECK FOR RUN-ONS

1 To see if a sentence is a run-on, read it aloud and listen for a break marking two complete thoughts. Your voice will probably drop and pause at the break.

2 To check an entire paper read it aloud from the *last* sentence to the *first*. Doing so will help you hear and see each complete thought.

3 Be on the lookout for words that can lead to run-on sentences:

I	he, she, it	they	this	then
you	we	there	that	next

4 Correct run-on sentences by using one of the following methods:
- A period and a capital letter
- A comma and a joining word (*and, but, for, or, nor, so, yet*)
- A semicolon
- Subordination (as explained above and on page 387)

ℚ Review Test 1

Correct the following run-ons by using either (1) a period and a capital letter or (2) a comma and the joining word *and*, *but*, *for*, or *so*. Do not use the same method of correction for each sentence.

and

Example   Fred pulled the cellophane off the cake, the icing came along with
it.

1. I put fifty cents in the soda machine all I got was an empty cup.
2. I tore open a catsup packet a bright red streak flew across the front of my new white sweater.
3. Some people like to talk Roland just wants to watch TV.
4. The theater's parking lot was full we missed the first ten minutes of the movie.
5. Helen bites her nails she tries to keep her hands hidden.
6. The waiter cheerfully filled our coffee cups three times we left him a generous tip.
7. I love to wander through old cemeteries I enjoy reading the gravestones and taking pictures of them.
8. Travel to the stars has long been a dream of humanity the technology to achieve that dream will soon be available.
9. Elena no longer has to worry about missing the bus she rides to work in a van pool.
10. The baby wouldn't stop crying all the passengers on the bus gave the mother dirty looks.

ℚ Review Test 2

Follow the directions given for Review Test 1.

H

Example   Tony hated going to a new barber. He was afraid his hair would be
butchered.

1. My puppy loves me he also loves French toast and popcorn.
2. I began to shake on the examining table the nurse reached out and held my hand.

3. Molly microwaved her egg too long it exploded all over the inside of the oven.

4. Some young children are afraid of the water others can be taught to swim early.

5. People often spend too much money on vacations they wouldn't pay nine dollars for a hamburger at home.

6. Matthew uses his one-room apartment for everything it is an office, bedroom, kitchen, and den.

7. Sunlight shone through the blue bottle on the windowsill a bright blue light slashed across the floor.

8. The skateboard shot out from under her the front wheel had hit a crack in the sidewalk.

9. Crazy Bill melted a block of dry ice in a tub he wanted to take a bath without getting wet.

10. Revolutionary armies did not fight on rainy days paper cartridges would get wet and gunpowder would not fire.

Review Test 3

On separate paper, write six sentences, each of which has two complete thoughts. Use a period and a capital letter between the thoughts in two of the sentences. Use a comma and a joining word (*and, but, or, nor, for, so, yet*) to join the thoughts in another two sentences. Use a semicolon to join the thoughts in the final two sentences.

Review Test 4

Write for five minutes about something that makes you angry. Don't worry about spelling, punctuation, finding exact words, or organizing your thoughts. Just focus on writing as many words as you can without stopping.

After you have finished, go back and make whatever changes are needed to correct any run-on sentences in your writing.

Standard English Verbs

INTRODUCTORY PROJECT

Underline what you think is the correct form of the verb in each of the sentences below.

That radio station once (play, played) top-forty hits.
It now (play, plays) classical music.

When Jean was a little girl, she (hope, hoped) to become a movie star.
Now she (hope, hopes) to be accepted at law school.

At first, my father (juggle, juggled) with balls of yarn.
Now that he is an expert, he (juggle, juggles) raw eggs.

On the basis of the above examples, see if you can complete the following statements.

1. The first sentence in each pair refers to an action in the (past time, present time), and the regular verb has an _____ ending.
2. The second sentence in each pair refers to an action in the (past time, present time), and the regular verb has an _____ ending.

Answers are on page 459.

Many people have grown up in communities where nonstandard verb forms are used in everyday life. Such forms include *they be, it done, we has, you was, she don't,* and *it ain't.* Community dialects have richness and power but are a drawback in college and the world at large, where standard English verb forms must be used. Standard English helps ensure clear communication among English-speaking people everywhere, and it is especially important in the world of work.

This chapter compares the community dialect and the standard English forms of a regular verb and three common irregular verbs.

REGULAR VERBS: DIALECT AND STANDARD FORMS

The chart below compares community dialect (nonstandard) and standard English forms of the regular verb *talk.*

	TALK	
Community Dialect (Do not use in your writing)	***Standard English*** (Use for clear communication)	

Present Tense		
~~I talks~~ ~~we talks~~	I talk	we talk
you talks you talks	you talk	you talk
~~he, she, it talk~~ ~~they talks~~	he, she, it talks	they talk

Past Tense		
~~I talk~~ ~~we talk~~	I talked	we talked
you talk you talk	you talked	you talked
~~he, she, it talk~~ ~~they talk~~	he, she, it talked	they talked

One of the most common nonstandard forms results from dropping the endings of regular verbs. For example, people might say "Rose work until ten o'clock tonight" instead of "Rose works until ten o'clock tonight." Or they'll say "I work overtime yesterday" instead of "I worked overtime yesterday." To avoid such nonstandard usage, memorize the forms shown above for the regular verb *talk.* Then use the activities that follow to help make the inclusion of verb endings a writing habit.

Present Tense Endings

The verb ending -s or -es is needed with a regular verb in the present tense when the subject is *he, she, it,* or any one person or thing.

He	He lifts weights.
She	She runs.
It	It amazes me.
One person	Their son Ted swims.
One person	Their daughter Terry dances.
One thing	Their house jumps at night with all the exercise.

Practice 1

All but one of the ten sentences that follow need -s or -es endings. Cross out the nonstandard verb forms and write the standard forms in the spaces provided. Mark the one sentence that needs no change with a *C*.

ends   **Example**   The sale ~~end~~ tomorrow.

_____   1. Tim drive too fast for me.

_____   2. Our washing machine always get stuck at the rinse cycle.

_____   3. Louis announce all the college basketball games over the campus radio station.

_____   4. Whenever I serve meat loaf, my daughter make a peanut butter sandwich.

_____   5. My grandfather brush his teeth with baking soda.

_____   6. While watching television in the evening, Kitty usually fall asleep.

_____   7. Mom always wakes me by saying, "Get up, the day is growing older."

_____   8. On my old car radio, a static sound come from every station but one.

_____   9. My little sister watch fireworks with her hands over her ears.

_____   10. The cook at the sushi bar wrap raw pieces of fish around fillings of vinegar-flavored rice.

Practice 2

Rewrite the short selection below, adding present tense -*s* verb endings wherever needed.

My little sister want to be a country singer when she grow up. She constantly hum and sing around the house. Sometimes she make quite a racket. When she listen to music on the radio, for example, she sing very loudly in order to hear herself over the radio. And when she take a shower, her voice ring through the whole house, because she think nobody can hear her from there.

_____

_____

_____

_____

_____

_____

_____

_____

_____

_____

_____

_____

Past Tense Endings

The verb ending -*d* or -*ed* is needed with a regular verb in the past tense.

Yesterday we finished painting the house.

I completed the paper an hour before class.

Fred's car stalled on his way to work this morning.

Practice 1

All but one of the ten sentences that follow need *-d* or *-ed* endings. Cross out the nonstandard verb forms and write the standard forms in the spaces provided. Mark the one sentence that needs no change with a *C*.

jumped   **Example**   The cat ~~jump~~ on my lap when I sat down.

_____   1. The hammer missed the nail and thump my thumb.

_____   2. In a prim Indiana town, a couple was actually jail for kissing in public.

_____   3. While ironing my new shirt this morning, I burn a hole right through it.

_____   4. Fran wrapped the gag gift in waxed paper and tie it with dental floss.

_____   5. Pencil marks dotted Matt's bedroom wall where he measure his height each month.

_____   6. My brother was eating too fast and almost choked on a piece of bread.

_____   7. Nicole insist she had turned in her paper until she saw it sticking out of her notebook.

_____   8. The kids construct an obstacle course in the basement out of boxes and toys.

_____   9. The rain came down so hard it level the young cornstalks in our garden.

_____   10. As Alfonso pulled up to the red light, he suddenly realize his brakes were not working.

Practice 2

Rewrite this selection, adding past tense *-d* or *-ed* verb endings where needed.

> My cousin Joel complete a course in home repairs and offer one day to fix several things in my house. He repair a screen door that squeak, a dining room chair that wobble a bit, and a faulty electrical outlet. That night when I open the screen door, it loosen from its hinges. When I seat myself in the chair Joel had fix, one of its legs crack off. Remembering that Joel had also fool around with the electrical outlet, I quickly call an electrician and ask him to stop by the next day. Then I pray the house would not burn down before he arrive.

_____

_____

_____

_____

_____

THREE COMMON IRREGULAR VERBS: DIALECT AND STANDARD FORMS

The following charts compare the nonstandard and standard dialects of the common irregular verbs *be, have,* and *do.* (For more on irregular verbs, see the next chapter, beginning on page 58.)

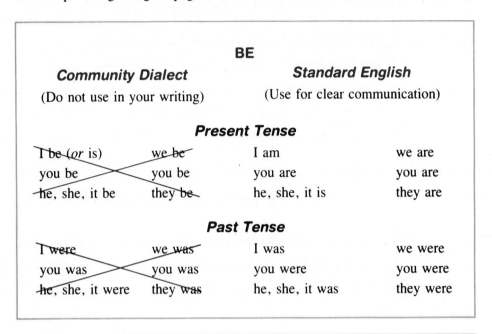

BE

Community Dialect		*Standard English*	
(Do not use in your writing)		(Use for clear communication)	

Present Tense

I be (*or* is)	we be	I am	we are
you be	you be	you are	you are
he, she, it be	they be	he, she, it is	they are

Past Tense

I were	we was	I was	we were
you was	you was	you were	you were
he, she, it were	they was	he, she, it was	they were

HAVE

Community Dialect		*Standard English*	
(Do not use in your writing)		(Use for clear communication)	

Present Tense

I has	we has	I have	we have
you has	you has	you have	you have
he, she, it have	they has	he, she, it has	they have

Past Tense

I has	we has	I had	we had
you has	you has	you had	you had
he, she, it have	they has	he, she, it had	they had

DO

Community Dialect	Standard English
(Do not use in your writing)	(Use for clear communication)

Present Tense

Community Dialect		Standard English	
I does	we does	I do	we do
you does	you does	you do	you do
he, she, it do	they does	he, she, it does	they do

Past Tense

Community Dialect		Standard English	
I done	we done	I did	we did
you done	you done	you did	you did
he, she, it done	they done	he, she, it did	they did

Note: Many people have trouble with one negative form of *do*. They will say, for example, ''She don't listen'' instead of ''She doesn't listen,'' or they will say ''This pen don't work'' instead of ''This pen doesn't work.'' Be careful to avoid the common mistake of using *don't* instead of *doesn't*.

Practice 1

Underline the standard form of the irregular verbs *be, have,* or *do*.

1. My psychology class (be, is) very dull.
2. For one thing, the instructor (have, has) a monotonous tone of voice.
3. While she (be, is) talking, students gaze out the windows or stare at their desks.
4. Several students even (do, does) their homework for other classes.
5. The instructor (do, does) not ask any questions in class.
6. So the students know they (do, does) not (has, have) to know any answers.
7. It (be, is) easy to spend the entire class half asleep.
8. Sometimes I think that the teacher (does, do) not even need to show up for class.
9. All she (have, has) to do is send in a tape recording of her lecture.
10. None of the students would know things (was, were) any different.

Practice 2

Cross out the nonstandard verb form in each sentence. Then write the standard form of *be*, *have*, or *do* in the space provided.

_____ 1. If you does your assignments on time, you may not understand my friend Albert.

_____ 2. Albert be the world's worst procrastinator.

_____ 3. Procrastinators be people who always put things off.

_____ 4. They has problems with deadlines of all kinds.

_____ 5. Albert were a procrastinator at the age of six.

_____ 6. The boy next door have a few friends over for lunch one day.

_____ 7. Albert's parents was upset when they learned Albert got there three hours late.

_____ 8. They done the neighbors a favor by taking Albert home at once.

_____ 9. Today, Albert still do everything at the last minute or even later.

_____ 10. He have plans to join Procrastinators Anonymous—when he gets around to it.

Practice 3

Fill in each blank with the standard form of *be*, *have*, or *do*.

My cousin Rita _____ decided to lose thirty pounds, so she _____ put herself on a rigid diet that _____ not allow her to eat anything that she enjoys. Last weekend, while the family _____ at Aunt Jenny's house for dinner, all Rita _____ to eat _____ a can of Diet Delight peaches. We _____ convinced that Rita meant business when she joined an exercise club whose members _____ to work out on enormous machines and _____ twenty sit-ups just to get started. If Rita _____ reach her goal, we _____ all going to be very proud of her. But I would not be surprised if she _____ not succeed, because this _____ her fourth diet this year.

℘ Review Test 1

Underline the standard verb form.

1. A cake in the oven (make, makes) the whole house smell good.
2. My brother deliberately (wear, wears) socks that clash with his clothes.
3. Our boss (don't, doesn't) want us to take any extra coffee breaks.
4. When I got home from shopping, I (realize, realized) I had lost a package.
5. My cheap ballpoint pen (skip, skips) whenever I try to write with it.
6. If they (was, were) my children, I wouldn't let them play near that creek.
7. We have to be quiet, because my mother (is, be) studying for her sociology test.
8. Max (watch, watched) the foam slide over the rim of his beer can.
9. When the sculptor (unveil, unveiled) his work, no one could figure out what it was.
10. *Consumer Reports* (did, done) a report last month on cars, and mine was the lowest-rated model on the list.

℘ Review Test 2

Cross out the nonstandard verb form in each of the sentences that follow. Then write the standard English verb form in the space at the left, as shown.

played   **Example**   For most of the morning, the children ~~play~~ quietly in the sandbox.

_____   1. Making promises be easier than keeping them.

_____   2. Baked potatoes doesn't have as many calories as I thought.

_____   3. The game were lost when the other team scored a fourth-quarter touchdown.

_____   4. Our psychology professor ride a motorcycle to school.

_____   5. At the end of the hike, we was covered with mosquito bites.

_____   6. Max the Mauler always scowl fiercely when his opponents enter the ring.

_____   7. Our cat stay outside the kitchen window all morning and watched me bake cookies.

_____   8. Many childhood diseases, such as scarlet fever and whooping cough, has almost vanished in America.

_____   9. Stanley turned the television on during the day because the house sound too quiet without it.

_____   10. That restaurant offers free nonalcoholic drinks to the person who be the driver for a group.

Irregular Verbs

INTRODUCTORY PROJECT

You may already have a sense of which common English verbs are regular and which are not. To test yourself, fill in the past tense and past participle of the verbs below. Five are regular verbs and so take *-d* or *-ed* in the past tense and past participle. Five are irregular verbs and will probably not sound right when you try to add *-d* or *-ed*. Put *I* for irregular in front of these verbs. Also, see if you can write in their irregular verb forms.

Present	Irregular	Past	Past Participle
fall	*I*	*fell*	*fallen*
1. scream			
2. write			
3. steal			
4. ask			
5. kiss			
6. choose			
7. ride			
8. chew			
9. think			
10. dance			

Answers are on page 460.

A BRIEF REVIEW
OF REGULAR VERBS

Every verb has four principal parts: the present, the past, the past participle, and the present participle. These parts can be used to build all the verb tenses (the times shown by a verb).

The past and past participle of a regular verb are formed by adding *-d* or *-ed* to the present. The *past participle* is the form of the verb used with the helping verbs *have, has,* or *had* (or some form of *be* with passive verbs). The *present participle* is formed by adding *-ing* to the present. Here are the principal forms of some regular verbs:

Present	*Past*	*Past Participle*	*Present Participle*
laugh	laughed	laughed	laughing
ask	asked	asked	asking
touch	touched	touched	touching
decide	decided	decided	deciding
explode	exploded	exploded	exploding

Most verbs in English are regular.

LIST OF IRREGULAR VERBS

Irregular verbs have irregular forms in the past tense and past participle. For example, the past tense of the irregular verb *grow* is *grew;* the past participle is *grown*.

Almost everyone has some degree of trouble with irregular verbs. When you are unsure about the form of a verb, you can check the list of irregular verbs on the following pages. (The present participle is not shown on this list because it is formed simply by adding *-ing* to the base form of the verb.) Or you can check a dictionary, which gives the principal parts of irregular verbs.

Present	Past	Past Participle
arise	arose	arisen
awake	awoke *or* awaked	awoke *or* awaked
be (am, are, is)	was (were)	been
become	became	become
begin	began	begun
bend	bent	bent
bite	bit	bitten
blow	blew	blown
break	broke	broken
bring	brought	brought
build	built	built
burst	burst	burst
buy	bought	bought
catch	caught	caught
choose	chose	chosen
come	came	come
cost	cost	cost
cut	cut	cut
do (does)	did	done
draw	drew	drawn
drink	drank	drunk
drive	drove	driven
eat	ate	eaten
fall	fell	fallen
feed	fed	fed
feel	felt	felt
fight	fought	fought
find	found	found
fly	flew	flown
freeze	froze	frozen
get	got	got *or* gotten
give	gave	given
go (goes)	went	gone
grow	grew	grown
have (has)	had	had
hear	heard	heard
hide	hid	hidden
hold	held	held
hurt	hurt	hurt
keep	kept	kept
know	knew	known
lay	laid	laid

Present	*Past*	*Past Participle*
lead	led	led
leave	left	left
lend	lent	lent
let	let	let
lie	lay	lain
light	lit	lit
lose	lost	lost
make	made	made
meet	met	met
pay	paid	paid
ride	rode	ridden
ring	rang	rung
rise	rose	risen
run	ran	run
say	said	said
see	saw	seen
sell	sold	sold
send	sent	sent
shake	shook	shaken
shrink	shrank	shrunk
shut	shut	shut
sing	sang	sung
sit	sat	sat
sleep	slept	slept
speak	spoke	spoken
spend	spent	spent
stand	stood	stood
steal	stole	stolen
stick	stuck	stuck
sting	stung	stung
swear	swore	sworn
swim	swam	swum
take	took	taken
teach	taught	taught
tear	tore	torn
tell	told	told
think	thought	thought
wake	woke *or* waked	woken *or* waked
wear	wore	worn
win	won	won
write	wrote	written

Practice 1

Cross out the incorrect verb form in the following sentences. Then write the correct form of the verb in the space provided.

___*began*___ **Example** When the mud slide started, the whole neighborhood ~~begun~~ going downhill.

_____ 1. The coach caught Otto when he come in two hours after curfew.

_____ 2. We standed out in the cold all night to buy tickets to the concert.

_____ 3. The Romans had builded a network of roads so the army could travel more quickly from place to place.

_____ 4. Our championship team has swam in every important meet this year.

_____ 5. I done everything the recipe said, but the sponge cake looked like a big yellow brownie.

_____ 6. The overweight recruit had fell every time he came to the tires on the obstacle course.

_____ 7. The linebacker hit me so hard that I thought my ribs were broke.

_____ 8. The tornado blowed the sign from the top of the bank, and it landed five blocks away in the motel swimming pool.

_____ 9. He had wrote the answers to all the questions before anyone else had finished the first page.

_____ 10. The poker players knowed they were in trouble when the stranger shuffled the cards with one hand.

Practice 2

For each of the italicized verbs in the following sentences, fill in the three missing forms in the order shown in the box:

a. Present tense, which takes an -s ending when the subject is *he, she, it,* or any *one person* or *thing* (see page 51)

b. Past tense

c. Past participle—the form that goes with the helping verb *have, has,* or *had*

Example My little nephew loves to _break_ things. Every Christmas he (a) _____ _breaks_ _____ his new toys the minute they're unwrapped. Last year he (b) _____ _broke_ _____ five toys in seven minutes and then went on to smash his family's new china platter. His mother says he won't be happy until he has (c) _____ _broken_ _____ their hearts.

1. Did you ever go to _sleep_ on a water bed? My cousin Nancy (a) _____ on one. Last year I spent the weekend at Nancy's apartment, and I (b) _____ on it. Since then I have (c) _____ on it several more times, without once getting seasick.

2. A dreadful little boy in my neighborhood loves to _ring_ my doorbell and run away. Sometimes he (a) _____ it several times a day. The last time he (b) _____ it over and over, I finally refused to answer the door. Then I found out that United Parcel had (c) _____ the doorbell to deliver a gift from my boyfriend.

3. Why does every teacher ask us to _write_ about our summer vacations? Most students (a) _____ about what really happened, but that is usually too dull. I (b) _____ an essay about being taken aboard an alien spacecraft. I bet it was the most interesting essay anybody has ever (c) _____ for my teacher's English class.

4. My sister never has to _stand_ in line for a movie very long. She always (a) _____ for a few minutes and then walks straight to the entrance. "I (b) _____ in line as long as I could," she tells the ticket taker. "In fact," she continues in a weak voice, "I have (c) _____ in line too long already. I feel faint." She is always ushered inside immediately.

5. As usual, Ron planned to _swim_ at least a hundred laps before breakfast. He knows that an Olympic hopeful (a) _____ while others sleep. That morning he (b) _____ with a deliberate stroke, counting the rhythm silently. He had (c) _____ this way daily for the last two years. It was a price he was willing to pay to be one of the best.

6. Stella expected her new blouse to *shrink* somewhat. All new clothes (a) _____ the first time they are laundered. Her blue jeans (b) _____ so much she could barely wriggle into them. Feeling anxious, she opened the door of the dryer and took out the dry clothes. Then she shook her head in dismay. The designer blouse had (c) _____ so much that it would probably now fit her daughter's teddy bear.

7. My friend Alice loves to *eat*. But no matter how much she (a) _____, she stays thin. Her husband, on the other hand, is fat. "Why?" he jokingly complains. "I (b) _____ very little today. In fact," he adds with a grin, "all my life I have (c) _____ just one meal a day. Of course, it usually lasts from morning till night."

8. David sat in his car at the rural crossroads and wondered which direction to *choose*. Should he (a) _____ left or right? He sighed and turned right, knowing that if he (b) _____ the wrong way, he would run out of gas before finding his way back to the highway. After several anxious minutes, he spotted an Exxon sign. He pulled into the service station, grateful that he had (c) _____ the right direction after all.

9. All the kids in the neighborhood waited each winter for Mahoney's pond to *freeze*. They knew that a sudden cold snap only (a) _____ the surface. It took at least a week of low temperatures before the pond (b) _____ more than a few inches deep. Mr. Mahoney checked the ice each day. When it had finally (c) _____ to a depth of six inches, he gave his permission for the children to skate on it.

10. The moment when a girl opens the door to *meet* a blind date is crucial. She (a) _____ "Mr. Right" or Mr. Teenage Frankenstein. A girl I once (b) _____ bragged that all her blind dates were terrific. My luck has been the opposite. I keep hoping for a cruise on the *Love Boat,* but every blind date I have (c) _____ has given me on a ride on the *Titanic*.

TROUBLESOME IRREGULAR VERBS

Three common irregular verbs that often give people trouble are *be*, *have*, and *do*. See pages 54–55 for a discussion of these verbs. Three sets of other irregular verbs that can lead to difficulties are *lie-lay*, *sit-set*, and *rise-raise*.

Lie- Lay

The principal parts of *lie* and *lay* are as follows:

Present	*Past*	*Past Participle*
lie	lay	lain
lay	laid	laid

To lie means *to rest* or *recline*. *To lay* means *to put something down*.

To Lie	*To Lay*
Tony *lies* on the couch.	I *lay* the mail on the table.
This morning he *lay* in the tub.	Yesterday I *laid* the mail on the counter.
He has *lain* in bed all week with the flu.	I have *laid* the mail where everyone will see it.

Practice

Underline the correct verb. Use a form of *lie* if you can substitute *recline*. Use a form of *lay* if you can substitute *place*.

1. Even though it looks cloudy, you'll get sunburned if you (lie, lay) here too long.
2. The investigators found a brass button (lying, laying) next to the dead victim's hand.
3. The Magna Carta (lay, laid) the foundation for the establishment of the English Parliament.
4. While cleaning out his desk, Paul found a package of cheese crackers that had (lain, laid) there all summer.
5. I (lay, laid) down on the couch and pressed my face into the pillow.

Sit- Set

The principal parts of *sit* and *set* are as follows:

Present	Past	Past Participle
sit	sat	sat
set	set	set

To sit means *to take a seat* or *to rest*. *To set* means *to put* or *to place*.

To Sit

I *sit* down during work breaks.

I *sat* in the doctor's office for three hours.

I have always *sat* in the last desk.

To Set

Tony *sets* out the knives, forks, and spoons.

His sister already *set* out the dishes.

They have just *set* out the dinner-ware.

Practice

Underline the correct form of the verb. Use a form of *sit* if you can substitute *rest*. Use a form of *set* if you can substitute *place*.

1. When I'm on a bus, I like (sitting, setting) in front.
2. The movers have (sat, set) all the smaller boxes on the kitchen table.
3. The aircraft carrier (sat, set) five miles offshore as helicopters shuttled back and forth to the island.
4. (Sit, Set) the plant on the windowsill so it will get the morning sun.
5. The boys practiced hunting by (sitting, setting) empty cans along the fence and shooting at them with BB guns.

Rise-Raise

The principal parts of *rise* and *raise* are as follows:

Present	Past	Past Participle
rise	rose	risen
raise	raised	raised

To rise means *to get up* or *to move up*. *To raise* (which is a regular verb with simple *-ed* endings) means *to lift up* or *to increase in amount*.

To Rise	*To Raise*
The soldiers *rise* at dawn.	I'm going to *raise* the stakes in the card game.
The crowd *rose* to applaud the batter.	I *raised* the shades to let in the sun.
Dracula has *risen* from the grave.	I would have quit if the company had not *raised* my salary.

Practice

Underline the correct verb. Use a form of *rise* if you can substitute *get up* or *move up*. Use a form of *raise* if you can substitute *lift up* or *increase*.

1. It is usually warmer upstairs because heat (rises, raises).
2. The new owner (rose, raised) the rent, so now I will have to look for another apartment.
3. We (rose, raised) at three o'clock in the morning to watch the meteor shower.
4. After four days of rain, the river had (risen, raised) over its banks and threatened to flood the highway.
5. A single sailboat made them (rise, raise) the drawbridge, stopping traffic in both directions for fifteen minutes.

✺ Review Test 1

Cross out the incorrect verb form. Then write the correct form of the verb in the space provided.

_____ 1. The spare key under the mat falled through a crack in the porch floor.

_____ 2. When he blowed out the dozens of candles on his cake, the old man used a hair dryer.

_____ 3. At the beauty shop, I heared a woman talking about me in the next booth.

_____ 4. Jim said he could have swam ten more laps if he hadn't gotten leg cramps.

_____ 5. After you have broke up with a boyfriend or girlfriend, it feels like every day is a cloudy and cold Monday morning.

_____ 6. People looked away from the homeless man who was laying on the sidewalk.

_____ 7. You should have saw Ann's face when she passed her driving test.

_____ 8. After I lended Dave money, I remembered he seldom pays people back.

_____ 9. There have been times I have awoke at night and not known where I was.

_____ 10. The health inspector come into the kitchen as the cook picked up a hamburger from the floor.

✺ Review Test 2

Write short sentences using the form noted for the following irregular verbs.

Example Past of _ride_ _The Lone Ranger rode into the sunset._

1. Present of _shake_ _____

2. Past participle of _write_ _____

3. Past participle of _begin_ _____

4. Past of _go_ _____

5. Past participle of _grow_ _____

6. Present of _speak_ _____

7. Past of _bring_ _____

8. Present of _do_ _____

9. Past participle of _give_ _____

10. Past of _drink_ _____

Subject-Verb Agreement

INTRODUCTORY PROJECT

As you read each pair of sentences below, place a check mark beside the sentence that you think uses the underlined word correctly.

There <u>was</u> many applicants for the position. _____

There <u>were</u> many applicants for the position. _____

The pictures in that magazine <u>is</u> very controversial. _____

The pictures in that magazine <u>are</u> very controversial. _____

Everybody usually <u>watch</u> the lighted numbers while riding in the elevator.

_____

Everybody usually <u>watches</u> the lighted numbers while riding in the elevator.

_____

On the basis of the above examples, see if you can complete the following statements.

1. In the first two pairs of sentences, the subjects are _____ and _____. Since both these subjects are plural, the verb must be plural.

2. In the last pair of sentences, the subject, *Everybody,* is a word that is always (singular, plural), and so that verb must be (singular, plural).

Answers are on page 461.

A verb must agree with its subject in number. A *singular subject* (one person or thing) takes a singular verb. A *plural subject* (more than one person or thing) takes a plural verb. Mistakes in subject-verb agreement are sometimes made in the following situations:

1   When words come between the subject and the verb
2   When a verb comes before the subject
3   With indefinite pronouns
4   With compound subjects
5   With *who, which,* and *that*

Each situation is explained on the following pages.

WORDS BETWEEN THE SUBJECT AND THE VERB

Words that come between the subject and the verb do not change subject-verb agreement. In the following sentence,

The breakfast cereals in the pantry are made mostly of sugar.

the subject (*cereals*) is plural and so the verb (*are*) is plural. The words *in the pantry* that come between the subject and the verb do not affect subject-verb agreement. To help find the subject of certain sentences, you should cross out prepositional phrases (explained on page 13):

One ~~of the crooked politicians~~ was jailed for a month.
The posters ~~on my little brother's wall~~ included rock singers, monsters, and blonde television stars.

Following is a list of common prepositions.

about	before	by	inside	over
above	behind	during	into	through
across	below	except	of	to
among	beneath	for	off	toward
around	beside	from	on	under
at	between	in	onto	with

Practice

Draw one line under the subject. Then lightly cross out any words that come between the subject and the verb. Finally, draw two lines under the correct verb in parentheses.

Example The price of the stereo speakers (is, are) too high for my wallet.

1. A trail of bloodstains (leads, lead) to the spot where the murder was committed.
2. The winter clothes in the hall closet (takes, take) up too much room.
3. A basket of fancy fruits and nuts (was, were) delivered to my house.
4. Floating logs in the river from the recent storm (poses, pose) a threat to navigation.
5. The heated air from the registers in the bedroom (dries, dry) up my throat during the night.
6. Workers at that automobile plant (begins, begin) each day with a period of exercise.
7. The earliest date on any of the cemetery gravestones (appears, appear) to be 1804.
8. I tug and pull, but the line of supermarket carts (seems, seem) welded together.
9. The garbled instructions for assembling the bicycle (was, were) almost impossible to follow.
10. Sleeping bags with the new synthetic insulation material (protects, protect) campers even in subzero temperatures.

VERB BEFORE THE SUBJECT

A verb agrees with its subject even when the verb comes *before* the subject. Words that may precede the subject include *there, here,* and, in questions, *who, which, what,* and *where.*

Inside the storage shed are the garden tools.
At the street corner were two panhandlers.
There are times I'm ready to quit my job.
Where are the instructions for the microwave oven?

If you are unsure about the subject, ask *who* or *what* of the verb. With the first sentence above, you might ask, "What are inside the storage shed?" The answer, garden *tools,* is the subject.

Practice

Draw one line under the subject. Then draw two lines under the correct verb in parentheses.

1. There (is, are) a scratching noise coming from behind this wall.
2. On the bottom of the jar of preserves (is, are) the berries.
3. Floating near the base of the dock (was, were) several discarded aluminum cans.
4. In the middle of the woods behind our home (sits, sit) an abandoned cabin.
5. There (was, were) so many students talking at once that the teacher shouted for quiet.
6. Outside the novelty shop at the mall (stands, stand) a life-size cutout of W.C. Fields.
7. Coming out of the fog toward the frightened boys (was, were) the menacing shape of a large dog.
8. In the rear of the closet (was, were) the basketball sneakers that I thought I had lost.
9. On the table in the doctor's office (is, are) some magazines that are five years old.
10. Lining one wall of the gym (was, were) a row of lockers for the team members.

INDEFINITE PRONOUNS

The following words, known as *indefinite pronouns,* always take singular verbs:

(*-one* words)	(*-body* words)	(*-thing* words)	
one	nobody	nothing	each
anyone	anybody	anything	either
everyone	everybody	everything	neither
someone	somebody	something	

Note: *Both* always takes a plural verb.

Practice

Write the correct form of the verb in the space provided.

keeps,
keep

1. Something always _____ me from getting to bed on time.

brags,
brag

2. Nobody I know _____ as much as Ernest.

pays,
pay

3. Neither of the jobs offered to me _____ more than four dollars an hour.

has, have

4. Both of the speakers _____ told us more than we care to know about the dangers of water pollution.

slips, slip

5. Someone in Inez's apartment house _____ an unsigned valentine under her door every year.

leans,
lean

6. Anything sitting on the old wooden floor _____ to one side.

expects,
expect

7. Each of my friends _____ to be invited to my new backyard pool.

was, were

8. Not one of the five starters _____ in the basketball game at the end.

stops, stop

9. Only one of all the brands of waxes _____ the rust on my car from spreading.

has, have

10. Just about everybody who hates getting up early for work _____ jumped out of bed at 6 A.M. to go on vacation.

COMPOUND SUBJECTS

Subjects joined by *and* generally take a plural verb.

> <u>Yoga</u> and <u>biking</u> <u>are</u> Lola's ways of staying in shape.
> <u>Ambition</u> and <u>good luck</u> <u>are</u> the keys to his success.

When subjects are joined by *either . . . or, neither . . . nor, not only . . . but also,* the verb agrees with the subject closer to the verb.

> Either the <u>restaurant manager</u> or his <u>assistants</u> <u>deserve</u> to be fired for the spoiled meat used in the stew.

The nearer subject, *assistants,* is plural, and so the verb is plural.

Practice

Write the correct form of the verb in the space provided.

saddens,
sadden

1. The shivering and crying of animals in pet stores _____ me very much.

belongs,
belong

2. The cooking utensils and dishes in the kitchen _____ to the landlord.

has, have

3. Her best friend and her coach _____ more influence on Sally than her parents.

continues,
continue

4. Crabgrass and dandelions _____ to spread across the lawn despite my efforts to wipe them out.

tears,
tear

5. Either the neighborhood kids or an automatic car-wash machine always _____ the antenna off my car.

WHO, WHICH, AND THAT

When *who, which,* and *that* are used as subjects, they take singular verbs if the word they stand for is singular and plural verbs if the word they stand for is plural. For example, in the sentence

Gary is one of those people <u>who</u> <u>are</u> very private.

the verb is plural because *who* stands for *people,* which is plural. On the other hand, in the sentence

Gary is a person <u>who</u> <u>is</u> very private.

the verb is singular because *who* stands for *person,* which is singular.

Practice

Write the correct form of the verb in the space provided.

has, have

1. The man who _____ volunteered to give blood just turned pale at the sight of the needle.

goes, go

2. The jacket that _____ with those pants is at the cleaners.

becomes,
become

3. Women who _____ police officers often have to prove themselves more capable than the men they work with.

looks, look 4. The museum has some paintings that _____ like the scribbling of schoolchildren.

is, are 5. The ceiling in Kevin's bedroom is covered with stars which _____ in the shape of the constellations.

⊘ Review Test 1

In the following sentences, underline the subject. Then complete each sentence using *is, are, was, were, have,* or *has.*

Example The <u>hot dogs</u> in that luncheonette *are hazardous to your health.*

1. In my glove compartment _____

2. The instructor and his favorite student _____
_____

3. I frequently see people who _____

4. Neither of the wrestlers _____

5. Scattered across the parking lot _____

6. The dust balls under my bed _____

7. There are _____

8. My friend and his brother _____

9. The newspapers that accumulate in my garage _____
_____

10. It was one of those movies that _____
_____

⊘ Review Test 2

Draw one line under the subject. Then draw two lines under the correct verb in parentheses.

1. The socks from the dryer (crackles, crackle) as I try to roll them into balls.
2. Nobody (walks, walk) on the streets of this neighborhood at night.
3. Phil is one of those people who (gets, get) on everybody's nerves.
4. A talking computerized car and several stunt people (was, were) the true stars of the movie.

5. There (is, are) billboards all along the road warning drivers to stay sober.

6. A paper plate fitted over the dog's head (prevents, prevent) the animal from biting its stitches.

7. Since I gained weight, neither my old suits nor my new shirt (fits, fit) me.

8. What (does, do) my marital status have to do with my qualifications for the job?

9. Sitting silently off in the distance in the bright moonlight (was, were) the wolf and his mate.

10. Neither the coach nor the quarterback (was, were) available to talk to the press after the game.

Review Test 3

There are ten mistakes in subject-verb agreement in the following passage. Cross out each incorrect verb and write the correct form above it. In addition, underline the subject of each of the verbs that must be changed.

After more than twenty years on television, there is few honors that *Sesame Street* has not won. The awards are deserved, for *Sesame Street* is one of the few shows on television which treats children with respect. Most children's programs consists of cheaply made cartoons that is based on the adventures of a superhero or a video-game character. Unfortunately, children's TV programs are generally so poor because quality kids' shows does not make the profits which the networks demand. Both the superhero story and the video-game story is easy to slap together. By contrast, the producers of *Sesame Street* spends enormous amounts of time and money researching how children learn. Another reason for the low profits are the nature of the audience. Because children have little money to spend on sponsors' products, each of the networks charge bottom rates for advertising during children's programs. *Sesame Street*, a nonprofit show, does not even accept ads. And income from the sale of *Sesame Street* products are used to do an even better job of producing the show.

Consi
Verb

two mistakes in verb tense in the following sel...

When Stereo Warehouse had a sale, Alex decided to buy a videocassette recorder. He thought he would plug the machine right in and start taping his favorite shows. When he arrived home, however, Alex discovers that hooking up a VCR could be complicated and confusing. The directions sounded as if they had been written for electrical engineers. After two hours of frustration, Alex gave up and calls a TV repair shop for help.

Now try to complete the following statement:

Verb tenses should be consistent. In the above selection, two verbs have to be changed because they are mistakenly in the (present, past) tense while all the other verbs in the selection are in the (present, past) tense.

Answers are on page 461.

KEEPING TENSES CONSISTENT

Do not shift tenses unnecessarily. If you begin writing a paper in the present tense, don't shift suddenly to the past. If you begin in the past, don't shift without reason to the present. Notice the inconsistent verb tenses in the following selection:

> Smoke <u>spilled</u> from the front of the overheated car. The driver <u>opens</u> up the hood, then <u>jumped</u> back as steam <u>billows</u> out.

The verbs must be consistently in the present tense:

> Smoke <u>spills</u> from the front of the overheated car. The driver <u>opens</u> up the hood, then <u>jumps</u> back as steam <u>billows</u> out.

Or the verbs must be consistently in the past tense:

> Smoke <u>spilled</u> from the front of the overheated car. The driver <u>opened</u> up the hood, then <u>jumped</u> back as steam <u>billowed</u> out.

Practice

In each selection one verb must be changed so that it agrees in tense with the other verbs. Cross out the incorrect verb and write the correct form in the space at the left.

looked   **Example**   I gave away my striped sweater after three people told me I ~~look~~ like a giant bee.

_____   1. I gasped and then shrieks when I discovered a dead mouse in the toe of my galoshes.

_____   2. The old woman looked delicate, but she ran quickly toward the bus and jumps onto the step.

_____   3. On vacation, I couldn't face another restaurant meal, so I purchase cheese and crackers and ate in my room.

_____   4. Before the rain stopped, mud slid down the hill and crashes into the houses in the valley.

_____   5. When my little brother found my new box of markers, he snatches one and made green circles all over our front steps.

_____   6. The basement looked as if it hadn't been cleaned in years. Dust cover everything, and the smell of mildew hung in the air.

————————   7. The outfielder tumbled, made a spectacular catch, and lifts the ball up for the umpire to witness.

————————   8. Annie talks aloud to her favorite soap opera character; she argued and fights with the woman over her decisions.

————————   9. At the pie-eating contest, Leo stuffed in the last piece of blueberry pie, swallows it all, and then flashed a purple grin for the photographer.

————————   10. The supermarket seemed empty on Sunday morning; shopping carts stood in long lines, bakery shelves were bare, and the lights over the meat counter glow dimly.

Review Test 1

Change verbs where needed in the following selection so that they are consistently in the past tense. Cross out each incorrect verb and write the correct form above it, as shown in the example. You will need to make ten corrections.

lived

[1]Years ago, I ~~live~~ in an old apartment house where I got little peace and quiet. [2]For one thing, I could hear the constant fights that went on in the adjoining apartment. [3]The husband yells about killing his wife, and she screamed right back about leaving him or having him arrested. [4]In addition, the people in the apartment above me have four noisy kids. [5]Sometimes it seem like a football game was going on upstairs. [6]The noise reach a high point when I got home from work, which also happened to be the time the kids return from school. [7]If the kids and neighbors were not disturbing me, I always had one other person to depend on—the superintendent, who visits my apartment whenever he felt like it. [8]He always had an excuse, such as checking the water pipes or caulking the windows. [9]But each time he came, I suspect he just wants to get away from his noisy family, which occupied the basement apartment. [10]I move out of that apartment as soon as I could afford to.

Review Test 2

Change verbs where needed in the following selection so that they are consistently in the past tense. Cross out each incorrect verb and write the correct form above it. You will need to make ten corrections in all.

[1]As a kid, I never really enjoyed the public swimming pool. [2]First, there were all sorts of rules that prevent me from having as much fun in the water as possible. [3]One was that children under the age of fourteen had to be accompanied by an adult. [4]I didn't like having to beg a parent or a neighbor to take me swimming every time I want to go. [5]Another rule was that girls are not allowed in the water without bathing caps. [6]The required bathing cap was so tight that it cause a heavy press mark on my forehead. [7]Also, it often gives me a headache. [8]Second, I wasn't a very good swimmer then. [9]Most of the time I find myself hanging on to the side of the pool. [10]And whenever I attempted a graceful dive, I end up doing a belly flop. [11]Finally, many of the kids tease me. [12]Some of them liked splashing water into my face, which force me to swallow chlorine and a dead bug or two. [13]Even worse was the boy who sneak up behind me all summer long to dump ice cubes in the back of my swimsuit.

Additional Information about Verbs

The purpose of this special chapter is to provide additional information about verbs. Some people will find the grammar terms here a helpful reminder of earlier school learning about verbs. For them, the terms will increase their understanding of how verbs function in English. Other people may welcome more detailed information about terms used elsewhere in the text. In either case, remember that the most common mistakes that people make when writing verbs have been treated in earlier sections of the book.

VERB TENSE

Verbs tell us the time of an action. The time that a verb shows is usually called *tense*. The most common tenses are the simple present, past, and future. In addition, there are nine other tenses that enable us to express more specific ideas about time than we could with the simple tenses alone. Shown on the next page are the twelve verb tenses and examples of each tense. Read them over to increase your sense of the many different ways of expressing time in English.

Tenses	Examples
Present	I *work*. Jill *works*.
Past	Howard *worked* on the lawn.
Future	You *will work* overtime this week.
Present perfect	Gail *has worked* hard on the puzzle. They *have worked* well together.
Past perfect	They *had finished* the work before their shift ended.
Future perfect	The volunteers *will have worked* many unpaid hours.
Present progressive	I *am* not *working* today. You *are working* the second shift. The clothes dryer *is* not *working* properly.
Past progressive	She *was working* outside. The plumbers *were working* here this morning.
Future progressive	The sound system *will be working* by tonight.
Present perfect progressive	Married life *has* not *been working* out for that couple.
Past perfect progressive	I *had been working* overtime until recently.
Future perfect progressive	My sister *will have been working* at that store for eleven straight months by the time she takes a vacation next week.

The perfect tenses are formed by adding *have, has,* or *had* to the past participle (the form of the verb that ends, usually, in *-ed*). The progressive tenses are formed by adding *am, is, are, was,* or *were* to the present participle (the form of the verb that ends in *-ing*). The perfect progressive tenses are formed by adding *have, has,* or *had* plus *been* to the present participle.

Certain tenses are explained in more detail on the following pages.

Present Perfect
(*have* or *has* + past participle)

The present perfect tense expresses an action that began in the past and has recently been completed or is continuing in the present.

The city has just agreed on a contract with the sanitation workers.

Tony's parents have lived in that house for twenty years.

Lola has watched *Star Trek* reruns since she was a little girl.

Past Perfect
(*had* + past participle)

The past perfect tense expresses a past action that was completed before another past action.

Lola had learned to dance by the time she was five.

The class had just started when the fire bell rang.

Bad weather had never been a problem on our vacations until last year.

Present Progressive
(*am, is,* or *are* + the *-ing* form)

The present progressive tense expresses an action still in progress.

I am taking an early train into the city every day this week.

Karl is playing softball over at the field.

The vegetables are growing rapidly.

Past Progressive
(*was* or *were* + the *-ing* form)

The past progressive expresses an action that was in progress in the past.

I was spending twenty dollars a week on cigarettes before I quit.

Last week, the store was selling many items at half price.

My friends were driving over to pick me up when the accident occurred.

Practice

For the sentences that follow, fill in the present or past perfect or the present or past progressive of the verb shown. Use the tense that seems to express the meaning of each sentence best.

> **Example**   park   This summer, Mickey _____*is parking*_____ cars at a French restaurant.

dry
1. The afternoon sun was so hot it _____ our jeans in less than an hour.

plan
2. My parents _____ a trip to the seashore until they heard about the sharks.

grow
3. This year, Aunt Anita _____ tomatoes; she must have two hundred already.

throw
4. The pitcher _____ the ball to second; unfortunately, the runner was on third.

carve
5. Everyone at the dinner table continued to complain about the way Henry _____ the Thanksgiving turkey.

open
6. The excited child _____ all her birthday presents before her father could load his camera.

care
7. Erica answered a baby-sitter ad and now _____ for three children, two dogs, and twenty houseplants.

watch
8. Helen is a television athlete; she _____ almost every football and baseball game televised this year.

crack
9. The shelf over the washer and dryer _____ because of all the heavy cookbooks Rita stacked on it.

try
10. Last winter my brothers _____ to get a job bagging groceries at the supermarket.

VERBALS

Verbals are words formed from verbs. Verbals, like verbs, often express action. They can add variety to your sentences and vigor to your writing style. The three kinds of verbals are *infinitives*, *participles*, and *gerunds*.

Infinitive

An infinitive is *to* plus the base form of the verb.

I started *to practice*.
Don't try *to lift* that table.
I asked Russ *to drive* me home.

Participle

A participle is a verb form used as an adjective (a descriptive word). The present participle ends in *-ing*. The past participle ends in *-ed* or has an irregular ending.

Favoring his *cramped* leg, the *screaming* boy waded out of the pool.
The *laughing* child held up her *locked* piggy bank.
Using a shovel and a bucket, I scooped water out of the *flooded* basement.

Gerund

A gerund is the *-ing* form of a verb used as a noun.

Studying wears me out.
Playing basketball is my main pleasure during the week.
Through *jogging*, you can get yourself in shape.

Practice

In the space beside each sentence, identify the italicized word as a participle (*P*), an infinitive (*I*), or a gerund (*G*).

_____   1. Carmen preferred the *reclining* chair for his bad back.

_____   2. Doctors believe that *walking* is one of the most beneficial forms of exercise.

_____   3. The quiet night and bright campfire inspired us *to tell* ghost stories.

_____   4. It isn't *flying* that makes Elsa anxious but the airline food.

_____   5. *Scratching* its back against a tree, the bear looked deceptively harmless.

_____   6. *To make* the room more cheerful, Alice painted the dark cabinets yellow.

_____   7. *Observing* gorillas' mating behavior is part of that zookeeper's job.

_____   8. During the movie, Bert continued *to crunch* loudly on his popcorn.

_____   9. My brother's *receding* hairline makes him look older than he really is.

_____   10. In the drainage ditch, the boys found a wooden crate *containing* dozens of spiders.

ACTIVE AND PASSIVE VERBS

When the subject of a sentence performs the action of a verb, the verb is in the *active voice*. When the subject of a sentence receives the action of a verb, the verb is in the *passive voice*.

The passive form of a verb consists of a form of the verb *be* plus the past participle of the main verb. Look at the active and passive forms of the verbs below.

Active	*Passive*
Lola *ate* the vanilla pudding. (The subject, *Lola*, is the doer of the action.)	The vanilla pudding *was eaten by* Lola. (The subject, *pudding*, does not act. Instead, something happens to it.)
The plumber *replaced* the hot water heater. (The subject, *plumber*, is the doer of the action.)	The hot water heater *was replaced by* the plumber. (The subject, *heater*, does not act. Instead, something happens to it.)

In general, active verbs are more effective than passive ones. Active verbs give your writing a simpler and more vigorous style. The passive form of verbs is appropriate, however, when the performer of the action is unknown or is less important than the receiver of the action. For example:

My house was vandalized last night.
(The performer of the action is unknown.)
Mark was seriously injured as a result of your negligence.
(The receiver of the action, *Mark*, is being emphasized.)

Practice

Change the sentences on the next page from the passive to the active voice. Note that you may have to add a subject in some cases.

Examples   The moped bicycle was ridden by Tony.
Tony rode the moped bicycle.

The basketball team was given a standing ovation.
The crowd gave the basketball team a standing ovation.

(Here a subject had to be added.)

1. The bus was boarded by a man with a live parrot on his shoulder.

   _____

2. The stained-glass window was broken by a large falling branch.

   _____

3. Baseballs for hospitalized children were autographed by the entire team.

   _____

4. The hotel was destroyed by a fire that started with a cigarette.

   _____

5. The pressures of dealing with life and death must be faced by doctors.

   _____

6. The missile was directed to its target by a sophisticated laser system.

   _____

7. The kitchen shelves were covered by a thick layer of yellowish grease.

   _____

8. All the wrapping paper was stuffed into the wastebasket by the compulsively
   neat child.

   _____

9. Most of the escaped convicts were captured within a mile of the jail by the
   state police.

   _____

10. Prizes were awarded by the judges for hog-calling and stone-skipping.

    _____

Review Test

On separate paper, write three sentences for each of the following forms:

1. Present perfect tense
2. Past perfect tense
3. Present progressive tense
4. Past progressive tense
5. Infinitive
6. Participle
7. Gerund
8. Passive voice (when the performer of the action is unknown or is less
   important than the receiver of an action—see page 86)

Misplaced Modifiers

INTRODUCTORY PROJECT

Because of misplaced words, each of the sentences below has more than one possible meaning. In each case, see if you can explain both the intended meaning and the unintended meaning. Also, circle the words that you think create the confusion because they are misplaced.

1. The farmers sprayed the apple trees wearing masks.

   Intended meaning: _____

   Unintended meaning: _____

2. The woman reached out for the faith healer who had a terminal disease.

   Intended meaning: _____

   Unintended meaning: _____

Answers are on page 462.

WHAT MISPLACED MODIFIERS ARE
AND HOW TO CORRECT THEM

Misplaced modifiers are words that, because of awkward placement, do not describe the words the writer intended them to describe. Misplaced modifiers often confuse the meaning of a sentence. To avoid them, place words as close as possible to what they describe.

Misplaced Words	*Correctly Placed Words*
They could see the Goodyear blimp *sitting on the front lawn*. (The Goodyear blimp was sitting on the front lawn?)	Sitting on the front lawn, they could see the Goodyear blimp. (The intended meaning—that the Goodyear blimp was visible from the front lawn—is now clear.)
We had a hamburger after the movie, *which was too greasy for my taste*. (The *movie* was too greasy for your taste?)	After the movie, we had a hamburger, which was too greasy for my taste. (The intended meaning—that the hamburger was greasy—is now clear.)
Our phone *almost* rang fifteen times last night. (The phone almost rang fifteen times, but in fact did not ring at all?)	Our phone rang almost fifteen times last night. (The intended meaning—that the phone rang a little under fifteen times—is now clear.)

Other single-word modifiers to watch out for include *only, even, hardly, nearly,* and *often.* Such words should be placed immediately before the word they modify.

Practice 1

Underline the misplaced word or words in each sentence. Then rewrite the sentence, placing related words together and thereby making the meaning clear.

Example   Anita returned the hamburger to the supermarket that was spoiled.
Anita returned the hamburger that was spoiled to the

supermarket.

1. The tiger growled at a passerby at the back of his cage.

   _____

   _____

2. Arthur spilled a full bottle on the table of soda.

   _____

   _____

3. We watched the fireworks standing on our front porch.

   _____

   _____

4. Jason almost has two hundred baseball cards.

   _____

   _____

5. The salesclerk exchanged the blue sweater for a yellow one with a smile.

   _____

   _____

6. Jenny kept staring at the man in the front row with curly hair.

   _____

   _____

7. I love the cookies from the bakery with the chocolate frosting.

   _____

   _____

8. The faculty decided to strike during their last meeting.

   _____

   _____

9. Larry looked on as his car burned with disbelief.

   _____

   _____

10. My cousin sent me instructions on how to get to her house in a letter.

    _____

    _____

Practice 2

Rewrite each sentence, adding the *italicized* words. Make sure that the intended meaning is clear and that two different interpretations are not possible.

Example   I borrowed a pen for the essay test. (Insert *that ran out of ink.*)
For the essay test, I borrowed a pen that ran out of ink.

1. I was thrilled to read that my first niece was born. (Insert *in a telegram.*)

   _____

   _____

2. My father agreed to pay for the car repairs. (Insert *over the phone.*)

   _____

   _____

3. I found a note on the kitchen bulletin board. (Insert *from Jeff.*)

   _____

   _____

4. The children ate the whole bag of cookies. (Insert *almost.*)

   _____

   _____

5. Jon read about how the American Revolution began. (Insert *during class.*)

   _____

   _____

Review Test 1

Place an *M* for *misplaced* or a *C* for *correct* in front of each sentence.

_____   1. I keep a dollar under the car seat for emergencies.

_____   2. I keep a dollar for emergencies under the car seat.

_____   3. This morning, I planned my day in the shower.

_____   4. In the shower this morning, I planned my day.

_____   5. While roller-skating, Ben ran over a dog's tail.

_____   6. Ben ran over a dog's tail roller-skating.

_____   7. I could hear my neighbors screaming at each other through the apartment wall.

_____ 8. Through the apartment wall, I could hear my neighbors screaming at each other.

_____ 9. For our anniversary, my husband gave me a scarf, which I exchanged for another scarf.

_____ 10. My husband gave me a scarf for our anniversary, which I exchanged for another scarf.

_____ 11. Roger visited the old house, still weak with the flu.

_____ 12. Roger, still weak with the flu, visited the old house.

_____ 13. While still weak with the flu, Roger visited the old house.

_____ 14. My teenage son nearly grew three inches last year.

_____ 15. My teenage son grew nearly three inches last year.

_____ 16. The teacher explained how to study for the final exam at the end of her lecture.

_____ 17. The teacher explained how to study at the end of her lecture for the final exam.

_____ 18. At the end of her lecture, the teacher explained how to study for the final exam.

_____ 19. On the radio, we heard that a volcano erupted this morning.

_____ 20. We heard that a volcano erupted on the radio this morning.

Review Test 2

Underline and then correct the five misplaced modifiers in the following passage.

¹The young teenagers who almost hang out in our town library every night are becoming a major nuisance. ²They show up every weeknight and infuriate the otherwise mild librarians throwing spitballs and paper airplanes. ³Some of the kids hide out behind stacks of bookcases; others indulge in continual adolescent flirting games. ⁴The noise many of these teenagers make is especially offensive to some of the older library patrons, who often give looks to the clusters of young people that are disapproving. ⁵One time there was so much noise that a librarian lost her temper and yelled at some boys to be quiet or leave the library at the top of her lungs. ⁶The worst recent offense took place when a soaking-wet dog was led into the middle of the library by a junior high school boy with a stubby tail and the meanest-looking face one could ever imagine.

Dangling Modifiers

INTRODUCTORY PROJECT

Because of dangling words, each of the sentences below has more than one possible meaning. In each case, see if you can explain both the intended meaning and the unintended meaning.

1. Munching leaves from a tall tree, the children were fascinated by the eighteen-foot-tall giraffe.

   Intended meaning: _____

   Unintended meaning: _____

2. Arriving home after ten months in the service, the neighbors threw a block party for Michael.

   Intended meaning: _____

   Unintended meaning: _____

Answers are on pages 462–463.

WHAT DANGLING MODIFIERS ARE AND HOW TO CORRECT THEM

A modifier that opens a sentence must be followed immediately by the word it is meant to describe. Otherwise, the modifier is said to be *dangling*, and the sentence takes on an unintended meaning. For example, in the sentence

While sleeping in his backyard, a Frisbee hit Bill on the head.

the unintended meaning is that the *Frisbee* was sleeping in his backyard. What the writer meant, of course, was that *Bill* was sleeping in his backyard. The writer should have placed *Bill* right after the modifier:

While sleeping in his backyard, *Bill* was hit on the head by a Frisbee.

The sentence could also be corrected by placing the subject within the opening word group:

While *Bill* was sleeping in his backyard, a Frisbee hit him on the head.

Other sentences with dangling modifiers follow. Read the explanations of why they are dangling and look carefully at the ways they are corrected.

Dangling	*Correct*
Having almost no money, my survival depended on my parents. (*Who* has almost no money? The answer is not *survival* but *I*. The subject *I* must be added.)	Having almost no money, *I* depended on my parents for survival. *Or:* Since *I* had almost no money, I depended on my parents for survival.
Riding his bike, a German shepherd bit Tony's ankle. (*Who* is riding the bike? The answer is not *German shepherd*, as it unintentionally seems to be, but *Tony*. The subject *Tony* must be added.)	Riding his bike, *Tony* was bitten on the ankle by a German shepherd. *Or:* While *Tony* was riding his bike, a German shepherd bit him on the ankle.
When trying to lose weight, all snacks are best avoided. (*Who* is trying to lose weight? The answer is not *snacks* but *you*. The subject *you* must be added.)	When trying to lose weight, *you* should avoid all snacks. *Or:* When *you* are trying to lose weight, avoid all snacks.

These examples make clear two ways of correcting a dangling modifier. Decide on a logical subject and do one of the following:

1 Place the subject *within* the opening word group:

Since *I* had almost no money, I depended on my parents for survival.

Note: In some cases an appropriate subordinating word such as *since* must be added, and the verb may have to be changed slightly as well.

2 Place the subject right *after* the opening word group:

Having almost no money, *I* depended on my parents for survival.

Sometimes even more rewriting is necessary to correct a dangling modifier. What is important to remember is that a modifier must be placed as close as possible to the word that it modifies.

Practice 1

Rewrite each sentence to correct the dangling modifier. Mark the one sentence that is correct with a *C*.

  1. Having turned sour, I would not drink the milk.

  _____

  _____

  2. At the age of five, my mother bought me a chemistry set.

  _____

  _____

  3. While it was raining, shoppers ran into the stores.

  _____

  _____

  4. Having brake trouble, I drove my car slowly.

  _____

  _____

5. Talking on the phone, my hot tea turned cold.

_____

_____

6. Piled high with dirty dishes, Pete hated to look at the kitchen sink.

_____

_____

7. Having locked my keys in the car, the police had to open it for me.

_____

_____

8. Because they were drooping, the children watered the plants.

_____

_____

9. After sitting through a long lecture, my foot was asleep.

_____

_____

10. Being late, stopping for coffee was out of the question.

_____

_____

Practice 2

Complete the following sentences. In each case, a logical subject should follow
the opening words.

Example   Checking the oil stick, _I saw that my car was a quart low._

1. While taking a bath, _____

2. Before starting the car, _____

3. Frightened by the noise in the basement, _____

4. Realizing it was late, _____

5. Though very expensive, _____

○ Review Test 1

Place a *D* for *dangling* or a *C* for *correct* in front of each sentence. Remember that the opening words are a dangling modifier if they are not followed immediately by a logical subject.

————— 1. Burning quickly, the fire fighters turned several hoses on the house.

————— 2. Because it was burning quickly, the fire fighters turned several hoses on the house.

————— 3. While focusing the camera, several people wandered out of view.

————— 4. While I focused the camera, several people wandered out of view.

————— 5. When I peered down from the thirtieth floor, the cars looked like toys.

————— 6. When peering down from the thirtieth floor, the cars looked like toys.

————— 7. Suddenly sick, I drove Helen to the doctor's office.

————— 8. When Helen suddenly became sick, I drove her to the doctor's office.

————— 9. Thundering loudly, the dog trembled.

————— 10. As it thundered loudly, the dog trembled.

————— 11. In a sentimental frame of mind, the music brought tears to Beth's eyes.

————— 12. As Beth was in a sentimental frame of mind, the music brought tears to her eyes.

————— 13. Knowing Phil preferred pizza, our choice of restaurant was Italian.

————— 14. Knowing Phil preferred pizza, we chose an Italian restaurant.

————— 15. Because Phil preferred pizza, our choice of restaurant was Italian.

————— 16. The pancake was browned on one side, so Mark flipped it over.

————— 17. Browned on one side, Mark flipped the pancake over.

————— 18. Hanging by her teeth, the acrobat's body swung back and forth.

————— 19. Hanging by her teeth, the acrobat swung back and forth.

————— 20. As she hung by her teeth, the acrobat's body swung back and forth.

Review Test 2

Underline and then (using your own paper) correct the five dangling modifiers in the passage.

¹Have you ever thought about what life was like for the first generation of your family to come to America? ²Or have you wondered what your grandparents did for fun when they were your age? ³Family stories tend to be told for two or three generations and then disappear because no one ever records them. ⁴By using a tape recorder, these stories can be saved for the future. ⁵Here are some hints for conducting interviews with older members of your family. ⁶Thinking hard about what you really want to know, good questions can be prepared in advance. ⁷Try to put the people you interview at ease by reassuring them that you value what they have to say. ⁸Nervous about the tape recorder, stories might not come so easily to them otherwise. ⁹Remember that most people have never been interviewed before. ¹⁰Listening carefully to everything the person says, your interview will be more successful. ¹¹By respecting their feelings, your older relatives will be delighted to talk with you. ¹²The tapes you make will be valued by your family for many years to come.

Faulty Parallelism

INTRODUCTORY PROJECT

Read aloud each pair of sentences below. Put a check mark beside the sentence that reads more smoothly and clearly and sounds more natural.

Pair 1

I use my TV remote control to change channels, to adjust the volume, and for turning the set on and off.

I use my TV remote control to change channels, to adjust the volume, and to turn the set on and off.

Pair 2

One option the employees had was to take a cut in pay; the other was longer hours of work.

One option the employees had was to take a cut in pay; the other was to work longer hours.

Pair 3

The refrigerator has a cracked vegetable drawer, one of the shelves is missing, and a strange freezer smell.

The refrigerator has a cracked vegetable drawer, a missing shelf, and a strange freezer smell.

Answers are on page 463.

PARALLELISM EXPLAINED

Words in a pair or a series should have a parallel structure. By balancing the items in a pair or a series so that they have the same structure, you will make your sentences clearer and easier to read. Notice how the parallel sentences that follow read more smoothly than the nonparallel ones.

Nonparallel (Not Balanced)	*Parallel (Balanced)*
Fran spends her free time reading, listening to music, and she works in the garden.	Fran spends her free time reading, listening to music, and working in the garden. (A balanced series of *-ing* words: *reading, listening, working.*)
After the camping trip I was exhausted, irritable, and wanted to eat.	After the camping trip I was exhausted, irritable, and hungry. (A balanced series of descriptive words: *exhausted, irritable, hungry.*)
My hope for retirement is to be healthy, to live in a comfortable house, and having plenty of money.	My hope for retirement is to be healthy, to live in a comfortable house, and to have plenty of money. (A balanced series of *to* verbs: *to be, to live, to have.*)
Nightly, Fred puts out the trash, checks the locks on the doors, and the burglar alarm is turned on.	Nightly, Fred puts out the trash, checks the locks on the doors, and turns on the burglar alarm. (Balanced verbs and word order: *puts out the trash, checks the locks, turns on the burglar alarm.*)

Balanced sentences are not a skill you need worry about when writing first drafts. But when you rewrite, you should try to put matching words and ideas into matching structures. Such parallelism will improve your writing style.

Practice 1

The unbalanced part of each sentence is italicized. Rewrite this part so that it matches the rest of the sentence.

Example   In the afternoon, I changed two diapers, ironed several shirts, and *was watching* soap operas.   _____ *watched* _____

1. Annie put the coin into the slot machine, pulled its arm, and *was waiting* to strike it rich.

   _____

2. Studying a little each day is more effective than *to cram*.

   _____

3. Many old people fear loneliness, *becoming ill,* and poverty.

   _____

4. When he sleeps, Joseph snores, *mumbling sounds occur,* and rolls a lot.

   _____

5. My pet peeves are screeching chalk, *buses that are late,* and dripping sinks.

   _____

6. As smoke billowed around her, Paula knew her only choices were to jump or *suffocation*.

   _____

7. The principal often pestered students, yelled at teachers, and *was interrupting* classes.

   _____

8. People immigrate to America with hopes of finding freedom, happiness, and *in order to become financially secure*.

   _____

9. Once inside the zoo gates, Julio could hear the lions roaring, *the chirping of many birds,* and the elephants trumpeting.

   _____

10. As a child I had nightmares about a huge monster that came out of a cave, *was breathing fire,* and wanted to barbecue me.

   _____

Practice 2

Complete the following statements. The first two parts of each statement are parallel in form; the part that you add should be parallel in form as well.

Example Three things I like about myself are my sense of humor, my thoughtfulness, and _my self-discipline._ _____

1. Celebrating my birthday means sleeping late, eating a good dinner, and

   _____.

2. Whether to get a tan, to read a book, or _____

   _____ were some of the tougher decisions Chris had to

   make over summer vacation.

3. Despite the salesman's pitch, I could see that his "wonderful" used car had

   thin tires, rusting fenders, and _____

   _____.

4. Trying to realize that it was only a machine, Tina sat down in front of the

   computer, took a deep breath, and _____

   _____.

5. Three qualities I look for in a friend are loyalty, a sense of humor, and

   _____.

Review Test 1

Cross out the unbalanced part of each sentence. Then rewrite the unbalanced part so that it matches the other item or items in the sentence.

Example I enjoy watering the grass and ~~to work~~ in the garden.
   working _____

1. When someone gives you advice, do you listen, laugh, or are you just ignoring it?

   _____

2. After finding our apartment, we signed a lease, made a deposit, and preparations to move in.

_____

3. The little girl came home from school with a tear-streaked face, a black eye, and her shirt was torn.

_____

4. Jackie watched television, was talking on the phone, and studied all at the same time.

_____

5. My Halloween shopping list included one bottle of blue nail polish, fake blood, and a wig that was colored purple.

_____

6. Carmen went to class prepared to take notes, to volunteer answers, and with questions to ask.

_____

7. By getting an early start, taking a shortcut, and because we drove at a constant fifty-five miles per hour, we arrived an hour ahead of time.

_____

8. When I got back from vacation, my refrigerator contained rotting vegetables, milk that was soured, and moldy cheese.

_____

9. The guide demonstrated how colonial Americans made iron tools, crushed grain for flour, and were making their own cloth.

_____

10. When my roommate's rock records blast, I shut her door, put cotton in my ears, and am running the vacuum cleaner.

_____

Review Test 2

On separate paper, write five sentences of your own that use parallel structure. Each sentence should contain three items in a series. Do not use the same format for each sentence.

Review Test 3

There are six nonparallel parts in the following passage. The first is corrected for you as an example; find and correct the other five.

[1]Running, an outstanding form of exercise, can be good for you mentally,

emotionally.

physically, and ~~it can put be good for your emotions~~. [2]A beginning runner should keep three things in mind: the warm-up session, the time you're running, and the cool-down period. [3]Never start a run without first having warmed up through stretching exercises. [4]Stretching before a run reduces muscle stiffness, decreases the possibility of injury, and it's a good method to gradually increase the heart rate. [5]During the run itself, move at a steady and comfortable pace. [6]Your breathing should be deep and with rhythm. [7]Be careful that you don't try to overdo it at first. [8]If you have been inactive for a long period of time, you can't expect to lose weight, to increase heart and lung capacity, and that you'll wind up feeling better all overnight. [9]Finally, remember to cool down after a run. [10]An adequate cool-down period allows time for the body to relax and the normalizing of the heart rate.

Pronoun Reference, Agreement, and Point of View

Pronouns are words that take the place of nouns (persons, places, or things). In fact, the word *pronoun* means *for a noun*. Pronouns are shortcuts that keep you from unnecessarily repeating words in writing. Here are some examples of pronouns:

> Martha shampooed *her* dog. (*Her* is a pronoun that takes the place of *Martha.*)
> As the door swung open, *it* creaked. (*It* replaces *door.*)
> When the motorcyclists arrived at McDonald's, *they* removed *their* helmets. (*They* and *their* replace *motorcyclists.*)

This section presents rules that will help you avoid three common mistakes people make with pronouns. The rules are as follows:

1 A pronoun must refer clearly to the word it replaces.
2 A pronoun must agree in number with the word or words it replaces.
3 Pronouns should not shift unnecessarily in point of view.

PRONOUN REFERENCE

A sentence may be confusing and unclear if a pronoun appears to refer to more than one word, or if the pronoun does not refer to any specific word. Look at this sentence:

> We never buy vegetables at that store, because they charge too much.

Who charges too much? There is no specific word that *they* refers to. Be clear:

> We never buy vegetables at that store, because the owners charge too much.

Here are sentences with other kinds of faulty pronoun reference. Read the explanations of why they are faulty and look carefully at the ways they are corrected.

Faulty	*Clear*
Lola told Gina that she had gained weight.	Lola told Gina, ''You've gained weight.''
(*Who* had gained weight: Lola or Gina? Be clear.)	(Quotation marks, which can sometimes be used to correct an unclear reference, are explained on page 169.)

Faulty	*Clear*
My older brother is an electrician, but I'm not interested in it. (There is no specific word that *it* refers to. It would not make sense to say, "I'm not interested in electrician.")	My older brother is an electrician, but I'm not interested in becoming one.
Our teacher did not explain the assignment, which made me angry. (Does *which* mean that the teacher's failure to explain the assignment made you angry, or that the assignment itself made you angry? Be clear.)	I was angry that the teacher did not explain the assignment.

Practice

Rewrite each of the following sentences to make clear the vague pronoun reference. Add, change, or omit words as necessary.

Example   Lana thanked Rita for the gift, which was very thoughtful of her.
   Lana thanked Rita for the thoughtful gift.

1. The defendant told the judge he was mentally ill.

_____

_____

2. Fran removed the blanket from the sofa bed and folded it up.

_____

_____

3. Before the demonstration, they passed out signs for us to carry.

_____

_____

4. Renni had to keep reminding her aunt that she had a dentist appointment.

_____

_____

5. Because I didn't rinse last night's dishes, it smells like a garbage can.

_____

_____

6. The students watched a film on environmental pollution, which really depressed them.

_____

_____

7. The veterinarian said that if I find a tick on my dog I should get rid of it immediately.

_____

_____

8. My sister removed the curtains from the windows so that she could wash them.

_____

_____

9. Richard said his chiropractor could help my sprained shoulder, but I don't believe in it.

_____

_____

10. I discovered when I went to sell my old textbooks that they've put out new editions, and nobody wants to buy mine.

_____

_____

PRONOUN AGREEMENT

A pronoun must agree in number with the word or words it replaces. If the word a pronoun refers to is singular, the pronoun must be singular; if the word is plural, the pronoun must be plural. (Note that the word a pronoun refers to is known as the *antecedent*.)

Lola agreed to lend me (her) Billy Joel albums.

The gravediggers sipped coffee during (their) break.

In the first example, the pronoun *her* refers to the singular word *Lola;* in the second example, the pronoun *their* refers to the plural word *gravediggers*.

Practice

Write the appropriate pronoun (*they, their, them, it*) in the blank space in each of the following sentences.

Example   My credit cards got me into debt, so I burned _____*them*_____.

1. The two girls in identical dresses were surprised when _____ saw each other at the prom.
2. It annoys me when disc jockeys play _____ favorite songs all the time.
3. I put my photo album in a safe place, and now I can't find _____.
4. I used to collect baseball cards and comic books, but then I gave _____ to my little brother.
5. When the children are watching television, it's impossible to get _____ attention.

Indefinite Pronouns

The following words, known as *indefinite pronouns*, are always singular.

(*-one* words)	(*-body* words)	
one	nobody	each
anyone	anybody	either
everyone	everybody	neither
someone	somebody	

Either of the apartments has its drawbacks.

One of the girls lost her skateboard.

Everyone in the class must hand in his paper tomorrow.

In each example, the pronoun is singular because it refers to one of the indefinite pronouns. There are two important points to remember about indefinite pronouns.

Point 1:   In the last example above, if the job applicants were all female, the pronoun would be *her*. If the students were a mixed group of men and women, the pronoun form would be *his or her:*

Everyone in the class must hand in *his or her* paper tomorrow.

Some writers follow the traditional practice of using *his* to refer to both men and women. Some use *his or her* to avoid an implied sexual bias. Perhaps the best practice, though, is to avoid using either *his* or the somewhat awkward *his or her*. This can be done by rewriting a sentence in the plural:

All students in the class must hand in their papers tomorrow.

Here are some examples of sentences that can be rewritten in the plural.

A young child is seldom willing to share her toys with others.
Young children are seldom willing to share their toys with others.

Anyone who does not wear his seat belt will be fined.
People who do not wear their seat belts will be fined.

A newly elected politician should not forget his or her campaign promises.
Newly elected politicians should not forget their campaign promises.

Point 2:   In informal spoken English, *plural* pronouns are often used with the indefinite pronouns. Instead of saying

Everybody has *his or her* own idea of an ideal vacation.

we are likely to say

Everybody has *their* own idea of an ideal vacation.

Here are other examples:

Everyone in the class must pass in *their* papers.
Everybody in our club has *their* own idea about how to raise money.
No one in our family skips *their* chores.

In such cases, the indefinite pronouns are clearly plural in meaning. Also, the use of such plurals helps people to avoid the awkward *his or her*. In time, the plural pronoun may be accepted in formal speech or writing. Until that happens, however, you should use the grammatically correct singular form in your writing.

Practice

Underline the correct pronoun.

Example Neither of those houses has (<u>its</u>, their) own garage.

1. Neither of the men was aware that (his, their) voice was being taped.
2. One of the waiters was fired for failing to turn over all (his, their) tips.
3. We have three dogs, and each of them has (its, their) own bowl.
4. During the intermission, everyone had to wait a while for (her, their) turn to get into the ladies' room.
5. All the boxes of old clothing need to have labels attached to (it, them).
6. Mr. Alvarez refuses to let anyone ride in his car without using (his or her, their) seat belt.
7. It seems that neither of the mothers is comfortable answering (her, their) teenager's questions about sex.
8. If anybody objects to the new men's-club rules, (he, they) should speak up now.
9. Nobody on the women's basketball team had enough nerve to voice (her, their) complaints to the coach.
10. Before moving into this development, each homeowner must agree in writing to keep (his or her, their) pet on a leash.

PRONOUN POINT OF VIEW

Pronouns should not shift their point of view unnecessarily. When writing a paper, be consistent in your use of first-, second-, or third-person pronouns.

Type of Pronoun	Singular	Plural
First-person pronouns	I (my, mine, me)	we (our, us)
Second-person pronouns	you (your)	you (your)
Third-person pronouns	he (his, him) she (her) it (its)	they (their, them)

Note: Any person, place, or thing, as well as any indefinite pronoun like *one, anyone, someone,* and so on (page 109), is a third-person word.

For instance, if you start writing in the first person *I*, don't jump suddenly to the second person *you*. Or if you are writing in the third person *they*, don't shift unexpectedly to *you*. Look at the examples.

Inconsistent

One reason that *I* like living in the city is that *you* always have a wide choice of sports events to attend. (The most common mistake people make is to let a *you* slip into their writing after they start with another pronoun.)

Someone dieting should have the help of friends; *you* should also have plenty of willpower.

Students who work while *they* are going to school face special problems. For one thing, *you* seldom have enough study time.

Consistent

One reason that *I* like living in the city is that *I* always have a wide choice of sports events to attend.

Someone dieting should have the help of friends; *one* (or *he or she*) should also have plenty of will-power.

Students who work while *they* are going to school face special problems. For one thing, *they* seldom have enough study time.

Practice

Cross out inconsistent pronouns in the following sentences and write the correction above the error.

Example   I work much better when the boss doesn't hover over ~~you~~ with
instructions on what to do.
me

1. A good horror movie makes my bones feel like ice and gets your blood running cold.
2. Many men and women have problems meeting people, especially if you don't go to singles' bars.
3. Even though Tom is careful about his health, you can't prevent an occasional cold.
4. If students attend class regularly and study hard, you should receive a good grade.

5. I like to shop in my hometown because all the store owners know you.

6. Every year we make resolutions to improve, and every year one finds excuses for not carrying them out.

7. Andy enjoys watching soap operas because then you can worry about someone else's problems instead of your own.

8. Our math class is so confusing that you don't even know what to study for the tests.

9. Mrs. Almac enjoys working the three-to-eleven shift because that way you can still have a large part of your day free.

10. All of us at work voted to join the union because we felt it would protect your rights.

Review Test 1

Underline the correct word in the parentheses.

1. Debbie twisted the channel selector on the television so hard that (it, the selector) broke.

2. During the boring movie, people started to squirm in (his or her, their) seats.

3. I love living alone because (you, I) never have to answer to anyone else.

4. Almost all the magazines I subscribe to arrive with (its, their) covers torn.

5. My mother is angry with my sister because (she, my sister) has a drinking problem.

6. I like driving on that turnpike because (they, state officials) don't allow billboards there.

7. Neither one of the umpires wanted to admit that (he, they) had made a mistake.

8. When Ed went to the bank for a home improvement loan, (they, the loan officers) asked him for three credit references.

9. Even if you graduate from that business school, (they, the placement officers) don't guarantee they will find you a job.

10. Not one of the women in the audience was willing to raise (her, their) hand to volunteer to be sawed in half on stage.

✐ Review Test 2

Cross out the pronoun error in each sentence and write the correction in the space provided at the left. Then circle the letter that correctly describes the type of error that was made.

Examples   *People*   ~~Anyone~~ turning in their papers late will be penalized.
Mistake in: a. pronoun reference   (b.) pronoun agreement

_____*Paul*_____   When Clyde takes his son Paul to the park, ~~he~~ enjoys himself.
Mistake in: (a.) pronoun reference   b. pronoun point of view

_____*we*_____   From where we stood, ~~you~~ could see three states.
Mistake in: a. pronoun agreement   (b.) pronoun point of view

_____   1. A good salesperson knows you should be courteous to customers.
Mistake in: a.   pronoun agreement   b.   pronoun point of view

_____   2. Neither of the girls who flunked bothered to bring their report card home.
Mistake in: a.   pronoun reference   b.   pronoun agreement

_____   3. When Lola tried to return her dress, they refused to accept it.
Mistake in: a.   pronoun agreement   b.   pronoun reference

_____   4. Nobody seems to add or subtract without their pocket calculators anymore.
Mistake in: a.   pronoun agreement   b.   pronoun point of view

_____   5. Denise went everywhere with Nita until she moved to Texas last year.
Mistake in: a.   pronoun agreement   b.   pronoun reference

_____   6. It seems everyone watches the lighted numbers whenever they ride on an elevator.
Mistake in: a.   pronoun agreement   b.   pronoun point of view

_____   7. In baking desserts, people should follow the directions carefully or you are likely to end up with something strange.
Mistake in: a.   pronoun reference   b.   pronoun point of view

————— 8. When Jerry added another card to the delicate structure, it fell down.

Mistake in: a. pronoun reference b. pronoun point of view

————— 9. Anyone who wants to join the car pool should leave their names with me.

Mistake in: a. pronoun agreement b. pronoun reference

————— 10. Any working mother knows that you need at least a twenty-five-hour day.

Mistake in: a. pronoun agreement b. pronoun point of view

Hint: Rewrite items 4, 6, and 9 in the plural.

Pronoun Types

INTRODUCTORY PROJECT

In each pair, put a check beside the sentence that you think uses pronouns correctly.

Andy and *I* enrolled in a computer course. _____

Andy and *me* enrolled in a computer course. _____

The police officer pointed to my sister and *me*. _____

The police officer pointed to my sister and *I*. _____

Lola prefers men *whom* take pride in their bodies. _____

Lola prefers men *who* take pride in their bodies. _____

The players are confident that the league championship is *theirs'*. _____

The players are confident that the league championship is *theirs*. _____

Them concert tickets are too expensive. _____

Those concert tickets are too expensive. _____

Our parents should spend some money on *themself* for a change. _____

Our parents should spend some money on *themselves* for a change.

_____

Answers are on page 464.

116

This section describes some common types of pronouns: subject and object pronouns, relative pronouns, possessive pronouns, demonstrative pronouns, and reflexive pronouns.

SUBJECT AND OBJECT PRONOUNS

Pronouns change their form depending upon the place that they occupy in a sentence. Here is a list of subject and object pronouns:

Subject Pronouns	Object Pronouns
I	me
you	you (no change)
he	him
she	her
it	it (no change)
we	us
they	them

Subject Pronouns

The subject pronouns are subjects of verbs.

They are getting tired. (*They* is the subject of the verb *are getting*.)
She will decide tomorrow. (*She* is the subject of the verb *will decide*.)
We women organized the game. (*We* is the subject of the verb *organized*.)

Several rules for using subject pronouns, and mistakes people sometimes make, are explained starting below.

Rule 1:   Use a subject pronoun in a sentence with a compound (more than one) subject.

Incorrect	Correct
Nate and *me* went shopping yesterday.	Nate and *I* went shopping yesterday.
Him and *me* spent lots of money.	*He* and *I* spent lots of money.

If you are not sure what pronoun to use, try each pronoun by itself in the sentence. The correct pronoun will be the one that sounds right. For example, "*Me* went shopping yesterday" does not sound right; "*I* went shopping yesterday" does.

Note that the pronoun is normally placed in the second position: "Nate and I," *not* "I and Nate."

Rule 2:   Use a subject pronoun after forms of the verb *be*. Forms of *be* include *am, are, is, was, were, has been, have been,* and others.

> It was *I* who telephoned.
> It may be *they* at the door.
> It is *she*.

The sentences above may sound strange and stilted to you, since they are seldom used in conversation. When we speak with one another, forms such as "It was me," "It may be them," and "It is her" are widely accepted. In formal writing, however, the grammatically correct forms are still preferred. You can avoid having to use the pronoun form after *be* simply by rewording a sentence. Here is how the preceding examples could be reworded:

> *I* was the one who telephoned.
> *They* may be at the door.
> *She* is here.

Rule 3:   Use subject pronouns after *than* or *as*. The subject pronoun is used because a verb is understood after the pronoun.

> You read faster than I (read). (The verb *read* is understood after *I*.)
> Tom is as stubborn as I (am). (The verb *am* is understood after *I*.)
> We don't go out as much as they (do). (The verb *do* is understood after *they*.)

Avoid mistakes by simply adding the "missing" verb at the end of the sentence.

Object Pronouns

The object pronouns (*me*, *him*, *her*, *us*, *them*) are the objects of verbs or prepositions. (Prepositions are connecting words like *for*, *at*, *about*, *to*, *before*, *by*, *with*, and *of*. See also page 13.)

> Rita chose *me*. (*Me* is the object of the verb *chose*.)
> We met *them* at the ball park. (*Them* is the object of the verb *met*.)
> Don't mention UFOs to *us*. (*Us* is the object of the preposition *to*.)
> I live near *her*.   (*Her* is the object of the preposition *near*.)

People are sometimes uncertain about what pronoun to use when two objects follow the verb.

Incorrect	*Correct*
I spoke to George and *he*.	I spoke to George and *him*.
She pointed at Linda and *I*.	She pointed at Linda and *me*.

Hint: If you are not sure what pronoun to use, try each pronoun by itself in the sentence. The correct pronoun will be the one that sounds right. For example, ''I spoke to he'' doesn't sound right; ''I spoke to him'' does.

Practice 1

Underline the correct subject or object pronoun in each of the following sentences. Then show whether your answer is a subject or an object pronoun by circling the *S* or *O* in the margin. The first one is done for you as an example.

S Ⓞ   1. I left the decision to (her, she).

S *O*   2. (She, Her) and Louise look enough alike to be sisters.

S *O*   3. Just between you and (I, me), these rolls taste like sawdust.

S *O*   4. The certified letter was addressed to both (she, her) and (I, me).

S *O*   5. If (he, him) and Vic are serious about school, why are they missing so many classes?

S *O*   6. Practically everyone is better at crossword puzzles than (I, me).

S *O*   7. It was (they, them) who left the patio furniture outside during the rainstorm.

S *O*   8. The creature that climbed out of the coffin scared Boris and (I, me) half to death.

S *O*   9. (We, Us) students are organizing a surprise party for a teacher who is retiring.

S *O*   10. When we were little, my sister and (I, me) invented a secret language our parents couldn't understand.

Practice 2

Write in a subject or object pronoun that fits in the space provided. Try to use as many different pronouns as possible. The first one is done for you as an example.

1. Lola ran after Sue and _____*me*_____ to return our suntan lotion.

2. The referee disqualified Ben and _____ for fighting.

3. I have seldom met two people as boring as _____.

4. If you and _____ don't lose patience, we'll finish sanding this floor by tonight.

5. Our professor told _____ students that our final exam would be a take-home test.

6. Ernie and _____ drove on the interstate highway for ten hours with only one stop.

7. We don't use our VCR as much as _____.

8. You know better than _____ how to remove lipstick stains.

9. Maggie and _____ spent several hours yesterday looking for the lost puppy.

10. Since we wore identical costumes, duplicate prizes for originality were presented to the Sawyer twins and _____.

RELATIVE PRONOUNS

Relative pronouns do two things at once. First, they refer to someone or something already mentioned in the sentence. Second, they start a short word group which gives additional information about this someone or something. Here is a list of relative pronouns, followed by some example sentences:

who	which
whose	that
whom	

The only friend *who* really understands me is moving away.
The child *whom* Ben and Arlene adopted is from Korea.
Chocolate, *which* is my favorite food, upsets my stomach.
I guessed at half the questions *that* were on the test.

In the example sentences, *who* refers to *friend*, *whom* refers to *child*, *which* refers to *chocolate,* and *that* refers to *questions*. In addition, each of these relative pronouns begins a group of words that describes the person or thing being referred to. For example, the words *whom Ben and Arlene adopted* tell which child the sentence is about, and the words *which is my favorite food* give added information about chocolate.

Points to Remember about Relative Pronouns

Point 1: *Whose* means *belonging to whom*. Be careful not to confuse *whose* with *who's,* which means *who is*.

Point 2: *Who, whose,* and *whom* all refer to people. *Which* refers to things. *That* can refer to either people or things.

I don't know *whose* book this is.

Don't sit on the chair *which* is broken.

Let's elect a captain *that* cares about winning.

Point 3: *Who, whose, whom,* and *which* can also be used to ask questions. When they are used in this way, they are called *interrogative* pronouns:

Who murdered the secret agent?

Whose fingerprints were on the bloodstained knife?

To *whom* have the detectives been talking?

Which suspect is going to confess?

Note: In informal usage, *who* is generally used instead of *whom* as an interrogative pronoun. Informally, we can say or write, ''*Who* are you rooting for in the game?'' or ''*Who* did the teacher fail?'' More formal usage would use *whom:* ''Whom are you rooting for in the game?'' ''Whom did the teacher fail?''

Point 4: *Who* and *whom* are used differently. *Who* is a subject pronoun. Use *who* as the subject of a verb:

Let's see *who* will be teaching the course.

Whom is an object pronoun. Use *whom* as the object of a verb or a preposition:

Dr. Kelsey is the teacher *whom* I like best.

I haven't decided for *whom* I will vote.

You may want to review the material on subject and object pronouns on pages 117–119.

Here is an easy way to decide whether to use *who* or *whom*. Find the first verb after the place where the *who* or *whom* will go. See if it already has a subject. If it does have a subject, use the object pronoun *whom*. If there is no subject, give it one by using the subject pronoun *who*. Notice how *who* and *whom* are used in the sentences that follow:

I don't know *who* sideswiped my car.

The suspect *whom* the police arrested finally confessed.

In the first sentence, *who* is used to give the verb *sideswiped* a subject. In the second sentence, the verb *arrested* already has a subject, *police*. Therefore, *whom* is the correct pronoun.

Practice 1

Underline the correct pronoun in each of the following sentences.

1. Some of the coupons (who, which) I brought to the supermarket had expired.
2. On a bright, sunny day, some office buildings (who, that) have glass walls look like giant icicles.
3. My sister, (who, whom) loves ballet, walks around the house on her toes.
4. The new highway (who, which) just opened in May was closed three months later for repairs.
5. The supervisor (who, whom) everybody dislikes was just given thirty days' notice.

Practice 2

Write five sentences using *who*, *whose*, *whom*, *which*, and *that*.

POSSESSIVE PRONOUNS

Possessive pronouns show ownership or possession.

Clyde shut off the engine of *his* motorcycle.
The keys are *mine*.

Here is a list of possessive pronouns:

my, mine	our, ours
your, yours	your, yours
his	their, theirs
her, hers	
its	

Points to Remember about Possessive Pronouns

Point 1: A possessive pronoun *never* uses an apostrophe. (See also page 164.)

Incorrect	**Correct**
That coat is *hers'*.	That coat is *hers*.
The card table is *theirs'*.	The card table is *theirs*.

Point 2: Do not use any of the following nonstandard forms to show possession.

Incorrect	**Correct**
I met a friend of *him*.	I met a friend of *his*.
Can I use *you* car?	Can I use *your* car?
Me sister is in the hospital.	*My* sister is in the hospital.
That magazine is *mines*.	That magazine is *mine*.

Practice

Cross out the incorrect pronoun form in each of the sentences that follow. Write the correct form in the space at the left.

_____My_____ **Example** ~~Me~~ car has broken down again.

_____ 1. Are these shears yours' or mine?

_____ 2. Only relatives of him are allowed to visit while he is in the hospital.

_____ 3. My sisters think that every new dress I buy is theirs' too.

_____ 4. Are you going to eat all of you hamburger, or can I have half?

_____ 5. I'm sure this thermos is mines because of the dents and broken strap.

DEMONSTRATIVE PRONOUNS

Demonstrative pronouns point to or single out a person or thing. There are four demonstrative pronouns:

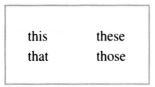

this	these
that	those

Generally speaking, *this* and *these* refer to things close at hand; *that* and *those* refer to things farther away.

Is anyone using *this* spoon?

I am going to throw away *these* magazines.

I just bought *that* white Volvo at the curb.

Pick up *those* toys in the corner.

Note: Do not use *them*, *this here*, *that there*, *these here*, or *those there* to point out. Use only *this*, *that*, *these*, or *those*.

Incorrect	*Correct*
Them tires are badly worn.	*Those* tires are badly worn.
This here book looks hard to read.	*This* book looks hard to read.
That there candy is delicious.	*That* candy is delicious.
Those there squirrels are pests.	*Those* squirrels are pests.

Practice 1

Cross out the incorrect form of the demonstrative pronoun and write the correct form in the space provided.

Those   **Example**   ~~Them~~ clothes need washing.

_____ 1. This here town isn't big enough for both of us, Tex.

_____ 2. Let's hurry and get them seats before someone else does.

_____ 3. That there dress looked better on the hanger than it does on you.

_____ 4. Let me try one of those there candies before they're all gone.

_____ 5. Watch out for them potholes the next time you drive my car.

Practice 2

Write four sentences using *this*, *that*, *these*, and *those*.

_____

_____

_____

_____

REFLEXIVE PRONOUNS

Reflexive pronouns are ones that refer to the subject of a sentence. Here is a list of reflexive pronouns:

myself	ourselves
yourself	yourselves
himself	themselves
herself	
itself	

Sometimes the reflexive pronoun is used for emphasis:

You will have to wash the dishes *yourself*.
We *ourselves* are willing to forget the matter.
The president *himself* turns down his living room thermostat.

Points to Remember about Reflexive Pronouns

Point 1:   In the plural *-self* becomes *-selves*.

Lola washes *herself* in Calgon bath oil.
They treated *themselves* to a Bermuda vacation.

Point 2:   Be careful that you do not use any of the following incorrect forms as reflexive pronouns.

Incorrect	*Correct*
He believes in *hisself*.	He believes in *himself*.
We drove the children *ourself*.	We drove the children *ourselves*.
They saw *themself* in the fun house mirror.	They saw *themselves* in the fun house mirror.
I'll do it *meself*.	I'll do it *myself*.

Practice

Cross out the incorrect form of the reflexive pronoun and write the correct form in the space at the left.

themselves   **Example**   She believes that God helps those who help ~~themself~~.

_____   1.   Our neighbors keep to themself most of the time.

_____   2.   The restaurant owner herselve came out to apologize to us.

_____   3.   When my baby brother tries to dress hisself, the results are often funny.

_____   4.   The waiter was busy, so we poured ourself coffee from a nearby pot.

_____   5.   These housepainters seem to be making more work for theirselves than is necessary.

Review Test 1

Underline the correct word in the parentheses.

1. The waitress finally brought Dolores and (I, me) our order.
2. Since he worked on the project (hisself, himself), he should be able to answer our questions.
3. Hand me (that, that there) fiddle, and I'll play you a tune.
4. If it were up to (she, her), men wouldn't have the right to vote.
5. Roger, (who, whom) has worked here only two days, is ready to quit.
6. Vera dressed much more casually than (I, me) for the party.
7. You won't get very far on that bike unless you add more air to (its, it's) tires.

8. We'll be reading (this, this here) stack of books during the semester.

9. I have the address of a cousin of (his, him) to look up when I visit next month.

10. The ducks circled the lake until they were sure that no one was around but (theirselves, themselves).

Review Test 2

Cross out the pronoun error in each sentence and write the correct form in the space at the left.

_____/_____ **Example** Terry and ~~me~~ have already seen the movie.

_____ 1. The chili that Manny prepared was too spicy for we to eat.

_____ 2. I checked them wires, but I couldn't find any faulty connections.

_____ 3. The old Chevy, who has 110,000 miles on it, is still running well.

_____ 4. Until her and her daughter show up, it is senseless to begin this meeting.

_____ 5. Joel realized that he would have to change the tire hisself.

_____ 6. My husband is much more sentimental than me.

_____ 7. My dog won't be comfortable in this heat unless I have its' coat clipped.

_____ 8. The records are mines, but you can listen to them whenever you wish.

_____ 9. This here telephone works only if you have a credit card.

_____ 10. Vicky and me are going to the concert at the fairgrounds.

Review Test 3

On separate paper, write sentences that use correctly each of the following words or word groups.

Example   Peter and him   *The coach suspended Peter and him.*

1. yourselves
2. Lola and me
3. these
4. the neighbors and us
5. Victor and he
6. slower than I
7. its
8. which
9. you and I
10. Maria and them

Adjectives
and
Adverbs

INTRODUCTORY PROJECT

Write in an appropriate word to complete each of the sentences below.

1. The teenage years were a _____ time for me.

2. The mechanic listened _____ while I described my car problem.

3. Basketball is a _____ game than football.

4. My brother is the _____ person in our family.

Now see if you can complete the following sentences.

The word inserted in the first sentence is an (adjective, adverb); it describes the word *time*.

The word inserted in the second sentence is an (adjective, adverb); it ends in the two letters _____ and describes the word *listened*.

The word inserted in the third sentence is a comparative adjective; it is preceded by *more* or ends in the two letters _____.

The word inserted in the fourth sentence is a superlative adjective; it is preceded by *most* or ends in the three letters _____.

Answers are on page 465.

Adjectives and adverbs are descriptive words. Their purpose is to make the meanings of the words they describe more specific.

ADJECTIVES

What Are Adjectives?

Adjectives describe nouns (names of persons, places, or things) or pronouns.

Charlotte is a *kind* woman. (The adjective *kind* describes the noun *woman*.)
He is *tired*. (The adjective *tired* describes the pronoun *he*.)

Adjectives usually come before the word they describe (as in *kind woman*). But they also come after forms of the verb *be* (*is, are, was, were,* and so on). Less often, they follow verbs such as *feel, look, smell, sound, taste, appear, become,* and *seem*.

That bureau is *heavy*. (The adjective *heavy* describes the bureau.)
The children are *restless*. (The adjective *restless* describes the children.)
These pants are *itchy*. (The adjective *itchy* describes the pants.)

Using Adjectives to Compare

For most *short* adjectives, add *-er* when comparing two things and *-est* when comparing three or more things.

I am *taller* than my brother, but my father is the *tallest* person in the house.
The farm market sells *fresher* vegetables than the corner store, but the *freshest* vegetables are the ones grown in my own garden.

For most *longer* adjectives (two or more syllables), add *more* when comparing two things and *most* when comparing three or more things.

Backgammon is *more enjoyable* to me than checkers, but chess is the *most enjoyable* game of all.
My mother is *more talkative* than my father, but my grandfather is the *most talkative* person in the house.

Points to Remember about Adjectives

Point 1:   Be careful that you do not use both an *-er* ending and *more*, or both an *-est* ending and *most*:

Incorrect

Football is a *more livelier* game than baseball.

Tod Traynor was voted the *most likeliest* to succeed in our high school class.

Correct

Football is a *livelier* game than baseball.

Tod Traynor was voted the *most likely* to succeed in our high school class.

Point 2:   Pay special attention to the following four words, each of which has irregular forms.

	Comparative (Two)	Superlative (Three or More)
bad	worse	worst
good, well	better	best
little	less	least
much, many	more	most

Practice 1

Fill in the comparative or superlative forms for the following words. Two are done for you as examples.

	Comparative (Two)	Superlative (Three or More)
firm	firmer	firmest
organized	more organized	most organized
tough		
practical		
quiet		
aggressive		
clear		

Practice 2

Add to each sentence the correct form of the word in the margin.

Example *bad* The _____worst_____ day of my life was the one when my house caught fire.

good 1. I hope the _____ days of my life are still to come.

dirty 2. The water in Mudville is _____ than the name of the town.

considerate 3. If Tyrone were _____, he would have more friends.

bad 4. The announcement of a pop quiz gave me a _____ headache than this morning's traffic did.

sure 5. The _____ way to do a job right is to pay attention to details.

little 6. As hard as it is to believe, he is even a _____ dependable worker than his brother.

sincere 7. Making amends for shoplifting, young man, requires a _____ effort than a simple letter of apology.

silly 8. June is even _____ than her sister; she once burst out laughing at a wedding and had to run out of the church.

soft 9. I don't understand why people in commercials are so concerned with finding the _____ toilet paper.

fattening 10. Estella ordered a tossed salad as her main course, so she could have the _____ dessert on the menu.

ADVERBS

What Are Adverbs?

Adverbs describe verbs, adjectives, or other adverbs. They usually end in *-ly*.

Charlotte spoke *kindly* to the confused man. (The adverb *kindly* describes the verb *spoke*.)

The man said he was *completely* alone in the world. (The adverb *completely* describes the adjective *alone*.)

Charlotte listened *very* sympathetically to his story. (The adverb *very* describes the adverb *sympathetically*.)

A Common Mistake
with Adjectives and Adverbs

Perhaps the most common mistake that people make with adjectives and adverbs is to use an adjective instead of an adverb after a verb.

Incorrect	*Correct*
Tony breathed *heavy*.	Tony breathed *heavily*.
I rest *comfortable* in that chair.	I rest *comfortably* in that chair.
She learned *quick*.	She learned *quickly*.

Practice

Underline the adjective or adverb needed.

1. I need a vacation (bad, badly).
2. The crowd reacted (harsh, harshly) to the noisy demonstrators.
3. The truck groaned as it crept up the (steep, steeply) grade.
4. My boss tells me (frequent, frequently) that I do a good job.
5. Many (colorful, colorfully) flags fluttered gently around the monument.
6. If you think your decision was right, you'll sleep (peaceful, peacefully).
7. Walter the werewolf smiled at the (bright, brightly) moonlight shining through his bedroom window.
8. Nate was playing the stereo so (loud, loudly) that both the dog and the cat were cowering in the basement.
9. The surgeon stitched the wound very (careful, carefully), so that the scar would not be noticeable.
10. Dawn's new boyfriend complains (bitter, bitterly) that she doesn't take his feelings seriously.

Well and *Good*

Two words often confused are *well* and *good*. *Good* is an adjective; it describes nouns. *Well* is usually an adverb; it describes verbs. *Well* (rather than *good*) is also used when referring to a person's health.

I became a *good* swimmer. (*Good* is an adjective describing the noun *swimmer*.)

For a change, two-year-old Tommy was *good* during the church service. (*Good* is an adjective describing Tommy and comes after *was*, a form of the verb *be*.)

Maryann did *well* on that exam. (*Well* is an adverb describing the verb *did*.)

I explained that I wasn't feeling *well*. (*Well* is used in reference to health.)

Practice

Write *well* or *good* in the sentences that follow.

1. My parents and my in-laws get along _____.

2. The dog did a _____ job of chewing our sofa.

3. If Lee does _____ on the interview, he will get the job.

4. My idea of a _____ date is to talk over dinner.

5. Although I didn't feel _____, I tried to keep doing my work.

Review Test 1

Underline the correct word in the parentheses.

1. When I found out the landlord intended to increase my rent, I moved back in with my parents (immediate, immediately).

2. A little VW cut (sharp, sharply) in front of me on the turnpike and almost caused an acident.

3. For as long as I can remember, my teachers have tried to get me to write more (neat, neatly).

4. Judy's parents were deeply disturbed that her grades were (worse, more worse) than ever.

5. My grandfather says that teenagers acted just as (unpredicable, unpredictably) when he was a boy as they do today.

6. The plane taxied (rapid, rapidly) down the runway but then came to a complete stop.

7. After the carpenter fitted the oak floorboards, he sanded them to give them a (more fine, finer) finish.

8. Holding the purple felt-tipped pen (loose, loosely), Gina drew graceful spirals in her notebook.

9. Although Al thought his accounting test was the (difficultest, most difficult) test he had ever taken, he got an A on it.

10. I did so (good, well) on my first visit to the racetrack that I unwisely decided to try my luck a second time.

Review Test 2

Write a sentence that uses correctly each of the following adjectives and adverbs.

1. confident _____

2. vigorously _____

3. well _____

4. more impulsive _____

5. better _____

6. cleverly _____

7. worst _____

8. rough _____

9. most annoying _____

10. sweeter _____

Section 2: Mechanics

Paper Format

INTRODUCTORY PROJECT

Which of the paper openings below seems clearer and easier to read?

A

	Finding Faces
	It takes just a little imagination to find faces in the
	objects around you. For instance, clouds are sometimes
	shaped like faces. If you lie on the ground on a partly

B

	"finding faces"
	It takes just a little imagination to find faces in the objects
	around you. For instance, clouds are sometimes shaped like
	faces. If you lie on the ground on a partly cloudy day, cha-
	nces are you will be able to spot many well-known faces

What are three reasons for your choice?

_____

_____

_____

Answers are on page 465.

PAPER GUIDELINES

Here are guidelines to follow in preparing a paper for an instructor.

1 Use full-sized theme or typewriter paper, 8½ by 11 inches.

2 Keep wide margins (1 to 1½ inches) all around the paper. In particular, do not crowd the right-hand or bottom margins. The white space makes your paper more readable; also, the instructor has room for comments.

3 If you write by hand:

Use a blue or black pen (*not* a pencil).

Be careful not to overlap letters or to make decorative loops on letters.

On narrow-ruled paper, write on every other line.

Make all your letters distinct. Pay special attention to *a, e, i, o,* and *u*—five letters that people sometimes write illegibly.

Keep your capital letters clearly distinct from your small letters. You may even want to print all capital letters.

4 Center the title of your paper on the first line of page one. Do not put quotation marks around the title or underline the title. Capitalize all the major words in a title, including the first word. Small connecting words within a title, such as *of, for, the, in,* and *to,* are not capitalized.

5 Skip a line between the title and the first line of your text. Indent the first line of each paragraph about five spaces (half an inch) from the left-hand margin.

6 Make commas, periods, and other punctuation marks firm and clear. Leave a slight space after each period. When you type, leave a double space after a period.

7 If you break a word at the end of a line, break only between syllables (see page 198). Do not break words of one syllable.

8 Put your name, date, and course number where your instructor asks for them.

Also keep in mind these important points about the title and the first sentence of your paper:

9 The title should be several words that tell what the paper is about. The title is usually *not* a complete sentence.

10 Do not rely on the title to help explain the first sentence of your paper. The first sentence must stand independent of the title.

Practice 1

Identify the mistakes in format in the following lines from a student theme. Explain the mistakes in the spaces provided. One mistake is described for you as an example.

	"Being a younger sister"
	'When I was young, I would gladly have donated my
	older sister to another family. First of all, most of
	my clothes were hand-me-downs. I rarely got to buy anyth-
	ing new to wear. My sister took very good care of her clothes,
	which only made the problem worse. Also, she was very

1. *Break words only at syllable divisions (any-thing).* _____

2. _____

3. _____

4. _____

5. _____

6. _____

Practice 2

As already stated, a title should tell in several words what a paper is about. Often a title can be based on the sentence that expresses the main idea of a paper.

Following are five main-idea sentences from student papers. Write a suitable and specific title for each paper, basing the title on the main idea.

Example *Aging Americans as Outcasts* _____

Our society treats aging Americans as outcasts in many ways.

1. Title: _____

Pets offer a number of benefits to their owners.

2. Title: _____

Since I have learned to budget carefully, I no longer run out of money at the end of the week.

3. Title: _____

Studying regularly with a study group has helped me raise my grades.

4. Title: _____

Grandparents have a special relationship with their grandchildren.

5. Title: _____

My decision to eliminate junk food from my diet has been good for my health and my budget.

Practice 3

In four of the five following sentences, the writer has mistakenly used the title to help explain the first sentence. But as has been noted, you must *not* rely on the title to explain your first sentence. Rewrite the sentences so that they stand independent of the title. Put *Correct* under the one sentence that is independent.

Example Title: Flunking an Exam

First sentence: I managed to do this because of several bad habits.

Rewritten: *I managed to flunk an exam because of several bad habits.*

1. Title: The Best Children's Television Shows
    First sentence: They educate while they entertain, and they aren't violent.

    Rewritten: _____

    _____

2. Title: Women in the Workplace
    First sentence: They have made many gains there in the last decade.

    Rewritten: _____

    _____

3. Title: The Generation Gap
    First sentence: It results from differing experiences of various age groups.

    Rewritten: _____

    _____

4. Title: My Ideal Job
   First sentence: My idea of an ideal job would be to manage a rock group and make a lot of money.

   Rewritten: _____

   _____

5. Title: Important Accomplishments
   First sentence: One of them was to finish high school despite the divorce of my parents.

   Rewritten: _____

   _____

Review Test

Use the space provided below to rewrite the following sentences from a student paper, correcting the mistakes in format.

	"my nursing-home friends"
	I now count some of them among my good friends. I fi-
	rst went there just to keep a relative of mine company.
	That is when I learned some of them rarely got any
	visitors. Many were starved for conversation and friendship.
	At the time, I did not want to get involved. But what I

Capital Letters

INTRODUCTORY PROJECT

You probably know a good deal about the uses of capital letters. Answering the questions below will help you check your knowledge.

1. Write the full name of a person you know: _____

2. In what city and state were you born? _____

3. What is your present street address? _____

4. Name a country where you want to travel for a ''fling'': _____

5. Name a school that you attended: _____

6. Give the name of a store where you buy food: _____

7. Name a company where you or anyone you know works: _____

8. What day of the week gives you the best chance to relax? _____

9. What holiday is your favorite? _____

10. What brand of toothpaste do you use? _____

11. Give the brand name of a candy or chewing gum you like: _____

12. Name a song or a television show you enjoy: _____

13. Write the title of a magazine or newspaper you read: _____

Items 14–16: Three capital letters are needed in the lines below. Underline the words you think should be capitalized. Then write them, capitalized, in the spaces provided.

on Super Bowl Sunday, my roommate said, ''let's buy some snacks and invite a few friends over to watch the game.'' i knew my plans to write a term paper would have to be changed.

14. _____   15. _____   16. _____

Answers are on page 465.

MAIN USES OF CAPITAL LETTERS

Capital letters are used with:

1 The first word in a sentence or direct quotation
2 Names of persons and the word *I*
3 Names of particular places
4 Names of days of the week, months, and holidays
5 Names of commercial products
6 Titles of books, magazines, articles, films, television shows, songs, poems, stories, papers that you write, and the like
7 Names of companies, associations, unions, clubs, religious and political groups, and other organizations

Each use is illustrated on the pages that follow.

First Word in a Sentence or Direct Quotation

Our company has begun laying people off.
The doctor said, ''This may hurt a bit.''
''My husband,'' said Martha, ''is a light eater. When it's light, he starts to eat.''

Note: In the third example, *My* and *When* are capitalized because they start new sentences. But *is* is not capitalized, because it is part of the first sentence.

Names of Persons and the Word *I*

At the picnic, I met Tony Curry and Lola Morrison.

Names of Particular Places

After graduating from Gibbs High School in Houston, I worked for a summer at a nearby Holiday Inn on Clairmont Boulevard.

But: Use small letters if the specific name of a place is not given.

After graduating from high school in my hometown, I worked for a summer at a nearby hotel on one of the main shopping streets.

Names of Days of the Week, Months, and Holidays

This year Memorial Day falls on the last Thursday in May.

But: Use small letters for the seasons—summer, fall, winter, spring.

In the early summer and fall, my hay fever bothers me.

Names of Commercial Products

The consumer magazine rates highly Cheerios breakfast cereal, Howard Johnson's ice cream, and Jif peanut butter.

But: Use small letters for the *type* of product (breakfast cereal, ice cream, peanut butter, or whatever).

Titles of Books, Magazines, Articles, Films, Television Shows, Songs, Poems, Stories, Papers That You Write, and the Like

My oral report was on *The Diary of a Young Girl,* by Anne Frank.

While watching *The Young and the Restless* on television, I thumbed through *Cosmopolitan* magazine and *The New York Times.*

Names of Companies, Associations, Unions, Clubs, Religious and Political Groups, and Other Organizations

A new bill before Congress is opposed by the National Rifle Association.

My wife is Jewish; I am Roman Catholic. We are both members of the Democratic Party.

My parents have life insurance with Prudential, auto insurance with Allstate, and medical insurance with Blue Cross and Blue Shield.

Practice

Cross out the words that need capitals in the sentences that follow. Then write the capitalized forms of the words in the space provided. The number of spaces tells you how many corrections to make in each case.

Example   Rhoda said, "~~why~~ should I bother to *eat* this ~~hershey~~ bar? I should just apply it directly to my hips."   _____Why_____   _____Hershey_____

1. Sometimes i still regret not joining the boy scouts when I was in grade school.

   _____   _____   _____

2. After Carol went to smokenders in july, she threw away her last pack of marlboro cigarettes.

   _____   _____   _____

3. The sign in the front window of hanes ceramics says, "if you break it, you buy it."

   _____   _____   _____

4. In many new england towns, republicans outnumber democrats five to one.

   _____   _____   _____   _____

5. Dave was surprised to learn that both state farm and nationwide have insurance offices in the prudential building.

   _____   _____   _____   _____

   _____

6. At the dentist's office, I read an interesting article on the california condor in *national geographic* magazine.

   _____   _____   _____

7. The rose grower whom Manny works for said that the biggest rose-selling holidays are valentine's day and mother's day.

   _____   _____   _____   _____   _____

8. With a generous supply of cokes, fritos, and pretzels, the four mystery buffs settled in for a game of clue.

   _____   _____   _____

9. Bob's ford taurus was badly damaged when he struck a deer last saturday.

   _____   _____   _____

10. Though Julie Andrews excelled in the broadway version of *my fair lady,* Audrey Hepburn was cast in the female lead role in the movie version.

   _____   _____   _____   _____

OTHER USES OF CAPITAL LETTERS

Capital letters are also used with:

1   Names that show family relationships
2   Titles of persons when used with their names
3   Specific school courses
4   Languages
5   Geographic locations
6   Historical periods and events
7   Races, nations, and nationalities
8   Opening and closing of a letter

Each use is illustrated on the pages that follow.

Names That Show Family Relationships

Aunt Fern and Uncle Jack are selling their house.
I asked Grandfather to start the fire.
Is Mother feeling better?

But: Do not capitalize words like *mother, father, grandmother, grandfather, uncle, aunt,* and so on when they are preceded by *my* or another possessive word.

My aunt and uncle are selling their house.
I asked my grandfather to start the fire.
Is my mother feeling better?

Titles of Persons When Used with Their Names

I wrote an angry letter to Senator Blutt.
Can you drive to Dr. Stein's office?
We asked Professor Bushkin about his attendance policy.

But: Use small letters when titles appear by themselves, without specific names.

I wrote an angry letter to my senator.
Can you drive to the doctor's office?
We asked our professor about his attendance policy.

Specific School Courses

My courses this semester include Accounting I, Introduction to Data Processing, Business Law, General Psychology, and Basic Math.

But: Use small letters for general subject areas.

This semester I'm taking mostly business courses, but I have a psychology course and a math course as well.

Languages

Lydia speaks English and Spanish equally well.

Geographic Locations

I lived in the South for many years and then moved to the West Coast.

But: Use small letters in giving directions.

Go south for about five miles and then bear west.

Historical Periods and Events

One essay question dealt with the Battle of the Bulge in World War II.

Races, Nations, Nationalities

The census form asked whether I was Caucasian, Negro, Indian, Hispanic, or Asian.

Last summer I hitchhiked through Italy, France, and Germany.

The city is a melting pot for Koreans, Vietnamese, and Mexican Americans.

But: Use small letters when referring to *whites* or *blacks*.

Both whites and blacks supported our mayor in the election.

Opening and Closing of a Letter

Dear Sir: Sincerely yours,

Dear Madam: Truly yours,

Note: Capitalize only the first word in a closing.

Practice

Cross out the words that need capitals in the following sentences. Then write the capitalized forms of the words in the spaces provided. The number of spaces tells you how many corrections to make in each case.

1. The nervous game show contestant couldn't remember how long the hundred years' war lasted.

    _____   _____   _____

2. My sister and I always plead with aunt sophie to sing polish songs whenever she visits us.

    _____   _____   _____

3. While in Washington, we visited president kennedy's grave site at arlington cemetery.

    _____   _____   _____   _____

4. The readings for the first semester of world history end with the middle ages.

    _____   _____   _____   _____

5. The Miami area has many fine cuban restaurants, several spanish-language newspapers, and annual hispanic cultural festivals.

    _____   _____   _____

UNNECESSARY USE OF CAPITALS

Practice

Many errors in capitalization are caused by adding capitals where they are not needed. Cross out the incorrectly capitalized letters in the following sentences and write the correct forms in the spaces provided. The number of spaces tells you how many corrections to make in each sentence.

1. My Uncle, a self-made man, boasts that he never had the time to get a College Education.

   _____   _____   _____

2. In our High School, the American history teacher was also the Basketball Coach.

   _____   _____   _____   _____

3. A Shop at Westville Mall sells copies of all the trendy clothes shown on various television Musical Video shows.

   _____   _____   _____

4. Several Parents' Groups protested the Ads for the new horror movie, which showed Santa Claus as a Maniac with a knife.

   _____   _____   _____   _____

5. When I play a piece well, my Piano Teacher, who does not give many compliments, says, ''You must have had a lot of time to practice this Week.''

   _____   _____   _____

Review Test 1

Cross out the words that need capitals in the following sentences. Then write the capitalized forms of the words in the spaces provided. The number of spaces tells you how many corrections to make in each sentence.

Example During halftime of the ~~saturday~~ afternoon football game, my sister said, ''~~let's~~ get some hamburgers from ~~wendy~~'s or put a pizza in the oven.''

   _____Saturday_____   _____Let's_____   _____Wendy's_____

1. Although the ads claim, ''things go better with coke,'' i prefer root beer.

   _____   _____   _____

2. Millions of years ago, america's midwest was covered by a great inland sea.

   _____   _____

3. One of our thanksgiving traditions is sending a check to an organization such as care, which helps relieve world hunger.

   _____   _____

4. If you drive onto route 10 in tallahassee, florida, and stay on that road, you'll eventually end up in california.

   _____   _____   _____   _____

5. Just before english class this morning, Arlene titled her final paper ''my argument for an A.''

   _____   _____   _____

6. I read in the book *royal lives* that when an ancient egyptian king died, his servants were often killed and buried with him.

   _____   _____   _____

7. dear mr. Bradford:
   This is the third and final time I will write to complain about the leak in my bathroom.

   sincerely,
Anne Morrison

   _____   _____   _____

8. ''After age fifty,'' my grandma ida would say, ''time passes very quickly. it seems as though it's time for breakfast every fifteen minutes.''

   _____   _____   _____

9. Dr. Green, who teaches a course called cultural anthropology, spent last summer on an archeological dig in israel.

   _____   _____   _____

10. During the singing of ''the star-spangled banner,'' many fans at veterans' stadium drank sodas, read their programs, or chatted with each other.

   _____   _____   _____

   _____   _____   _____

Review Test 2

On separate paper, write:

- Seven sentences demonstrating the seven main uses of capital letters
- Eight sentences demonstrating the eight other uses of capital letters

Numbers
and
Abbreviations

INTRODUCTORY PROJECT

Put a check beside the item in each pair that you think uses numbers correctly.

I finished the exam by 8:55, but my grade was only 65 percent. _____

I finished the exam by eight-fifty-five, but my grade was only sixty-five per-cent. _____

9 people are in my biology lab, but there are 45 in my lecture group. _____

Nine people are in my biology lab, but there are forty-five in my lecture group. _____

Put a check beside the item in each pair that you think uses abbreviations correctly.

Both of my bros. were treated by Dr. Lewis after the mt. climbing accident. _____

Both of my brothers were treated by Dr. Lewis after the mountain climbing accident. _____

I spent two hrs. finishing my Eng. paper and handed it to my teacher, Ms. Peters, right at the deadline. _____

I spent two hours finishing my English paper and handed it to my teacher, Ms. Peters, right at the deadline. _____

Answers are on page 466.

NUMBERS

Rule 1:   Spell out numbers that take no more than two words. Otherwise, use numerals—the numbers themselves.

> Last year Tina bought nine new records.
> Ray struck out fifteen batters in Sunday's softball game.

But

> Tina now has 114 records in her collection.
> Already this season Ray has recorded 168 strikeouts.

You should also spell out a number that begins a sentence:

> One hundred fifty first-graders throughout the city showed flu symptoms today.

Rule 2:   Be consistent when you use a series of numbers. If some numbers in a sentence or paragraph require more than two words, then use numbers themselves throughout the selection.

> This past spring, we planted 5 rhodos, 15 azaleas, 50 summersweet, and 120 myrtle around our house.

Rule 3:   Use numbers to show dates, times, addresses, percentages, exact sums of money, and parts of a book.

> John Kennedy was killed on November 22, 1963.
> My job interview was set for 10:15. (*But:* Spell out numbers before *o'clock.* For example: The time was then changed to eleven o'clock.)
> Janet's new address is 118 North 35 Street.
> Almost 40 percent of my meals are eaten at fast-food restaurants.
> The cashier rang up a total of $18.35. (*But:* Round amounts may be expressed as words. For example: The movie has a five-dollar admission charge.)
> Read Chapter 6 in your math textbook and answer questions 1 to 5 on page 250.

Practice

Use the three rules to make the corrections needed in these sentences.

1. Almost every morning I get up at exactly six-fifteen.
2. But on Sunday mornings, I sleep until 9 o'clock.
3. The Challenger spaceship tragedy took place on January twenty-eight, 1986.
4. Joanne got really nervous when she saw there were only 6 other people in her English class.
5. Please send your complaints to seventeen hundred Pennsylvania Avenue.
6. 43 stores in the New England area were closed by a retail workers' strike.
7. Martin's computer system, including a printer, cost nine hundred and thirty dollars and twenty cents.
8. Pages sixty through sixty-four of my biology book are stuck together.
9. In Hollywood starlet Fifi LaFlamme's closet are twenty-seven evening gowns, fifty-two designer blouses, and 132 pairs of shoes.
10. Since over fifty percent of the class failed the midterm exam, the instructor decided not to count the grades.

ABBREVIATIONS

While abbreviations are a helpful time-saver in note-taking, you should avoid most abbreviations in formal writing. Listed below are some of the few abbreviations that can acceptably be used in compositions. Note that a period is used after most abbreviations.

1   Mr., Mrs., Ms., Jr., Sr., Dr. when used with proper names:

Mr. Rollin   Ms. Peters   Dr. Coleman

2   Time references:

A.M. or a.m.   P.M. or p.m.   B.C. or A.D.

3   First or middle initial in a signature:

T. Alan Parker   Linda M. Evans

4 Organizations, technical words, and trade names known primarily by their initials:

ABC   CIA   UNESCO   GM   STP   LTD

Practice

Cross out the words that should not be abbreviated and correct them in the spaces provided.

1. My no-wax flr. lost its shine in six mos.

   _____   _____

2. Sharon bought two bush. of ripe tomatoes at the farm mkt. on Rt. 73.

   _____   _____   _____

3. On Mon., NASA will announce its plans for a Sept. flight to Mars.

   _____   _____

4. The psych. class was taught by Dr. Aronson, a noted psychiatrist from Eng.

   _____   _____

5. Every Jan., our co. gives awards for the best employee suggestions of the previous yr.

   _____   _____   _____

6. Several baby opossums (each of which weighs less than an oz.) can fit into a tbsp.

   _____   _____

7. I didn't have time to study for my chem. test on Sun., but I studied for four hrs. yesterday.

   _____   _____   _____

8. The best part about owning three tel. sets is that I can watch ABC, NBC, and CBS at the same tm.

   _____   _____

9. Lawrence T. Johnson lost his lic. to practice medicine when the state board discovered he never went to med. school.

   _____   _____

10. Mick, a Vietnam vet., started his own photography bus. after graduating from a community coll.

    _____   _____   _____

✑ Review Test

Cross out the mistake or mistakes in numbers and abbreviations and correct them in the spaces provided.

1. Sears' 4-day sale starts this coming Thurs.

   _____   _____

2. One suspect had blue eyes and brn. hair and was over 6 ft. tall.

   _____   _____   _____

3. Answers to the chpt. questions start on p. two hundred and ninety-three.

   _____   _____   _____

4. With Dec. twenty-fifth only hrs. away, little Rhonda couldn't eat or sleep.

   _____   _____   _____

5. Over 200 children helped in the collection of seven hundred and thirty-two dollars for UNICEF.

   _____   _____

6. Eddy, who is now over 6 ft. tall, can no longer sleep comfortably in a twin bed.

   _____   _____

7. My 3 years of Spanish in h.s. helped me to get a job in the city health clinic.

   _____   _____   _____

8. The robber was sentenced to 10 yrs. in prison for holding up a bank on Pacific Blvd.

   _____   _____   _____

9. If a 1-lb. rock and a feather are dropped from a tall bldg. at the same time, they will hit the ground together.

   _____   _____   _____

10. I was pleased to find that the ins. co. gave me a ten percent discount on my homeowners' policy because I have a burglar alarm.

    _____   _____   _____

Section 3: Punctuation

End Marks

INTRODUCTORY PROJECT

Add the end mark needed in each of the following sentences.

1. All week I have been feeling depressed
2. What is the deadline for handing in the paper
3. The man at the door wants to know whose car is double-parked
4. That truck ahead of us is out of control

Answers are on page 466.

A sentence always begins with a capital letter. It always ends with a period, a question mark, or an exclamation point.

PERIOD (.)

Use a period after a sentence that makes a statement.

More single parents are adopting children.
It has rained for most of the week.

Use a period after most abbreviations.

Mr. Brady	B.A.	Dr. Ballard
Ms. Peters	A.M.	Tom Ricci, Jr.

QUESTION MARK (?)

Use a question mark after a *direct* question.

When is your paper due?
How is your cold?
Tom asked, "When are you leaving?"
"Why doesn't everyone take a break?" Rosa suggested.

Do not use a question mark after an *indirect* question (a question not in the speaker's exact words).

She asked when the paper was due.
He asked how my cold was.
Tom asked when I was leaving.
Rosa suggested that everyone take a break.

EXCLAMATION POINT (!)

Use an exclamation point after a word or sentence that expresses strong feeling.

Come here!
Ouch! This pizza is hot!
That truck just missed us!

Note: Be careful not to overuse exclamation points.

Practice

Add a period, question mark, or exclamation point, as needed, to each of the following sentences.

1. Is it possible for a fish to drown

2. Thomas Jefferson was a redhead

3. I asked Jill for the time of day, but she wouldn't give it to me

4. When Eva learned she had won the lottery, she jumped up and down, yelling, "I don't believe it "

5. Because Americans watch so much television, one writer has called us a nation of "videoits "

6. I questioned whether the police officer's report was accurate

7. If you had one year left to live, what would you do with the rest of your life

8. The last thing I heard before waking up in the hospital was someone screaming, "Look out for that truck "

9. On the plane from New York to Chicago, Dominic said, "Must I turn my watch back one hour—or forward "

10. In the first paper for her English class, Claire wrote that she wanted to "learn how not to be redundant and repeat myself "

Apostrophe

INTRODUCTORY PROJECT

1. You're the kind of person who believes he's going to be a big success without doing any hard work, but the world doesn't work that way.

    What is the purpose of the apostrophe in *You're, he's,* and *doesn't?*

    _____

2. the eagle's nest
    Fred's feet
    my mother's briefcase
    the children's drawings
    Babe Ruth's bat

    What is the purpose of the *'s* in all the examples above?

    _____

3. The piles of old books in the attic were starting to decay. One book's spine had been gnawed away by mice.
    Two cars were stolen yesterday from the mall parking lot. Another car's antenna was ripped off.

    In the sentence pairs above, why is the *'s* used in each second sentence but not in the first?

    _____

Answers are on page 466.

The two main uses of the apostrophe are:

1 To show the omission of one or more letters in a contraction
2 To show ownership or possession

Each use is explained on the pages that follow.

APOSTROPHE IN CONTRACTIONS

A contraction is formed when two words are combined to make one word. An apostrophe is used to show where letters are omitted in forming the contraction. Here are two contractions:

have + not = haven't (the *o* in *not* has been omitted)
I   + will = I'll (the *wi* in *will* has been omitted)

The following are some other common contractions:

I + am	= I'm		it + is	= it's
I + have	= I've		it + has	= it's
I + had	= I'd		is + not	= isn't
who + is	= who's		could + not	= couldn't
do + not	= don't		I + would	= I'd
did + not	= didn't		they + are	= they're
let + us	= let's		there + is	= there's

Note: *will* + *not* has an unusual contraction: *won't*.

Practice 1

Combine the following words into contractions. One is done for you.

she + is   = ___*she's*___   you + will   = _____

you + have = _____   we + would = _____

have + not = _____   could + not   = _____

he + has   = _____   they + will   = _____

we + are   = _____   does + not   = _____

Practice 2

Write the contraction for the words in parentheses.

Example   He (could not) _____ *couldn't* _____ come.

1. I (did not) _____ like the movie, but the popcorn (was not)
    _____ bad.

2. (We are) _____ good friends, but that (does not) _____
    mean we have to agree all the time.

3. (You are)_____ taking the wrong approach with Len, as he
    (can not) _____ stand being lectured.

4. This (is not) _____ the first time (you have) _____
    embarrassed me in public.

5. (We would) _____ love to have you stay for dinner if you
    (do not) _____ mind eating leftovers.

Note: Even though contractions are common in everyday speech and in written
dialogue, usually it is best to avoid them in formal writing.

Practice 3

Write five sentences using the apostrophe in different contractions.

1. _____

2. _____

3. _____

4. _____

5. _____

Four Contractions to Note Carefully

Four contractions that deserve special attention are *they're, it's, you're,* and
who's. Sometimes these contractions are confused with the possessive words
their, its, your, and *whose.* The chart on the following page shows the difference
in meaning between the contractions and the possessive words.

Contractions	*Possessive Words*
they're (means *they are*)	their (means *belonging to them*)
it's (means *it is* or *it has*)	its (means *belonging to it*)
you're (means *you are*)	your (means *belonging to you*)
who's (means *who is*)	whose (means *belonging to whom*)

Note: Possessive words are explained further on page 164.

Practice

Underline the correct form (the contraction or the possessive word) in each of the following sentences. Use the contraction whenever the two words of the contraction (*they are, it is, you are, who is*) would also fit.

1. (It's, Its) going to be a long time before (you're, your) going to get any more help from me.
2. I don't know (who's, whose) fault it is that the car battery is dead, but I know (who's whose) the primary suspect.
3. (You're, Your) feeling nauseated because you did not open any windows while staining (you're, your) living-room floor.
4. (They're, There) are some people who insist on acting gloomy no matter how well (they're, their) lives are going.
5. (It's, Its) hard to be pleasant to neighbors who always keep (they're, their) stereo on too loud.

APOSTROPHE TO SHOW
OWNERSHIP OR POSSESSION

To show ownership or possession, we can use such words as *belongs to, owned by,* or (most commonly) *of.*

> the knapsack *that belongs to* Lola
> the house *owned by* my mother
> the sore arm *of* the pitcher

But the apostrophe plus *s* (if the word does not end in *-s*) is often the quickest and easiest way to show possession. Thus we can say:

> Lola's knapsack
> my mother's house
> the pitcher's sore arm

Points to Remember

1   The *'s* goes with the owner or possessor (in the examples given, *Lola*, *mother*, and *pitcher*). What follows is the person or thing possessed (in the examples given, *knapsack*, *house*, and *sore arm*). An easy way to determine the owner or possessor is to ask the question "Whom does it belong to?" In the first example, the answer to the question "Whom does the knapsack belong to?" is *Lola*. Therefore, the *'s* goes with *Lola*.

2   There should always be a break between the word and the *'s*.

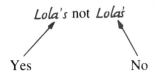

Yes   No

Practice 1

Rewrite the italicized part of each of the sentences listed below, using the *'s* to show possession. Remember that the *'s* goes with the owner or possessor.

Examples   *The motorcycle owned by Clyde* is a frightening machine.
Clyde's motorcycle
_____

The roommate of my brother is a sweet and friendly person.
My brother's roommate
_____

1. The *demonstration of the chef* stimulated our appetites.

_____

2. A strange man just drove away in *the car of Phil*.

_____

3. *The law of Murphy* states, "Anything that can go wrong, will go wrong."

_____

4. All the financial-planning information has been stored in the *memory of the computer*.

_____

5. Because *the mother of my wife* is in jail for forgery, I call her my mother-outlaw.

_____

6. Where is the rest of *the meat loaf of yesterday,* which I was planning to eat for lunch?

———————————————————————————————————

7. *The promotion of my sister* to vice president of the company was well earned.

———————————————————————————————————

8. *The bratty little brother of Maria* has grown up to become a charming young man.

———————————————————————————————————

9. The judges reversed *the call of the referee* after they viewed the videotaped replay.

———————————————————————————————————

10. Thousands of gallons of crude oil spilled into the ocean when *the hull of the tanker* ruptured in the storm.

———————————————————————————————————

Practice 2

Underline the word in each sentence that needs an *'s.* Then write the word correctly in the space at the left. One is done for you as an example.

horse's   1. The trainer removed a nail from the horse hoof.

————   2. My brother appetite is like a bottomless pit.

————   3. Arnie pulled his young son hand away from the kerosene heater.

————   4. The comedian trademarks were long cigars and red socks.

————   5. No matter when you dial the landlord number, nobody answers the phone.

————   6. The assistant manager always takes credit for Ted ideas.

————   7. We all froze when the bank teller wig fell off.

————   8. Some people never feel other people problems are their concern.

————   9. Nita hires an accountant to prepare her dance studio tax returns each year.

————   10. The screen door slammed on the little girl fingers.

Practice 3

Add an *'s* to each of the following words to make them the possessors or owners of something. Then write sentences using the words. Your sentences can be serious or playful. One is done for you as an example.

1. Cary ___*Cary's*___
   Cary's hair is bright red.

2. teacher _____

   _____

3. insect _____

   _____

4. husband _____

   _____

5. salesperson _____

   _____

Apostrophe versus Possessive Pronouns

Do not use an apostrophe with possessive pronouns. They already show ownership. Possessive pronouns include *his*, *hers*, *its*, *yours*, *ours*, and *theirs*.

Correct	*Incorrect*
The bookstore lost its lease.	The bookstore lost its' lease.
The racing bikes were theirs.	The racing bikes were theirs'.
The change is yours.	The change is yours'.
His problems are ours, too.	His' problems are ours', too.
His skin is more tanned than hers.	His' skin is more tanned than hers'.

Apostrophe versus Simple Plurals

When you want to make words plural, just add an *s* at the end of the word. Do *not* add an apostrophe. For example, the plural of the word *movie* is *movies*, not *movie's* or *movies'*. Look at this sentence:

When Sally's cat began catching birds, the neighbors called the police.

The words *birds* and *neighbors* are simple plurals, meaning more than one bird, more than one neighbor. The plural is shown by adding *-s* only. (More information about plurals starts on page 208.) On the other hand, the *'s* after *Sally* shows possession—that Sally owns the cat.

Practice

Insert an apostrophe where needed to show possession in the following sentences. Write *plural* above words where the *-s* ending simply means more than one thing.

                    plural   *plural*   *plural*

Example Originally the cuffs of men's pants were meant for cigar ashes.

1. The pizza parlors aroma seeped through the vents to our apartment upstairs.
2. Looking at the rabbits bones gave Teddy the shivers.
3. Karens tomato plants are taller than the six-foot stakes she used to support them.
4. Because of the lakes high bacteria level, officials prohibited boating, swimming, and fishing there.
5. I have considered applying for many positions, but an exterminators job is not one of them.
6. The candlelights glow fell gently on the pale, white plates and ruby-red goblets.
7. Crackers layered with cheese and apple slices are my fathers favorite snacks.
8. The police officers report of the accident is very different from the statements of the drivers involved.
9. Seabirds skidding along the oceans edge at midnight looked like miniature moonlight surfers.
10. The mothers prayers were answered when the batteries in her daughters radio died just as the "Heavy Metal Jamboree" was beginning.

Apostrophe with Words Ending in *-s*

If a word ends in *-s*, show possession by adding only an apostrophe. Most plurals end in *-s* and so show possession simply by adding the apostrophe.

James' promotion   my boss' temper

Ms. Travers' apartment   the students' graduation

Francis' idea   the workers' grievances

Practice

Add an apostrophe where needed.

1. The rhinoceros temper has a short fuse.
2. My two sisters feet are the same size, so they share their shoes.
3. When the cast was removed, Charles leg was as thin as his arm.
4. The Tylers new television set was mistakenly delivered to our house.
5. The photo album that was lost contained my parents wedding pictures.

Review Test 1

In each sentence cross out the two words that need apostrophes. Then write the words correctly in the spaces provided.

_____   1. That authors latest horror novel isnt so horrifying.
_____

_____   2. "I dont get it," I confessed after hearing Pams long and complicated joke.
_____

_____   3. Luckily, the motorcycles gas tank hadnt been scratched in the collision.
_____

_____   4. Whos been stealing the Sunday papers from my doorstep before Im awake?
_____

_____   5. The bouquet looks natural, but its one of the artificial ones Sylvias mother
_____   made.

——————   6. I too would like to take a shower, if theres any water left by the time youre
——————   finished.

——————   7. Olivia watched sadly as the highway departments bulldozer demolished the
——————   house shed grown up in.

——————   8. All the raffle winners tickets will be checked before well award the prizes.

——————

——————   9. Ive heard that electric ''bug zappers'' dont kill more than a few mosquitoes
——————   and do kill many beneficial insects.

——————   10. The authorities guess is that a radical protest group put the toxic chemical
——————   in the towns water supply.

Review Test 2

Rewrite the following sentences, changing the underlined words into either (1) a contraction or (2) a possessive.

1. Mel should have taken the advice of the bouncer and left the bar peacefully.

   _____

   _____

2. The weather forecast of today assured us that it is definitely going to be sunny, cloudy, or rainy.

   _____

   _____

3. The enthusiasm of my brother Manny for baseball is so great that he will even wear his glove and cap when he watches a game on TV.

   _____

   _____

4. Many parents think the influence of television is to blame for the poor performance of their children in school.

   _____

   _____

5. I was shocked by the announcement of my friend that he was going to marry a girl he had dated for only two months.

   _____

   _____

Quotation Marks

Read the following scene and underline all the words enclosed within quotation marks. Your teacher may also have you dramatize the scene, with one person reading the narration and two persons acting the two speaking parts of the bartender and the gorilla. The two speakers should imagine the scene as part of a stage play and try to make their words seem as real and true-to-life as possible.

A gorilla walked into a bar. "Bartender," he said, "I'll have a very dry martini."

"Coming right up," said the bartender. As the bartender mixed the drink, he muttered to himself, "There must be a better way to make a living."

The gorilla lit up a cigar and enjoyed the drink. Then he called out, "Bartender, that was an excellent martini. Please make me another, and let me have the bill."

The bartender brought the drink and also presented a bill for twenty-five dollars. "You know," the bartender said, gathering up his courage, "we don't get many gorillas in here."

"At your prices," said the gorilla, "no wonder."

1. On the basis of the above selection, what is the purpose of quotation marks?

   _____

2. Do commas and periods that come after a quotation go inside or outside the quotation marks?

   _____

Answers are on page 467.

The two main uses of quotation marks are:

1 To set off the exact words of a speaker or writer
2 To set off the titles of short works

Each use is explained on the pages that follow.

QUOTATION MARKS TO SET OFF THE WORDS OF A SPEAKER OR WRITER

Use quotation marks when you want to show the exact words of a speaker or writer:

''Who left the cap off the toothpaste?'' Lola demanded.
(Quotation marks set off the exact words that Lola spoke.)

Ben Franklin wrote, ''Keep your eyes wide open before marriage, half shut afterward.''
(Quotation marks set off the exact words that Ben Franklin wrote.)

''You're never too young,'' my Aunt Fern often tells me, ''to have a heart attack.''
(Two pairs of quotation marks are used to enclose the aunt's exact words.)

Maria complained, ''I look so old some days. Even makeup doesn't help. I feel as though I'm painting a corpse!''
(Note that the end quotes do not come until the end of Maria's speech. Place quotation marks before the first quoted word of a speech and after the last quoted word. As long as no interruption occurs in the speech, do not use quotation marks for each new sentence.)

Punctuation Hint: In the four examples above, notice that a comma sets off the quoted part from the rest of the sentence. Also observe that commas and periods at the end of a quote always go *inside* quotation marks.

Complete the following statements that explain how capital letters, commas, and periods are used in quotations. Refer to the four examples as guides.

● Every quotation begins with a _____ letter.
● When a quotation is split (as in the sentence about Aunt Fern), the second part does not begin with a capital letter unless it is a _____ sentence.
● _____ are used to separate the quoted part of a sentence from the rest of the sentence.
● Commas and periods that come at the end of a quote go _____ quotation marks.

The answers are *capital*, *new*, *Commas*, and *inside*.

Practice 1

Insert quotation marks where needed in the sentences that follow.

1. The chilling bumper sticker read, You can't hug children with nuclear arms.
2. One day we'll look back on this argument, and it will seem funny, Bruce assured Rosa.
3. Hey, lady, this is an express line! shouted the cashier to the woman with a full basket.
4. My grandfather was fond of saying, Happiness is found along the way, not at the end of the road.
5. When will I be old enough to pay the adult fare? the child asked.
6. The trouble with Easy Street is that it's a blind alley, said our minister.
7. The sign on the classroom wall read, When you come to the end of your rope, make a knot and hold on.
8. I'm not afraid to die, said Woody Allen. I just don't want to be there when it happens.
9. My son once told me, Sometimes I wish I were little again. Then I wouldn't have to make so many decisions.
10. I don't feel like cooking tonight, Eve said to Adam. Let's just have fruit.

Practice 2

Rewrite the following sentences, adding quotation marks where needed. Use a capital letter to begin a quote and use a comma to set off a quoted part from the rest of the sentence.

Example   I'm getting tired Sally said.
             "I'm getting tired," Sally said.
_____

1. Simon said take three giant steps forward.

    _____

2. Please don't hang up before leaving a message stated the telephone recording.

    _____

3. Clark Kent asked a man on the street where is the nearest phone booth?

    _____

4. You'll be deaf if you play that music any louder my father shouted.

    _____

5. Nothing can be done for your broken little toe, the doctor said. You have
    to wait for it to heal.

    _____

Practice 3

1. Write three quotations that appear in the first part of a sentence.

    Example   *"Let's go shopping," I suggested.*

    a. _____
    b. _____
    c. _____

2. Write three quotations that appear at the end of a sentence.

    Example   *Bob asked, "Have you had lunch yet?"*

    a. _____
    b. _____
    c. _____

3. Write three quotations that appear at the beginning and end of a sentence.

    Example   *"If the bus doesn't come soon," Mary said, "we'll freeze."*

    a. _____
    b. _____
    c. _____

Indirect Quotations

An indirect quotation is a rewording of someone else's comments rather than a word-for-word direct quotation. The word *that* often signals an indirect quotation.

Direct Quotation	*Indirect Quotation*
George said, "My son is a dare-devil."	George said that his son is a dare-devil.
(George's exact spoken words are given, so quotation marks are used.)	(We learn George's words *indirectly*, so no quotation marks are used.)
Carol's note to Arnie read, "I'm at the neighbors'. Give me a call."	Carol left a note for Arnie that said she would be at the neighbors' and he should give her a call.
(The exact words that Carol wrote in the note are given, so quotation marks are used.)	(We learn Carol's words *indirectly*, so no quotation marks are used.)

Practice 1

Rewrite the following sentences, changing words as necessary to convert the sentences into direct quotations. The first one is done for you as an example.

1. Agnes told me as we left work that Herb got a raise.
    Agnes said to me as we left work, "Herb got a raise."

2. I said that was hard to believe since Herb is a do-nothing.

    _____

3. Agnes replied that even so, he's gone up in the world.

    _____

4. I told her that she must be kidding.

    _____

5. Agnes laughed and said that Herb was moved from the first to the fourth floor today.

    _____

    _____

Practice 2

Rewrite the following sentences, converting each direct quotation into an indirect statement. In each case you will have to add the word *that* or *if* and change other words as well.

Example   The barber asked Fred, "Have you noticed how your hair is thinning?"

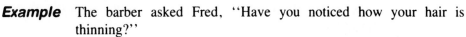

The barber asked Fred if he had noticed how his hair was thinning.

1. My doctor said, "You need to lose weight."

    _____

2. Lola asked Tony, "Don't you ever wash your car?"

    _____

3. The operator asked, "Have you tried to look up the number yourself?"

    _____

4. Janie whispered, "Harold's so boring he lights up a room when he leaves it."

    _____

5. The teacher said, "Movies are actually a series of still pictures."

    _____

QUOTATION MARKS TO SET OFF THE TITLES OF SHORT WORKS

Titles of short works are usually set off by quotation marks, while titles of long works are underlined. Use quotation marks to set off the titles of such short works as articles in books, newspapers, or magazines; chapters in a book; short stories, poems, and songs. On the other hand, you should underline the titles of books, newspapers, magazines, plays, movies, record albums, and television shows. See the examples on the next page.

Note: In printed form the titles of long works are set off by italics—slanted type that looks *like this.*

Quotation Marks	*Underlines*
the article "The Toxic Tragedy"	in the book <u>Who's Poisoning America</u>
the article "New Cures for Head-aches"	in the newspaper <u>The New York Times</u>
the article "When the Patient Plays Doctor"	in the magazine <u>Family Health</u>
the chapter "Connecting with Kids"	in the book <u>Straight Talk</u>
the story "The Dead"	in the book <u>Dubliners</u>
the poem "Birches"	in the book <u>The Complete Poems of Robert Frost</u>
the song "Some Enchanted Evening"	in the album <u>South Pacific</u>
	the television show <u>Hill Street Blues</u>
	the movie <u>Rear Window</u>

Practice

Use quotation marks or underlines as needed.

1. My sister just bought a videocassette recorder so she won't have to miss any more episodes of General Hospital.
2. Rita grabbed the National Enquirer and eagerly began to read the article I Had a Space Alien's Baby.
3. Our exam will cover two chapters, The Study of Heredity and The Origin of Diversity, in our biology textbook, Life.
4. The last song on the bluegrass program was called I Ain't Broke but I'm Badly Bent.
5. A three-page short story like Shirley Jackson's The Lottery is more exciting to me than a full-length action film like The Delta Force.
6. At last night's performance of Annie Get Your Gun, the audience joined the cast in singing There's No Business Like Show Business.
7. A typical article in Cosmopolitan will have a title like How to Hook a Man without Letting Him Know You're Fishing.
8. One way Joanne deals with depression is to get out her Man of La Mancha album and play the song The Impossible Dream.

9. I read the article How Good Is Your Breakfast? in Consumer Reports while munching a doughnut this morning.

10. According to a Psychology Today article titled Home on the Street, there are 36,000 people living on New York City's sidewalks.

OTHER USES OF QUOTATION MARKS

1 To set off special words or phrases from the rest of a sentence:

Many people spell the words ''all right'' as one word, ''alright,'' instead of correctly spelling them as two words.

I have trouble telling the difference between ''principal'' and ''principle.''

2 To mark off a quote within a quote. For this purpose, single quotes (' ') are used:

Ben Franklin said, ''The noblest question in the world is, 'What good may I do in it?' ''

''If you want to have a scary experience,'' Nick told Fran, ''read Stephen King's story 'The Mangler' in his book *Night Shift*.''

Review Test 1

Place quotation marks around the exact words of a speaker or writer in the sentences that follow.

1. Give me a break! Charlie shouted to no one in particular.

2. My mother always says, Some are wise, and some are otherwise.

3. Why do men continue to wear ties when they serve no purpose? asked Paul.

4. Take all you want, but eat all you take, read the cafeteria sign.

5. One of Mark Twain's famous lines is, Man is the only animal that blushes—or needs to.

6. My friend the radio announcer loses his voice every time we drive under a bridge, said the comedian.

7. The first time my daughter had a headache, she told me, Mommy, I have a pain in my brain.

8. If your parachute doesn't open, the skydiving instructor joked, bring it back, and we'll give you a new one.

9. The novelist ended a letter to his brother by saying, I'm sorry for writing such a long letter. I didn't have time for a shorter one.

10. The toughest place I ever worked was the Knuckle Room, Rodney Dangerfield explained. I looked in one of the finger bowls, and there were three fingers in it.

Review Test 2

1. Write a sentence in which you quote a favorite expression of someone you know. Identify the relationship of the person to you.

   Example *My brother Sam often says after a meal, "That wasn't bad at all."*

   _____

   _____

2. Write a quotation that contains the words *Tony asked Lola*. Write a second quotation that includes the words *Lola replied*.

   _____

   _____

   _____

3. Write a sentence that interests or amuses you from a book. Identify the title and author of the book.

   Example *In her book At Wit's End, Erma Bombeck advises, "Never go to a doctor whose office plants have died."*

   _____

   _____

   _____

4. Write a sentence that interests you from a newspaper. Identify the title and the author (if given) of the article.

   _____

   _____

   _____

5. Write a sentence that interests you from a magazine. Identify the title and the author of the article.

_____

_____

_____

Review Test 3

Go through the comics section of a newspaper to find a comic strip that amuses you. Be sure to choose a strip where two or more characters are speaking to each other. Write a full description that will enable people who have not read the comic strip to visualize it clearly and appreciate its humor. Describe the setting and action in each panel and enclose the words of the speakers in quotation marks.

Comma

INTRODUCTORY PROJECT

Commas often (though not always) signal a minor break or pause in a sentence. Each of the six pairs of sentences below illustrates one of six main uses of the comma. Read each pair of sentences aloud and place a comma wherever you feel a slight pause occurs.

1. a. Joel watched the eleven o'clock news a movie a *Honeymooners* rerun and the station sign-off.
   b. Please endorse your check write your account number on the back and fill out a deposit slip.

2. a. Even though I was safe indoors I shivered at the thought of the bitter cold outside.
   b. To start the car depress the accelerator and then turn the ignition key.

3. a. The opossum an animal much like the kangaroo carries its young in a pouch.
   b. George Derek who was recently arrested was a high school classmate of mine.

4. a. I had enrolled in the course during pre-registration but my name did not appear on the class list.
   b. A police cruiser blocked the busy intersection and an ambulance pulled up on the sidewalk near the motionless victims.

5. a. Emily said "Why is it so hard to remember your dreams the next day?"
   b. "After I left the interview" said David "I couldn't remember a word I had said."

6. a. Mike has driven over 1500000 accident-free miles in his job as a long-distance trucker.
   b. The Gates Trucking Company of 1800 Industrial Highway Jersey City New Jersey gave Mike an award on January 26 1990 for his superior safety record.

Answers are on page 468.

SIX MAIN USES OF THE COMMA

Commas are used mainly as follows:

1   To separate items in a series
2   To set off introductory material
3   On both sides of words that interrupt the flow of thought in a sentence
4   Between two complete thoughts connected by *and, but, for, or, nor, so, yet*
5   To set off a direct quotation from the rest of a sentence
6   For certain everyday material

You may find it helpful to remember that the comma often marks a slight pause, or break, in a sentence. Read aloud the sentence examples given for each rule, and listen for the minor pauses or breaks that are signaled by commas.

1   Comma between Items in a Series

Use a comma to separate items in a series.

Magazines, paperback novels, and textbooks crowded the shelves.
Hard-luck Sam needs a loan, a good-paying job, and a close friend.
Pat sat in the doctor's office, checked her watch, and smoked nervously.
Lola bit into the ripe, juicy apple.
More and more people entered the crowded, noisy stadium.

Notes

a   The final comma in a series is optional, but often it is used.
b   A comma is used between two descriptive words in a series only if *and* inserted between the words sounds natural. You could say:

Lola bit into the ripe *and* juicy apple.
More and more people entered the crowded *and* noisy stadium.

But notice in the following sentences that the descriptive words do not sound natural when *and* is inserted between them. In such cases, no comma is used.

The model wore a light sleeveless blouse. (A light *and* sleeveless blouse doesn't sound right, so no comma is used.)
Dr. Van Helsing noticed two tiny puncture marks on his patient's neck. (Two *and* tiny puncture marks doesn't sound right, so no comma is used.)

Practice

Place commas between items in a series.

1. Many of the refugees wandered around without work food or a place to live.
2. Ice cream crushed candy Pepsi and popcorn formed a gluelike compound on the movie theater's floor.
3. Lewis dribbled twice spun to his left and lofted his patented hook shot over the outstretched arms of the Panthers' center.
4. I discovered gum wrappers pennies and a sock hidden under the seats when I vacuumed my car.
5. We finally drove across the Arizona-New Mexico border after eight hours four hundred miles and three rest stops.

2 Comma after Introductory Material

Use a comma to set off introductory material.

Fearlessly, Lola picked up the slimy slug.

Just to annoy Tony, she let it crawl along her arm.

Although I have a black belt in karate, I decided to go easy on the demented bully who had kicked sand in my face.

Mumbling under her breath, the woman picked over the tomatoes.

Note: If the introductory material is brief, the comma is sometimes omitted. In the activities here, you should include the comma.

Practice

Place commas after introductory material.

1. When all is said and done a lot more is said than done.
2. If you mark your suitcase with colored tape it will be easier to find at the baggage counter.
3. Feeling brave and silly at the same time Anita volunteered to go onstage and help the magician.
4. As the bride smiled and strolled past me down the aisle I saw a bead of sweat roll from her forehead down her cheek. Remembering my own wedding I knew she wasn't sweating from the heat.
5. Using metallic cords from her Christmas presents young Ali made several bracelets for herself. After that she took a long ribbon and tied a bow around her dog's head.

3 Comma around Words
Interrupting the Flow of Thought

Use a comma on both sides of words that interrupt the flow of thought in a sentence.

> The car, cleaned and repaired, is ready to be sold.
> Martha, our new neighbor, used to work as a bouncer at Rexy's Tavern.
> Taking long walks, especially after dark, helps me sort out my thoughts.

Usually you can "hear" words that interrupt the flow of thought in a sentence. However, if you are not sure if certain words are interrupters, remove them from the sentence. If it still makes sense without the words, you know that the words are interrupters and that the information they give is nonessential. Such nonessential information is set off with commas. In the following sentence,

> Susie Hall, who is my best friend, won a new car in the *Reader's Digest* sweepstakes.

the words *who is my best friend* are extra information, not needed to identify the subject of the sentence, *Susie Hall.* Put commas around such nonessential information. On the other hand, in the sentence

> The woman who is my best friend won a new car in the *Reader's Digest* sweepstakes.

the words *who is my best friend* supply essential information needed for us to identify the woman. If the words were removed from the sentence, we would no longer know which woman won the sweepstakes. Commas are not used around such essential information.

Here is another example:

> *The Shining,* a novel by Stephen King, is the scariest book I've ever read.

Here the words *a novel by Stephen King* are extra information, not needed to identify the subject of the sentence, *The Shining.* Commas go around such nonessential information. On the other hand, in the sentence

> Stephen King's novel *The Shining* is the scariest book I've ever read.

the words *The Shining* are needed to identify the novel. Commas are not used around such essential information.

Most of the time you will be able to ''hear'' words that interrupt the flow of thoughts in a sentence and will not have to think about whether the words are essential or nonessential.*

Practice

Use commas to set off interrupting words.

1. The dancer aided by members of the chorus hobbled across the stage toward the wings.
2. Mr. and Mrs. Anderson who were married on the Fourth of July named their first child ''Freedom.''
3. All trees even the most gigantic are only 1 percent living tissue; the rest is deadwood.
4. The repairman unaware of the grease on his shoes left a black trail from our front door to the washing machine.
5. John Adams and Thomas Jefferson the second and third presidents of the United States died on the same day in 1826.

4   Comma between Complete Thoughts Connected by a Joining Word

Use a comma between two complete thoughts connected by *and, but, for, or, nor, so, yet.*

My parents threatened to throw me out of the house, so I had to stop playing the drums.

The polyester bed sheets had a gorgeous design on them, but they didn't feel as comfortable as plain cotton sheets.

The teenage girls walked the hot summer streets, and the teenage boys drove by in their shined-up cars.

---

* Some instructors refer to nonessential or extra information that is set off by commas as a *nonrestrictive clause.* Essential information that interrupts the flow of thought is called a *restrictive clause.* No commas are used to set off a restrictive clause.

Notes

a The comma is optional when the complete thoughts are short ones:

Hal relaxed but Bob kept working.
The soda was flat so I poured it away.
We left school early for the furnace broke down.

b Be careful not to use a comma in sentences having *one* subject and a *double* verb. The comma is used only in sentences made up of two complete thoughts (two subjects and two verbs). In the sentence

Mary lay awake that stormy night and listened to the thunder crashing.

there is only one subject (*Mary*) and a double verb (*lay* and *listened*). No comma is needed. Likewise, the sentence

The quarterback kept the ball and plunged across the goal line for a touchdown.

has only one subject (*quarterback*) and a double verb (*kept* and *plunged*); therefore, no comma is needed.

Practice

Place a comma before a joining word that connects two complete thoughts (two subjects and two verbs). Remember, do *not* place a comma within sentences that have only one subject and a double verb. Mark sentences that are correct with a *C*.

1. Kate arrived for the sale before the store opened but a large crowd was already there.
2. Our large lecture class was canceled so we spent an hour in the student center.
3. Eddie is building a kayak in his garage and plans to take it down the Columbia River next year.
4. I desperately need more storage space for I can't seem to throw anything away.
5. The helicopter hovered overhead and lowered a rescue line to the downed pilot.

6. Carlos was a very successful businessman but none of his children wanted to follow in his footsteps.

7. One of the men got ready to leave work at four but put his coat away upon seeing his boss.

8. The family expected Valerie to go to college but she went to work after eloping with her boyfriend.

9. Bobby had pleaded with his parents to buy him a personal computer for his schoolwork but he spends most of his time playing games on it.

10. The doctor examined me for less than ten minutes and then presented me with a bill for ninety dollars.

5 Comma with Direct Quotations

Use a comma to set off a direct quotation from the rest of a sentence.

> ''Please take a number,'' said the deli clerk.
>
> Fred told Martha, ''I've just signed up for a Dale Carnegie course.''
>
> ''Those who sling mud,'' a famous politician once said, ''usually lose ground.''
>
> ''Reading this book,'' complained Stan, ''is about as interesting as watching paint dry.''

Note: Commas and periods at the end of a quotation go inside quotation marks. See also page 169.

Practice

Use commas to set off quotations from the rest of the sentence.

1. Frowning, the swimming instructor said ''Your arms look fine, but you keep forgetting to kick.''

2. ''The best way to get rid of a temptation'' Oscar Wilde advised ''is to yield to it.''

3. The poster in the chemistry lab read ''If you're smoking a cigarette, you shouldn't be in this room.''

4. ''We're the last ones in the world to let you down'' stated the undertaker's sign.

5. ''Did you really think'' the judge asked the defendant ''you could kill both your parents and then ask for mercy because you're an orphan?''

3. The witness said she had seen the face of the robber, only for an instant.

4. After watching my form, on the high diving board, Mr. Riley, my instructor, asked me if I had insurance.

5. Rosa flew first to Los Angeles, and then she went to visit her parents, in Mexico City.

6. The tall, thin man who bought the red socks, is a nightclub comedian.

7. Onions, radishes, and potatoes, seem to grow better in cooler climates.

8. Whenever Larry is in Las Vegas, you can find him at the blackjack table, or the roulette wheel.

9. While I watched in disbelief, my car rolled down the hill, and through the front window of a Chinese restaurant.

10. The question, sir, is not, whether you committed the crime, but, when you committed the crime.

Review Test 1

Insert commas where needed. In the space provided under each sentence, summarize briefly the rule that explains the use of the comma or commas.

1. As the usher turned his head two youngsters darted into the movie theater.

_____

2. This car I strongly suspect is out to get me.

_____

3. I found my father's dusty water-stained yearbook behind some pipes in the basement.

_____

4. "Be careful what you wish for" an old saying goes "or you may get it."

_____

5. My final mortgage payment on December 3 2011 seems light-years away.

_____

6. We sat together on the riverbank watched the sun disappear and made plans for our divorce.

_____

7. I panicked when I saw the flashing red lights behind me but the policeman just wanted to pass.

_____

8. The burly umpire his shoes and trousers now covered with dirt pulled off his mask and angrily ejected the St. Louis manager from the game.

_____

9. "Knock off the noise" Sam yelled to the children. "I'm talking long distance to your grandmother."

_____

10. Rubbing her eyes and clearing her throat Stella tried to sound human as she answered the early-morning phone call.

_____

Review Test 2

1. Write a sentence telling of three items you want to get the next time you go to the store. _____

_____

2. Write a sentence that describes three things you would like to get done this week. _____

_____

3. Write two sentences, starting the first one with _If I found a hundred-dollar bill_ and the second one with _Also_. _____

_____

_____

_____

4. Write two sentences describing how you relax after getting home from school or work. Start the first sentence with _After_ or _When_. Start the second sentence with _Next_. _____

_____

_____

_____

5. Write a sentence about a selfish or generous person you know. Use the words _a selfish person_ or _a generous person_ right after his or her name.

_____

_____

6. Write a sentence that tells something about your favorite magazine or television show. Use the words *which is my favorite magazine* or *which is my favorite television show* after the name of the magazine or show.

_____

_____

7. Write two complete thoughts about foods you enjoy. Use *and* to join the two complete thoughts. _____

_____

8. Write two complete thoughts about a person you know. The first thought should tell of something you like about the person. The second thought should tell of something you don't like. Join the thoughts with *but*.

_____

_____

_____

9. Invent a line that Lola might say to Tony. Use the words *Lola said* in the sentence. _____

_____

10. Write a remark that you made to someone today. Use the words *I said* somewhere in the middle of the sentence. _____

_____

Review Test 3

On separate paper, write six sentences, with each sentence demonstrating one of the six main comma rules.

Other Punctuation Marks

INTRODUCTORY PROJECT

Every sentence below needs one of the following punctuation marks:

    ;   —   -   ( )   :

See if you can insert the correct mark in each case. Use each mark once.

1. The following singers were nominated by the Grammy Awards Committee for Best Male Artist Kenny Rogers, Bruce Springsteen, Stevie Wonder, Phil Collins, and Lionel Ritchie.
2. A life size statue of her cat adorns the living room of Diana's penthouse.
3. Sigmund Freud, the pioneer psychoanalyst 1856–1939, was a habitual cocaine user.
4. As children, we would put pennies on the railroad track we wanted to see what they would look like after being run over by a train.
5. The stuntwoman was battered, broken, barely breathing but alive.

Answers are on page 469.

COLON (:)

The colon is a mark of introduction. Use the colon at the end of a complete statement to do the following:

1   Introduce a list.

My little brother has three hobbies: playing video games, racing his Hot Wheels cars all over the floor, and driving me crazy.

2   Introduce a long quotation.

Janet's paper was based on a passage from George Eliot's novel *Middlemarch:* "If we had a keen vision and feeling of all ordinary human life, it would be like hearing the grass grow and the squirrel's heart beat, and we should die of that roar which lies on the other side of silence. As it is, the quickest of us walk about well wadded with stupidity."

3   Introduce an explanation.

There are two ways to do this job: the easy way and the right way.

Two minor uses of the colon are after the opening in a formal letter (*Dear Sir or Madam:*) and between the hour and the minute when writing the time (*The bus will leave for the game at 11:45*).

Practice

Place colons where needed.

1.   Roger is on a "see-food" diet if he sees food, he eats it.
2.   Brenda had some terrible problems last summer her mother suffered a heart attack, her husband lost his job, and one of her children was arrested for shoplifting.
3.   Andy Rooney wrote in one of his columns "Doctors should never talk to ordinary people about anything but medicine. When doctors talk politics, economics, or sports, they reveal themselves to be ordinary mortals, idiots just like the rest of us. That isn't what any of us wants our doctors to be."

SEMICOLON (;)

The semicolon signals more of a pause than the comma alone but not quite the full pause of a period. Use a semicolon to do the following:

1 Join two complete thoughts that are not already connected by a joining word such as *and, but, for,* or *so.*

The chemistry lab blew up; Professor Thomas was fired.
I once stabbed myself with a pencil; a black mark has been under my skin ever since.

2 Join two complete thoughts that include a transitional word such as *however, otherwise, moreover, furthermore, therefore,* or *consequently.*

I cut and raked the grass; moreover, I weeded the lawn.
Sally finished typing the paper; however, she forgot to bring it to class.

Note: The first two uses of the semicolon are treated in more detail on pages 43–44.

3 Mark off items in a series when the items themselves contain commas.

This fall I won't have to work on Labor Day, September 7; Veterans' Day, November 11; or Thanksgiving Day, November 26.
At the final Weight Watchers' meeting, prizes were awarded to Sally Johnson, for losing 20 pounds; Irving Ross, for losing 26 pounds; and Betty Mills, the champion loser, who lost 102 pounds.

Practice

Place semicolons where needed.

1. Manny worked four extra hours at his job last night consequently he has been like a zombie in class today.
2. We could tell it was still raining all the puddles looked as if they were being shot at.
3. The winners at the county fair's beard contest were Fred Billings, sixty-seven, longest beard Robert Anderson, forty-five, best-groomed Matt Shepherd, eighty-two, whitest and Jack McGonical, seventy-eight, fullest.

DASH (—)

A dash signals a degree of pause longer than a comma but not as complete as a period. Use the dash to set off words for dramatic effect.

> I suggest—no, I insist—that you stay for dinner.
> The prisoner walked toward the electric chair—grinning.
> A meaningful job, a loving wife, and a car that wouldn't break down all the time—these are the things he wanted in life.

Practice

Place dashes where needed.

1. The members of the Polar Bear Club marched into the icy sea shivering.
2. Jill's attempt to walk her first since the operation was a disaster.
3. My sociology class meets at the worst possible time eight o'clock on Monday morning.

HYPHEN (-)

Use a hyphen in the following ways:

1 With two or more words that act as a single unit describing a noun.

> The society ladies nibbled at the deep-fried grasshoppers.
> A white-gloved waiter then put some snails on their table.

Note: Your dictionary will often help when you are unsure about whether to use a hyphen between words.

2 To divide a word at the end of a line of writing or typing.

> Although it had begun to drizzle, the teams decided to play the championship game that day.

Notes

a Always divide a word between syllables. Use your dictionary (see page 198) to be sure of correct syllable divisions.

b Do not divide words of one syllable.

c Do not divide a word if you can avoid dividing it.

Practice

Place hyphens where needed.

1. Why do I always find myself behind a slow moving car when I'm in a no passing zone?
2. To convince herself that she was still on a diet, Paula ordered a sugar free cola with her double cheese pizza.
3. Twirling his moustache, the hard hearted villain chuckled as he tied the teary eyed heroine to the railroad tracks.

PARENTHESES ( )

Use parentheses to do the following:

1 Set off extra or incidental information from the rest of a sentence.

The chapter on drugs in our textbook (pages 142–178) contains some frightening statistics.

The normal body temperature of a cat (101 to 102°) is 3° higher than the temperature of its owner.

2 Enclose letters or numbers that signal items in a series.

Three steps to follow in previewing a textbook are to (1) study the title, (2) read the first and last paragraphs, and (3) study the headings and subheadings.

Note: Do not use parentheses too often in your writing.

Practice

Add parentheses where needed.

1. Only a minority of Americans 31 percent can remember what life was like before television.
2. That instructor's office hours 3 to 4 P.M. are impossible for any student with an afternoon job.
3. Since I am forgetful, I often 1 make lists and then 2 check off items I have done. Now where did I put my list?

✐ Review Test 1

At the appropriate spot, place the punctuation mark shown in the margin.

Example   ;   The singles dance was a success; I met several people I wanted to see again.

:
1. That catalogue lists some unusual items a sausage stuffer, an electric foot warmer, and a remote-control car starter.

—
2. My brother's jokes none of which I can repeat are unfunny and tasteless.

-
3. These days, many two career couples have decided not to have children.

( )
4. The section on space travel in my daughter's science book Chapters 10–11 is sadly out of date.

:
5. In his book *The Prophet,* Kahlil Gibran wrote "You are good when you walk to your goal firmly and with bold steps. Yet you are not evil when you go thither limping. Even those who limp go not backward."

;
6. The frightened hamster darted from room to room finally, it crawled under a dresser.

—
7. MasterCard bills, the mortgage payment, and car repairs no wonder my paycheck doesn't last till the end of the month.

-
8. Someone once defined a self confident person as one who does crossword puzzles in pen instead of pencil.

( )
9. Three ways to save money on home repairs are 1 get several estimates, 2 avoid costly designer products, and 3 do it yourself.

;
10. I ordered several items from Sears: two suitcases, one maroon and one blue an extra-large, machine-washable sweater and a canvas gym bag.

✐ Review Test 2

On separate paper, write two sentences for each of the following punctuation marks: colon, semicolon, dash, hyphen, parentheses.

Section 4: Word Use

Dictionary Use

INTRODUCTORY PROJECT

The dictionary is an indispensable tool, as will be apparent if you try to answer the following questions *without* using the dictionary.

1. Which one of the following words is spelled incorrectly?

   fortutious   macrobiotics   stratagem

2. If you wanted to hyphenate the following word correctly, at which points would you place the syllable divisions?

   h i e r o g l y p h i c s

3. What common word has the sound of the first *e* in the word *chameleon?*
4. Where is the primary accent in the following word?

   o c t o g e n a r i a n

5. What are two separate meanings of the word *earmark?*

Your dictionary is a quick and sure authority on all these matters: spelling, syllabication, pronunciation, and word meanings. And as the chapter ahead will show, it is also a source for many other kinds of information as well.

Answers are on page 470.

The dictionary is a valuable tool. To take advantage of it, you need to understand the main kinds of information that a dictionary gives about a word. Look at the information provided for the word *dictate* in the following entry from the *American Heritage Dictionary*, paperback edition.*

Spelling and syllabication   *Pronunciation*   *Part of speech*

dic•tate (dĭk′tāt′, dĭk-tāt′) *v.* **-tat•ed, -tat•ing.**
1. To say or read aloud for transcription.——*Meanings*
2. To prescribe or command with authority.
—*n.* (dĭk′tāt′). An order; directive. [< Lat.
dictare.] —**dic•ta′tion** *n.*

Etymology

Other form of the word

SPELLING

The first bit of information, in the boldface (heavy type) entry itself, is the spelling of *dictate*. You probably already know the spelling of *dictate*, but if you didn't, you could find it by pronouncing the syllables in the word carefully and then looking it up in the dictionary.

Use your dictionary to correct the spelling of the following words:

wellcome _____   persisttant _____

quiting _____   proformance _____

consentration _____   oppurtinity _____

perfessional _____   desision _____

recieving _____   roomate _____

aranged _____   envolvment _____

extremly _____   diferance _____

consentrate _____   catagory _____

exciteing _____   priveledge _____

SYLLABICATION

The second bit of information that the dictionary gives, also in the boldface entry, is the syllabication of *dic•tate*. Note that a dot separates each syllable (or part) of the word.

Use your dictionary to mark the syllable divisions in the following words. Also indicate how many syllables are in each word.

v e n t u r e	(_____ syllables)
o b s e s s i o n	(_____ syllables)
e n e r g e t i c	(_____ syllables)
m i c r o o r g a n i s m	(_____ syllables)

Noting syllable divisions will enable you to *hyphenate* a word: divide it at the end of one line of writing and complete it at the beginning of the next line. You can correctly hyphenate a word only at a syllable division, and you may have to check your dictionary to make sure of a particular word's syllable divisions.

PRONUNCIATION

The third bit of information in the dictionary entry is the pronunciation of *dictate:* (dĭk'tāt') or (dĭk-tāt'). You already know how to pronounce *dictate,* but if you did not, the information within the parentheses would serve as your guide. Use your dictionary to complete the following exercises that relate to pronunciation.

Vowel Sounds

You will probably use the pronunciation key in your dictionary mainly as a guide to pronouncing different vowel sounds (vowels are the letters *a, e, i, o,* and *u*). Here is the pronunciation key that appears on every other page of the paperback *American Heritage Dictionary:*

ă pat ā pay â care ä father ĕ pet ē be ĭ pit ī tie î pier ŏ pot ō toe ô paw, for oi noise o͝o took o͞o boot ou out th thin *th* this ŭ cut û urge yo͞o abuse zh vision ə about, item, edible, gallop, circus

The key tells you, for example, that the sound of the short *a* is pronounced like the *a* in *pat,* the sound of the long *a* is like the *a* in *pay,* and the sound of the short *i* is like the *i* in *pit.*

Now look at the pronunciation key in your dictionary. The key is probably located in the front of the dictionary or at the bottom of every page. What common word in the key tells you how to pronounce each of the following sounds?

ĕ _____   ō _____

ī _____   ŭ _____

ŏ _____   o͞o _____

(Note that the long vowel always has the sound of its own name.)

The Schwa (ə)

The symbol ə looks like an upside-down *e*. It is called a *schwa,* and it stands for the unaccented sound in such words as *about, item, edible, gallop,* and *circus.* More approximately, it stands for the sound *uh*—like the *uh* that speakers sometimes make when they hesitate in their speech. Perhaps it would help to remember that *uh,* as well as ə, could be used to represent the schwa sound.

Here are some of the many words in which the sound appears: *socialize* (sō′shə līz or sō′shuh līz); *legitimate* (lə jĭt′ə mĭt or luh jĭt′uh mĭt); *oblivious* (ə blĭv′ē əs or uh blĭv′ē uhs). Open your dictionary to any page, and you will almost surely be able to find three words that make use of the schwa in the pronunciation in parentheses after the main entry. Write three such words and their pronunciations in the following spaces:

1. _____

2. _____

3. _____

Accent Marks

Some words contain both a primary accent, shown by a heavy stroke (′), and a secondary accent, shown by a lighter stroke (′). For example, in the word *vicissitude* (vĭ sĭs′ĭ to͞od′), the stress, or accent, goes chiefly on the second syllable (sĭs′), and, to a lesser extent, on the last syllable (to͞od′).

Use your dictionary to add stress marks to the following words:

notorious (nō tôr ē əs)   enterprise (ĕn tər prīz)

instigate (ĭn stĭ gāt)   irresistible (ĭr ĭ zĭs tə bəl)

equivocate (ĭ kwĭv ə kāt)   probability (prŏb ə bĭl ĭ tē)

millennium (mə lĕn ē əm)   representative (rĕp rĭ zĕn tə tĭv)

Full Pronunciation

Use your dictionary to write out the full pronunciation (the information given in parentheses) for each of the following words:

1. magnate _____

2. semblance _____

3. satiate _____

4. bastion _____

5. celestial _____

6. extraneous _____

7. edifice _____

8. incipient _____

9. fallacious _____

10. ostracize _____

11. phlegmatic _____

12. proximity _____

13. anachronism _____

14. felicitous _____

15. extemporaneous

_____

Now practice pronouncing each word. Use the pronunciation key in your dictionary as an aid to sounding out each syllable. Do *not* try to pronounce a word all at once; instead, work on mastering *one syllable at a time*. When you can pronounce each of the syllables in a word successfully, then say them in sequence, add the accent, and pronounce the entire word.

OTHER INFORMATION ABOUT WORDS

Parts of Speech

The dictionary entry for *dictate* includes the abbreviation *v.* This means that the meanings of *dictate* as a verb will follow. The abbreviation *n.* is then followed by the meaning of *dictate* as a noun.

At the front of your dictionary, you will probably find a key that will explain the meanings of abbreviations used in the dictionary. Use the key to fill in the meanings of the following abbreviations:

pl. = _____

sing. = _____

adj. = _____

adv. = _____

Principal Parts of Irregular Verbs

Dictate is a regular verb and forms its principal parts by adding *-d, -d,* and *-ing* to the stem of the verb. When a verb is irregular, the dictionary lists its principal parts. For example, in the entry for *begin* the present tense comes first (the entry itself, *begin*). Next comes the past tense (*began*), and then the past participle (*begun*)—the form of the verb used with such helping words as *have, had,* and *was.* Then comes the present participle (*beginning*)—the *-ing* form of the word.

Look up the principal parts of the following irregular verbs and write them in the spaces provided. The first one has been done for you.

Present	*Past*	*Past Participle*	*Present Participle*
see	*saw*	*seen*	*seeing*
choose			
know			
speak			

Plural Forms of Irregular Nouns

The dictionary supplies the plural forms of all irregular nouns (regular nouns form the plural by adding *-s* or *-es*). Give the plural of each of the following nouns:

thief   _____

cavity   _____

hero   _____

thesis   _____

Note: See page 215 for more information about plurals.

Meanings

When there is more than one meaning to a word, the meanings are numbered in the dictionary, as with the verb *dictate.* In many dictionaries, the most common meanings are presented first. The introductory pages of your dictionary will explain the order in which meanings are presented.

Use the sentence context to try to explain the meaning of the underlined word in each of the following sentences. Write your definition in the space provided. Then look up and record the dictionary meaning of the word. Be sure you pick out the meaning that fits the word as it is used in the sentence.

1. Honesty is a cardinal rule in my family.

   Your definition: _____

   Dictionary definition: _____

   _____

2. The union strike put management in a ticklish situation.

   Your definition: _____

   Dictionary definition: _____

   _____

3. Ben probably lacks confidence because his parents constantly railed at him.

   Your definition: _____

   Dictionary definition: _____

   _____

Etymology

Etymology refers to the history of a word. Many words have origins in foreign languages, such as Greek (Gk) or Latin (L). Such information is usually enclosed in brackets and is more likely to be present in a hardbound desk dictionary than in a paperback one.

Good desk dictionaries include the following:

The American Heritage Dictionary
The Random House College Dictionary
Webster's New Collegiate Dictionary
Webster's New World Dictionary

A good desk dictionary will tell you, for example, that the word *cannibal* derives from the name of the man-eating tribe, the Caribs, that Christopher Columbus discovered on Cuba and Haiti.

See if your dictionary says anything about the origins of the following words.

fanatic _____

magazine _____

anatomy _____

frankfurter _____

Usage Labels

As a general rule, use only standard English words in your writing. If a word is not standard English, your dictionary will probably give it a usage label like one of the following: *informal, nonstandard, slang, vulgar, obsolete, archaic, rare.*

Look up the following words and record how your dictionary labels them. Remember that a recent hardbound desk dictionary will always be the best source of information about usage.

cheap (meaning *stingy*) _____

hard-nosed _____

sass (meaning *to talk impudently*) _____

ain't _____

put-down _____

Synonyms

A *synonym* is a word that is close in meaning to another word. Using synonyms helps you avoid unnecessary repetition of the same word in a paper. A paperback dictionary is not likely to give you synonyms for words, but a good desk dictionary will. (You might also want to own a *thesaurus,* a book that lists synonyms and antonyms. An *antonym* is a word approximately opposite in meaning to another word.)

Consult a desk dictionary that gives synonyms for the following words, and write the synonyms in the spaces provided.

desire _____

ask _____

cry _____

Review Test

Use your dictionary to answer the following questions.

1. How many syllables are in the word *neurosurgery?* _____

2. Where is the primary accent in the word *elevation?* _____

3. In the word *evasion,* the *a* is pronounced like
   a. short *o*
   b. short *a*
   c. schwa
   d. long *a*

4. In the word *mobility,* the *y* is pronounced like
   a. schwa
   b. short *a*
   c. long *e*
   d. short *e*

5. In the word *data,* the second *a* is pronounced like
   a. short *a*
   b. schwa
   c. short *i*
   d. long *e*

Items 6–10: There are five misspelled words in the following sentence. Cross out each misspelled word and write the correct spelling in the spaces provided (items 6–10).

Some freinds and I are planning to go to the libary tommorow to do some research for an importent paper for our litrature class.

6. _____

7. _____

8. _____

9. _____

10. _____

Spelling
Improvement

Answers are on page 470.

INTRODUCTORY PROJECT

See if you can circle the word that is misspelled in each of the following pairs:

akward	*or*	awkward
exercise	*or*	exercize
business	*or*	buisness
worried	*or*	worryed
shamful	*or*	shameful
begining	*or*	beginning
partys	*or*	parties
sandwichs	*or*	sandwiches
heroes	*or*	heros

Poor spelling often results from bad habits developed in early school years. With work, such habits can be corrected. If you can write your name without misspelling it, there is no reason why you can't do the same with almost any word in the English language. Following are seven steps you can take to improve your spelling.

STEP 1: USING THE DICTIONARY

Get into the habit of using the dictionary. When you write a paper, allow yourself time to look up the spelling of all those words you are unsure about. Do not overlook the value of this step just because it is such a simple one. Just by using the dictionary, you can probably make yourself a 95 percent better speller.

STEP 2: KEEPING A PERSONAL SPELLING LIST

Keep a list of words you misspell and study the words regularly. Use the space on the inside front cover of this book as a starter. When you accumulate additional words, you may want to use a back page of your English notebook.

Hint: When you have trouble spelling long words, try to break each word down into syllables and see whether you can spell the syllables. For example, *misdemeanor* can be spelled easily if you can hear and spell in turn its four syllables: *mis-de-mean-or*. The word *formidable* can be spelled easily if you hear and spell in turn its four syllables: *for-mi-da-ble*. Remember, then: try to see, hear, and spell long words in terms of their syllable parts.

STEP 3: MASTERING COMMONLY CONFUSED WORDS

Master the meanings and spellings of the commonly confused words on pages 219–235. Your instructor may assign twenty words for you to study at a time and give you a series of quizzes until you have mastered all the words.

STEP 4: USING A TYPEWRITER WITH AN AUTOMATIC SPELLER

Some of the electronic typewriters on the market today will automatically find and correct your spelling errors. They include a built-in dictionary that beeps when you misspell or mistype a word. They can then erase your error and show you the correct spelling of a word.

These typewriters, like the pocket calculators of years ago, are the latest example of how technology can help the learning process. If you are a poor speller and want a helpful way to remove spelling and typing errors from your papers, seriously consider investing in such a machine. Smith-Corona, for example, has typewriters with an ''AutoSpell'' feature that cost about two hundred dollars at discount stores.

STEP 5: UNDERSTANDING BASIC SPELLING RULES

Explained briefly here are three rules that may improve your spelling. While exceptions sometimes occur, the rules hold true most of the time.

1 *Change y to i.* When a word ends in a consonant plus *y*, change *y* to *i* when you add an ending.

try + ed = tried	marry + es = marries
worry + es = worries	lazy + ness = laziness
lucky + ly = luckily	silly + est = silliest

2 *Final silent e.* Drop a final *e* before an ending that starts with a vowel (the vowels are *a, e, i, o,* and *u*).

hope + ing = hoping	sense + ible = sensible
fine + est = finest	hide + ing = hiding

Keep the final *e* before an ending that starts with a consonant.

use + ful = useful	care + less = careless
life + like = lifelike	settle + ment = settlement

3 ***Doubling a final consonant.*** Double the final consonant of a word when all the following are true:

a The word is one syllable or is accented on the last syllable.
b The word ends in a single consonant preceded by a single vowel.
c The ending you are adding starts with a vowel.

sob + ing = sobbing	big + est = biggest
drop + ed = dropped	omit + ed = omitted
admit + ing = admitting	begin + ing = beginning

Practice

Combine the following words and endings by applying the three rules above.

1. hurry + ed = _____
2. admire + ing = _____
3. deny + es = _____
4. jab + ing = _____
5. magnify + ed = _____

6. commit + ed = _____
7. dive + ing = _____
8. hasty + ly = _____
9. propel + ing = _____
10. nudge + es = _____

STEP 6: UNDERSTANDING PLURALS

Most words form their plurals by adding -s to the singular.

Singular	*Plural*
blanket	blankets
pencil	pencils
street	streets

Some words, however, form their plurals in special ways, as shown in the rules that follow.

1 Words ending in -s, -ss, -z, -x, -sh, or -ch usually form the plural by adding -es.

kiss	kisses	inch	inches
box	boxes	dish	dishes

2   Words ending in a consonant plus *y* form the plural by changing *y* to *i* and adding *-es*.

party	parties	county	counties
baby	babies	city	cities

3   Some words ending in *f* change the *f* to *v* and add *-es* in the plural.

leaf	leaves	life	lives
wife	wives	yourself	yourselves

4   Some words ending in *o* form their plurals by adding *-es*.

potato	potatoes	mosquito	mosquitoes
hero	heroes	tomato	tomatoes

5   Some words of foreign origin have irregular plurals. When in doubt, check your dictionary.

antenna	antennae	crisis	crises
criterion	criteria	medium	media

6   Some words form their plurals by changing letters within the word.

man	men	foot	feet
tooth	teeth	goose	geese

7   Combined words (words made up of two or more words) form their plurals by adding *-s* to the main word.

brother-in-law	brothers-in-law
passerby	passersby

Practice

Complete these sentences by filling in the plural of the word at the left.

bus   1. No _____ are permitted on the Channel Bridge.

grocery   2. Many of the _____ spilled out of the bags in my trunk when I braked suddenly.

potato   3. Baked _____ complement almost any main dish.

taxi   4. Just after I decided to take the crowded bus, four _____ passed us on Market Street.

themself   5. The owners of the failed curried-pizza restaurant have no one but _____ to blame.

theory   6. The essay question asked us to describe two _____ of evolution.

passerby   7. When I had a flat tire after work, several _____ stopped to ask if they could help.

alumnus   8. More presidents of the United States were _____ of Harvard than of any other university.

sandwich   9. The best short-order cook I ever met could make thirty bacon, lettuce, and tomato _____ in ten minutes.

mouse   10. During the sanitation workers' strike, _____ scurried along the street between bags of uncollected trash.

STEP 7: MASTERING A BASIC WORD LIST

Make sure you can spell all the words in the following list. They are some of the words used most often in English. Again, your instructor may assign twenty words for you to study at a time and give you a series of quizzes until you have mastered the words.

ability	among	bargain	cereal
absent	angry	beautiful	certain
accident	animal	because	change
across	another	become	cheap
address	**20** answer	before	chief
advertise	anxious	begin	children
advice	apply	being	church
after	approve	believe	cigarette
again	argue	between	clothing
against	around	**40** bottom	collect
all right	attempt	breathe	color
almost	attention	building	comfortable
a lot	awful	business	company
always	awkward	careful	condition
although	balance	careless	**60** conversation

	daily		intelligence		ought		started
	danger		interest		pain		state
	daughter		interfere		paper		straight
	decide		kitchen		pencil		street
	death		knowledge		people	200	strong
	deposit		labor		perfect		student
	describe		language		period		studying
	different		laugh		personal		suffer
	direction		leave		picture		success
	distance		length	160	place		surprise
	doubt		lesson		pocket		teach
	dozen		letter		possible		telephone
	during		listen		potato		theory
	each		loneliness		president		thought
	early	120	making		pretty		thousand
	earth		marry		problem		through
	education		match		promise		ticket
	either		matter		property		tired
	English		measure		psychology		today
80	enough		medicine		public		together
	entrance		middle		question		tomorrow
	everything		might		quick		tonight
	examine		million		raise		tongue
	exercise		minute		ready		touch
	expect		mistake		really	220	travel
	family		money		reason		truly
	flower		month		receive		understand
	foreign		morning		recognize		unity
	friend		mountain		remember		until
	garden		much	180	repeat		upon
	general		needle		restaurant		usual
	grocery		neglect		ridiculous		value
	guess		newspaper		said		vegetable
	happy		noise		same		view
	heard	140	none		sandwich		visitor
	heavy		nothing		send		voice
	height		number		sentence		warning
	himself		ocean		several		watch
	holiday		offer		shoes		welcome
100	house		often		should		window
	however		omit		since		would
	hundred		only		sleep		writing
	hungry		operate		smoke		written
	important		opportunity		something		year
	instead		original		soul	240	yesterday

Review Test

Use the three spelling rules to spell the following words.

1. admire   + able = _____

2. drop   + ing   = _____

3. big   + est   = _____

4. gamble   + ing   = _____

5. luxury   + es   = _____

6. immediate + ly   = _____

7. imply   + es   = _____

8. plan   + ed   = _____

9. involve   + ment = _____

10. refer   + ed   = _____

Items 11–14:   Circle the correctly spelled plural in each pair.

11. partys   parties
12. yourselfs   yourselves
13. mosquitos   mosquitoes
14. crisis   crises

Items 15–20:   Circle the correctly spelled word (from the basic word list) in each pair.

15. tommorow   tomorrow
16. height   hieght
17. needel   needle
18. visiter   visitor
19. hungry   hungery
20. writting   writing

Omitted Words and Letters

INTRODUCTORY PROJECT

Some people drop small connecting words such as *of,* *and,* or *in* when they write. They may also drop the *-s* endings of plural nouns. See if you can find and circle the six places with dropped letters or words in the passage below.

Two glass bottle of apple juice lie broken the supermarket aisle. Suddenly, a toddler who has gotten away from his parents appears at the head of the aisle. He spots the broken bottles and begins to run toward them. His chubby body lurches along like wind-up toy and his arm move excitedly up and down. Luckily, alert shopper quickly reacts to the impending disaster and blocks the toddler's path. Then the shopper waits with crying, frustrated little boy until his parents show up.

Answers are on page 470.

Be careful not to leave out words or letters when you write. The omission of words like *a, an, of, to,* or *the* or the *-s* ending needed on nouns or verbs may confuse and irritate your readers. They may not want to read what they regard as careless work.

FINDING OMITTED WORDS AND LETTERS

Finding omitted words and letters, like finding many other sentence-skills mistakes, is a matter of careful proofreading. You must develop your ability to look carefully at a page to find places where mistakes may exist.

The exercises here will give you practice in finding omitted words and omitted *-s* endings on nouns. Another section of this book (pages 50–52) gives you practice in finding omitted *-s* endings on verbs.

Practice

Add the missing words (*a, an, the, of,* or *to*) as needed.

Example   Some people regard television as *a* tranquilizer that provides temporary
relief from *the* pain and anxiety *of* modern life.

1. I grabbed metal bar on roof of subway car as the train lurched into station.

2. For most our country's history, gold was basis the monetary system.

3. Maggie made about a quart French-toast batter—enough soak few dozen slices.

4. Several pairs sneakers tumbled around in dryer and banged against glass door.

5. To err is human and to forgive is divine, but never make a mistake in the first place takes lot of luck.

6. Raccoons like wash their food in stream with their nimble, glovelike hands before eating.

7. When I got the grocery store, I realized I had left my shopping list in glove compartment my car.

8. Game shows are inexpensive way for networks make high profit.

9. Soap operas, on other hand, are very expensive to produce because the high salaries of many cast members.

10. One memorable Friday the thirteenth, a friend mine bought black cat, broke mirror, and walked under ladder. He had a wonderful day!

The Omitted -s Ending

The plural form of regular nouns usually ends in -s. One common mistake that some people make with plurals is to omit this -s ending. People who drop the ending from plurals when speaking also tend to do it when writing. This tendency is especially noticeable when the meaning of the sentence shows that a word is plural.

> Ed and Mary pay two hundred dollar a month for an apartment that has only two room.

The -s ending has been omitted from *dollars* and *rooms.*

The activities that follow will help you correct the habit of omitting the -s endings from plurals.

Practice 1

Add -s endings where needed.

Example   Bill beat me at several game_∧ of darts.

1. Many sightseer flocked around the disaster area like ghoul.

2. Martha has two set of twins, and all of their name rhyme.

3. Dozen of beetle are eating away at the rosebush in our yard.

4. Since a convention of dentist was in town, all the restaurant had waiting line.

5. Until the first of the year, worker in all department will not be permitted any overtime.

6. Blinking light, such as those on video game or police car, can trigger seizures in person with epilepsy.

7. Ray and his friends invented several game using an old rubber radiator hose and two plastic ball.

8. My thirteen-year-old has grown so much lately that she doesn't fit into the shoe and jean I bought for her a couple of month ago.

9. While cleaning out her desk drawers, Ann found a page of postage stamp stuck together and a couple of dried-up pen.

10. Worker fed large log and chunk of wood into the huge machine, which spit out chip and sawdust from its other end.

Practice 2

Write sentences that use plural forms of the following pairs of words.

Example   girl, bike   *The little girls raced their bikes down the street.*

1. college, student _____

  _____

2. shopper, bargain _____

  _____

3. car, driver _____

  _____

4. teacher, grade _____

  _____

5. vampire, victim _____

  _____

Note: People who drop the *-s* ending on nouns also tend to omit endings on verbs. Pages 50–53 will help you correct the habit of dropping endings on verbs.

𝒪 Review Test 1

In the spaces provided, write in the two small connecting words needed in each sentence. Also include the word that follows each connecting word.

———————— 1. When I opened freezer door, box of ice cream fell out.

————————

———————— 2. Hiking along trail next to the lake, we came to very muddy stretch.

————————

———————— 3. The newlyweds rented apartment with two rooms and bath.

————————

———————— 4. I had walk all the way up to our fifth-floor office because elevator was broken.

————————

———————— 5. Unfortunately, the road leading wealth is a lot longer than one leading to poverty.

————————

𝒪 Review Test 2

Add the two -s endings needed in each sentence.

———————— 1. The tallest building in the city has 67 floor and 75,010 doorknob.

————————

———————— 2. Student who receive the highest grades are usually the one who study the most.

————————

———————— 3. The trash cans by the picnic benches attracted dozen of bee.

————————

———————— 4. Grimy fingerprint had turned all the electric switch plate black.

————————

———————— 5. The fruit basket we received included instruction for ripening fresh fruit and a booklet of recipe.

————————

Commonly Confused Words

INTRODUCTORY PROJECT

Circle the five words that are used incorrectly in the following passage. Then see if you can write their correct spellings in the spaces provided.

If your a resident of a temperate climate, you may suffer from feelings of depression in the winter and early spring. Scientists are now studying people who's moods seem to worsen in winter, and there findings show that the amount of daylight a person receives is an important factor in "seasonal depression." When people get to little sunlight, their mood darkens. Its fairly easy to treat severe cases of seasonal depression; the cure involves spending a few hours a day in front of full-spectrum fluorescent lights that contain all the components of natural light.

1. _____

2. _____

3. _____

4. _____

5. _____

Answers are on page 471.

HOMONYMS

The commonly confused words (also known as *homonyms*) on the following pages have the same sounds but different meanings and spellings. Complete the activities for each set of words, and check off and study the words that give you trouble.

all ready   completely prepared
already   previously; before

> We were *all ready* to go, for we had eaten and packed *already* that morning.

Fill in the blanks: Phil was _____ for his driver's test, since he had _____ memorized the questions and regulations.

Write sentences using *all ready* and *already*.

_____

_____

brake   stop
break   come apart

> Dot slams the *brake* pedal so hard that I'm afraid I'll *break* my neck in her car.

Fill in the blanks: If you don't _____ your speed right while skiing, you can _____ a leg.

Write sentences using *brake* and *break*.

_____

_____

coarse rough
course part of a meal; a school subject; direction; certainly (with *of*)

During the *course* of my career as a waitress, I've dealt with some very *coarse* customers.

Fill in the blanks: The instructor in my electronics _____ is famous for using _____ language.

Write sentences using *coarse* and *course*.

_____

_____

hear perceive with the ear
here in this place

If I *hear* another insulting ethnic joke *here*, I'll leave.

Fill in the blanks: Unless you sit right _____ in one of the front rows, you won't be able to _____ a single thing the lecturer says.

Write sentences using *hear* and *here*.

_____

_____

hole   an empty spot
whole entire

If there is a *hole* in the tailpipe, I'm afraid we will have to replace the *whole* exhaust assembly.

Fill in the blanks: If you eat the _____ portion of chili, it will probably burn a _____ in your stomach.

Write sentences using *hole* and *whole*.

_____

_____

its   belonging to it
it's the shortened form for *it is* or *it has*

The kitchen floor has lost *its* shine because *it's* been used as a roller skating rink by the children.

Fill in the blanks: Our living-room carpet has lost _____ vivid color since _____ been exposed to so much sunlight.

Write sentences using *its* and *it's*.

_____

_____

knew past tense of *know*
new   not old

We *knew* that the *new* television comedy would be canceled quickly.

Fill in the blanks: As soon as we brought our _____ microwave home, we _____ it wouldn't fit where we planned to put it.

Write sentences using *knew* and *new*.

_____

_____

know to understand
no   a negative

I never *know* who might drop in even though *no* one is expected.

Fill in the blanks: I _____ there are _____ openings in your company at present, but please keep my résumé in case anything turns up.

Write sentences using *know* and *no*.

_____

_____

pair   a set of two
pear   a fruit

The dessert consisted of a *pair* of thin biscuits topped with vanilla ice cream and poached *pear* halves.

Fill in the blanks: We spotted a _____ of bluejays on our dwarf _____ tree.

Write sentences using *pair* and *pear*.

_____

_____

passed   went by; succeeded in; handed to
past   a time before the present; by, as in "I drove past the house."

After Edna *passed* the driver's test, she drove *past* all her friends' houses and honked the horn.

Fill in the blanks: Norman couldn't understand why he'd been _____ over for the promotion because his _____ performance at work had been so good.

Write sentences using *passed* and *past*.

_____

_____

peace   calm
piece   a part

The *peace* of the little town was shattered when a *piece* of a human body was found in the town dump.

Fill in the blanks: We ate in _____ until my two brothers started fighting over who would get the last _____ of blueberry pie.

Write sentences using *peace* and *piece*.

_____

_____

plain   simple
plane   aircraft

The *plain* box contained a very expensive model *plane* kit.

Fill in the blanks: The _____ truth is that unless you can land this _____ within the next twenty minutes, it will run out of fuel and crash.

Write sentences using *plain* and *plane*.

_____

_____

principal   main; a person in charge of a school; amount of money borrowed
principle   a law or standard

My *principal* goal in child rearing is to give my daughter strong *principles* to live by.

Fill in the blanks: My _____ reason for turning down the part-time job is that it's against my _____s to work on weekends.

Write sentences using *principal* and *principle*.

_____

_____

Note: It might help to remember that the *e* in *principle* is also in *rule*—the meaning of *principle*.

right   correct; opposite of *left*; something to which one is entitled
write   what you do in English

It is my *right* to refuse to *write* my name on your petition.

Fill in the blanks: The instructor said if the students' outlines were not _____, they would have to _____ them again.

Write sentences using *right* and *write*.

_____

_____

than used in comparisons
then at that time

>   I glared angrily at my boss, and *then* I told him our problems were more serious *than* he suspected.

Fill in the blanks: Felix hiked seven miles and _____ chopped firewood; he was soon more tired _____ he'd been in years.

Write sentences using *than* and *then.*

_____

_____

Note: It might help to remember that *then* is also a time signal.

their   belonging to them
there   at that place; a neutral word used with verbs like *is, are, was, were, have,* and *had*
they're the shortened form of *they are*

>   The tenants *there* are complaining because *they're* being cheated by *their* landlords.

Fill in the blanks: The music next door is so loud that I'm going over _____ to tell my neighbors to turn _____ stereo down before _____ arrested for disturbing the peace.

Write sentences using *their, there,* and *they're.*

_____

_____

_____

threw   past tense of *throw*
through   from one side to the other; finished

> When a character in a movie *threw* a cat *through* the window, I had to close my eyes.

Fill in the blanks: When Lee was finally _____ studying for her

psychology final, she _____ her textbook and notes in her closet.

Write sentences using *threw* and *through*.

_____

_____

to   a verb part, as in *to smile;* toward, as in "I'm going to heaven."
too   overly, as in "The pizza was too hot"; also, as in "The coffee was hot, too."
two   the number 2

> Lola drove *to* the store *to* get some ginger ale. (The first *to* means *toward;* the second *to* is a verb part that goes with *get.*)
>
> The sport jacket is *too* tight; the slacks are tight, *too.* (The first *too* means *overly;* the second *too* means *also.*)
>
> The *two* basketball players leaped for the jump ball. (2)

Fill in the blanks: My _____ daughters are _____

young _____ wear much makeup.

Write sentences using *to, too,* and *two.*

_____

_____

_____

wear   to have on
where   in what place

I work at a nuclear reactor, *where* one must *wear* a radiation-detection badge at all times.

Fill in the blanks: At the college _____ Ann goes, almost all the students _____ very casual clothes to class.

Write sentences using *wear* and *where*.

_____ __

_____

weather   atmospheric conditions
whether   if it happens that; in case; if

Because of the threatening *weather*, it's not certain *whether* or not the game will be played.

Fill in the blanks: After I hear the _____ report, I'll decide _____ I'll drive or take a train to my sister's house.

Write sentences using *weather* and *whether*.

_____

_____

whose   belong to whom
who's   the shortened form for *who is* and *who has*

The man *who's* the author of the latest diet book is a man *whose* ability to cash in on the latest craze is well known.

Fill in the blanks: The cousin _____ visiting us is the one _____ car was just demolished by a tractor trailer.

Write sentences using *whose* and *who's*.

_____

_____

your   belonging to you
you're   the shortened form of *you are*

> Since *your* family has a history of heart disease, *you're* the kind of person who should take extra health precautions.

Fill in the blanks: If _____ not going to eat any more, could I have what's left on _____ plate?

Write sentences using *your* and *you're*.

_____

_____

OTHER WORDS FREQUENTLY CONFUSED

Following is a list of other words that people frequently confuse. Complete the activities for each set of words, and check off and study the ones that give you trouble.

a   Both *a* and *an* are used before other words to mean, approximately, *one*.
an

Generally you should use *an* before words starting with a vowel (*a, e, i, o, u*):

    an absence   an exhibit   an idol   an offer   an upgrade

Generally you should use *a* before words starting with a consonant (all other letters):

    a pen   a ride   a digital clock   a movie   a neighbor

Fill in the blanks: When it comes to eating, I am lucky; I can eat like _____ elephant and stay as thin as _____ snake.

Write sentences using *a* and *an*.

_____

_____

accept   receive; agree to
except   exclude; but

If I *accept* your advice, I'll lose all my friends *except* you.

Fill in the blanks: Everyone _____ my parents was delighted when I decided to _____ the out-of-town job offer.

Write sentences using *accept* and *except*.

_____

_____

advice   a noun meaning *an opinion*
advise   a verb meaning *to counsel, to give advice*

Jake never listened to his parents' *advice*, and he ended up listening to a cop *advise* him of his rights.

Fill in the blanks: My father once gave me some good _____;
never _____ people on anything unless they ask you to.

Write sentences using *advice* and *advise*.

_____

_____

affect   a verb meaning *to influence*
effect   a verb meaning *to bring about something;* a noun meaning *result*

My sister Sally cries for *effect*, but my parents caught on and her act no longer *affects* them.

Fill in the blanks: Some school officials think suspension _____*s*
students positively, but many students think its main _____ is time off from school.

Write sentences using *affect* and *effect*.

_____

_____

among implies three or more
between implies only two

We selfishly divided the box of candy *between* the two of us rather than *among* all the members of the family.

Fill in the blanks: _____ my souvenirs from high school is a scrapbook with a large pink rose pressed _____ two of its pages.

Write sentences using *among* and *between*.

_____

_____

beside along the side of
besides in addition to

Fred sat *beside* Martha. *Besides* them, there were ten other people at the Tupperware party.

Fill in the blanks: Elena refused to sit _____ Carlos in class because he always fidgeted, and, _____, he couldn't keep his mouth shut.

Write sentences using *beside* and *besides*.

_____

_____

can refers to the ability to do something
may refers to permission or possibility

If you *can* work overtime on Saturday, you *may* take Monday off.

Fill in the blanks: Joanne certainly _____ handle the project, but she _____ not have time to complete it by the deadline.

Write sentences using *can* and *may*.

_____

_____

clothes   articles of dress
cloths   pieces of fabric

I tore up some old *clothes* to use as polishing *cloths*.

Fill in the blanks: I keep a bag of dust _____ in the corner of

my _____ closet.

Write sentences using *clothes* and *cloths*.

_____

_____

desert   a stretch of dry land; to abandon one's post or duty
dessert   last part of a meal

Don't *desert* us now; order a sinful *dessert* along with us.

Fill in the blanks: I know my willpower will _____ me whenever

there are brownies for _____.

Write sentences using *desert* and *dessert*.

_____

_____

does   a form of the verb *do*
dose   an amount of medicine

Martha *does* not realize that a *dose* of brandy is not the best medicine for
the flu.

Fill in the blanks: A _____ of aspirin _____
wonders for Sally's arthritis.

Write sentences using *does* and *dose*.

_____

_____

fewer   used with things that can be counted
less   refers to amount, value, or degree

I missed *fewer* writing classes than Rafael, but I wrote *less* effectively than he did.

Fill in the blanks: Florence is taking _____ courses this semester because she has _____ free time than she did last year.

Write sentences using *fewer* and *less.*

_____

_____

former   refers to the first of two items named
latter   refers to the second of two items named

I turned down both the job in the service station and the job as a shipping clerk; the *former* involved irregular hours and the *latter* offered very low pay.

Fill in the blanks: My mother does both calisthenics and yoga; the _____ keeps her weight down while the _____ helps her relax.

Write sentences using *former* and *latter.*

_____

_____

Note: Be sure to distinguish *latter* from *later* (meaning *after some time*). Very often people will use the word *latter* when in fact they mean *later.*

learn   to gain knowledge
teach   to give knowledge

After Roz *learns* the new dance, she is going to *teach* it to me.

Fill in the blanks: My dog is very smart; she can _____ any new

trick I _____ her in just minutes.

Write sentences using *learn* and *teach*.

_____

_____

loose   not fastened; not tight-fitting
lose   misplace; fail to win

I am afraid I'll *lose* my ring: it's too *loose* on my finger.

Fill in the blanks: Those slippers are so _____ that every time I

take a step, I _____ one.

Write sentences using *loose* and *lose*.

_____

_____

quiet   peaceful
quite   entirely; really; rather

After a busy day, the children were not *quiet,* and their parents were *quite*
tired.

Fill in the blanks: After moving furniture all day, Vince was _____

exhausted, so he found a _____ place and lay down for a nap.

Write sentences using *quiet* and *quite*.

_____

_____

though   despite the fact that
thought   past tense of *think*

> *Though* I enjoyed the dance, I *thought* the cover charge of ten dollars was too high.

Fill in the blanks: Even _____ my paper was two weeks late, I _____ the instructor would accept it.

Write sentences using *though* and *thought*.

_____

_____

INCORRECT WORD FORMS

Following is a list of incorrect word forms that people sometimes use in their writing. Complete the activities for each word, and check off and study the words that give you trouble.

being that   Incorrect! Use *because* or *since*.

>   *because*
> I'm going to bed now ~~being that~~ I must get up early tomorrow.

Correct the following sentences.

1. Being that our stove doesn't work, we'll have tuna salad for dinner.
2. I never invite both of my aunts over together, being that they don't speak to each other.
3. I'm taking a day off tomorrow, being that it's my birthday.

can't hardly   Incorrect! Use *can hardly* or *could hardly*.
couldn't hardly

                        can
Small store owners ~~can't~~ hardly afford to offer large discounts.

Correct the following sentences.

1. I can't hardly concentrate when the teacher looks over my shoulder.
2. James couldn't hardly believe the bill for fixing his car's brakes.
3. You couldn't hardly hear the music, because the audience was so loud.

could of   Incorrect! Use *could have*.

         have
I could ~~of~~ done better in that test.

Correct the following sentences.

1. The sidewalk was so hot you could of toasted bread on it.
2. The moon was so bright you could of read by it.
3. The peach pie was so good that I could of eaten it all.

irregardless   Incorrect! Use *regardless*.

Regardless
~~Irregardless~~ of what anyone says, he will not change his mind.

Correct the following sentences.

1. Irregardless of your feelings about customers, you must treat them with courtesy.
2. Jay jogs every day irregardless of the weather.
3. Anyone can learn to read irregardless of age.

must of   Incorrect! Use *must have, should have, would have.*
should of
would of

     have
I should ~~of~~ applied for a loan when my credit was good.

Correct the following sentences.

1. I must of dozed off during the movie.
2. If Marty hadn't missed class yesterday, he would of known about today's test.
3. You should of told me to stop at the supermarket.

Review Test 1

These sentences check your understanding of *its, it's; there, their, they're; to, too, two;* and *your, you're.* Underline the correct word in the parentheses. Rather than guess, look back at the explanations of the words when necessary.

1. It seems whenever (your, you're) at the doctor's office, (your, you're) symptoms disappear.
2. The boss asked his secretary (to, too, two) rearrange the insurance files, placing each in (its, it's) proper sequence.
3. You'll get (your, you're) share of the pizza when (its, it's) cool enough (to, too, two) eat.
4. (Its, It's) a terrible feeling when (your, you're) (to, too, two) late (to, too, two) help someone.
5. (There, Their, They're) not only a disrespectful group of kids, but (there, their, they're) arrogant (to, too, two).
6. (Its, It's) a fact that (there, their, they're) are (to, too, two) many children being born in underdeveloped nations.
7. (There, Their, They're) is no valid reason for the (to, too, two) of you (to, too, two) have forgotten about turning in (your, you're) assignments.
8. If you (to, too, two) continue (to, too, two) drive so fast, (its, it's) likely you'll get ticketed by the police.
9. "My philosophy on guys is that (there, their, they're) just like buses," said Lola. "If you miss one, (there, their, they're) is always another one coming by in a little while."
10. "(Its, It's) about time you (to, too, two) showed up," the manager huffed. "(There, Their, They're) is already a line of customers waiting outside."

Review Test 2

The sentences that follow check your understanding of a variety of commonly confused words. Underline the correct word in the parentheses. Rather than guess, look back at the explanations of the words when necessary.

1. When (your, you're) (plain, plane) arrives, call us (weather, whether) (its, it's) late or not.

2. You (should have, should of) first found out (whose, who's) really (to, too, two) blame before coming in (hear, here) and making ridiculous and false accusations.

3. When Jack drove (threw, through) his old neighborhood, he (could hardly, couldn't hardly) recognize some of the places he (knew, new) as a child.

4. The (affect, effect) of having drunk (to, too, two) much alcohol last night was something like having (a, an) jackhammer drilling (among, between) my ears.

5. I was (quiet, quite) surprised to learn that in the (passed, past) Johnny Carson was (a, an) magician, Howard Cosell (a, an) lawyer, and Carol Burnett (a, an) usherette.

6. Of (coarse, course) (its, it's) important to get good grades while (your, you're) in school, but it (does, dose) not hurt to (know, now) the (right, write) people when (your, you're) looking for a job.

7. If (your, you're) interested in listening to a great album, take my (advice, advise) and pick up a copy of *Sgt. Pepper's Lonely Hearts Club Band;* (its, it's) been voted the most popular rock album in history.

8. (Being that, Since) Barry has failed all five quizzes and one major exam and didn't hand in the midterm paper, he (though, thought) it would be a good idea (to, too, two) drop the (coarse, course).

9. (Their, There, They're) is (know, no) greater feeling (than, then) that of walking (threw, through) a forest in the spring.

10. I spent the (hole, whole) day looking (threw, through) my anatomy notes, but when it came time to take the exam, I still (could hardly, couldn't hardly) tell the difference (among, between) the bones in my foot and the one in my head.

Review Test 3

On separate paper, write short sentences using the ten words shown below.

their	effect
your	passed
it's	here
then	brake
too (meaning *also*)	whose

Effective
Word Choice

Answers are on page 471.

INTRODUCTORY PROJECT

Put a check beside the sentence in each pair that you feel makes more effective use of words.

1. After the softball game, we wolfed down a few burgers and drank a couple of brews. _____

   After the softball game, we ate hamburgers and drank beer. _____

2. A little birdie told me you're getting married next month. _____

   Someone told me you're getting married next month. _____

3. The personality adjustment inventories will be administered on Wednesday. _____

   Psychological tests will be given on Wednesday. _____

4. The referee in the game, in my personal opinion, made the right decision in the situation. _____

   I think the referee made the right decision. _____

Now see if you can circle the correct number in each case:

Pair (1, 2, 3, 4) contains a sentence with slang; pair (1, 2, 3, 4) contains a sentence with a cliché; pair (1, 2, 3, 4) contains a sentence with pretentious words; and pair (1, 2, 3, 4) contains a wordy sentence.

Answers are on page 471.

Choose your words carefully when you write. Always take the time to think about your word choices, rather than simply using the first word that comes to mind. You want to develop the habit of selecting words that are appropriate and exact for your purposes. One way you can show your sensitivity to language is by avoiding slang, clichés, pretentious words, and wordiness.

SLANG

We often use slang expressions when we talk because they are so vivid and colorful. However, slang is usually out of place in formal writing. Here are some examples of slang expressions:

The party was a *real horror show*.
I don't want to *lay a guilt trip* on you.
Our boss is not *playing with a full deck*.
Dad *flipped out* when he learned that Jan had *totaled* the car.
Movies like *The Fly* really *gross me out*.
Carlos had to *pull an all-nighter* to get the paper done on time.
Working overtime for three days in a row was a *real bummer*.

Slang expressions have a number of drawbacks. They go out of date quickly, they become tiresome if used excessively in writing, and they may communicate clearly to some readers but not to others. Also, the use of slang can be an evasion of the specific details that are often needed to make one's meaning clear in writing. For example, in ''The party was a real horror show,'' the writer has not provided the specific details about the party necessary for us to understand the statement clearly. Was it the setting, the food and drink (or lack of same), the guests, the music, the hosts, the writer, or what that made the party such a dreadful experience? In general, then, you should avoid the use of slang in your writing. If you are in doubt about whether an expression is slang, it may help to check a recently published hardbound dictionary.

Practice

Rewrite the following sentences, replacing the italicized slang words with more formal ones.

Example   My friend had *wheels*, so we decided to *cut out* of the *crummy* dance.

We decided to use my friend's car to leave the boring dance.

1. If you keep *pigging out* like that, you're going to be a *blimp*.

   _____

   _____

2. My parents always *shoot me down* when I ask them for some *bucks* to buy new tapes.

   _____

   _____

3. First the home team *got creamed*, and then the visiting fans *trashed* the field.

   _____

   _____

4. If Ellen would *lighten up* and stop talking about her troubles, a date with her wouldn't be such a *downer*.

   _____

   _____

5. I'm going to have to *sweat out* the next couple of days, hoping the boss doesn't discover the *goof* I made.

   _____

   _____

CLICHÉS

Clichés are expressions that have been worn out through typical clichés are:

short but sweet	last but not least
drop in the bucket	work like a dog
had a hard time of it	all work and no play
word to the wise	it goes without saying
it dawned on me	at a loss for words
sigh of relief	taking a big chance
too little, too late	took a turn for the worse
singing the blues	easier said than done
in the nick of time	on top of the world
too close for comfort	time and time again
saw the light	

Clichés are common in speech but make your writing seem tired and stale. Also, they are often an evasion of the specific details that you must work to provide in your writing. You should, then, avoid clichés and try to express your meaning in fresh, original ways.

Practice 1

Underline the cliché in each of the following sentences. Then substitute specific, fresh words for the trite expression.

Example   My parents supported me through some <u>trying times</u>.
rough years

1. To make a long story short, my sister decided to file for divorce.

   _____

2. As quick as a wink, the baby tipped over the open box of oatmeal.

   _____

3. Any advice my friends give me goes in one ear and out the other.

_____

4. I felt like a million dollars when I got my first A on a college test.

_____

5. These days, well-paying jobs for high school graduates are few and far between.

_____

Practice 2

Write a short paragraph describing the kind of day you had. Try to put as many clichés as possible into your writing. For example, "I had a long hard day. I had a lot to get done, and I kept my nose to the grindstone." By making yourself aware of clichés in this way, you should lessen the chance that they will appear in your writing.

PRETENTIOUS WORDS

Some people feel they can improve their writing by using fancy and elevated words rather than more simple and natural words. They use artificial and stilted language that more often obscures their meaning than communicates it clearly. Here are some unnatural-sounding sentences:

The football combatants left the gridiron.
His instructional technique is a very positive one.
At the counter, we inquired about the arrival time of the aircraft.
I observed the perpetrator of the robbery depart from the retail establishment.

The same thoughts can be expressed more clearly and effectively by using plain, natural language, as below:

The football players left the field.
He is a good teacher.
At the counter, we asked when the plane would arrive.
I saw the robber leave the store.

Here is a list of some other inflated words and the simple words that could replace them.

Inflated Words	Simpler Words
subsequent to	after
finalize	finish
transmit	send
facilitate	help
component	part
initiate	begin
delineate	describe
manifested	shown
to endeavor	to try

Practice

Cross out the two artificial words in each sentence. Then substitute clear, simple language for the artificial words.

Example   Sally was ~~terminated~~ from her ~~employment~~.
Sally was fired from her job.

1. Please query one of our sales associates.

   _____

2. The climate is abominable today.

   _____

3. My parents desire me to obtain a college degree.

   _____

4. Do not protrude your arm out of the car, or an accident might ensue.

   _____

5. Many conflagrations are caused by the careless utilization of portable heaters.

   _____

WORDINESS

Wordiness—using more words than necessary to express a meaning—is often a sign of lazy or careless writing. Your readers may resent the extra time and energy they must spend when you have not done the work needed to make your writing direct and concise. Here are examples of wordy sentences:

> At this point in time in our country, the amount of violence seems to be increasing every day.
> I called to the children repeatedly to get their attention, but my shouts did not get any response from them.

Omitting needless words improves the sentences:

> Violence is increasing in our country.
> I called to the children repeatedly, but they didn't respond.

Here is a list of some wordy expressions that could be reduced to single words.

Wordy Form	*Short Form*
at the present time	now
in the event that	if
in the near future	soon
due to the fact that	because
for the reason that	because
is able to	can
in every instance	always
in this day and age	today
during the time that	while
a large number of	many
big in size	big
red in color	red
five in number	five
return back	return
good benefit	benefit
commute back and forth	commute
postponed until later	postponed

Practice

Rewrite the following sentences, omitting needless words.

Example   Starting as of the month of June, I will be working at the store on a full-time basis.

As of June, I will be working at the store full time.

1. It is a well-known and proven fact that there is no cure as yet for the common cold.

2. The main point that I will try to make in this paper is that our state should legalize and permit gambling.

3. Due to the fact that Rafael's car refused to start up, he had to take public transportation by bus to his place of work.

4. When I was just a little boy, I already knew in my mind that my goal was to be a stockbroker in the future of my life.

5. The exercises that Susan does every day of the week give her more energy with which to deal with the happenings of everyday life.

Review Test 1

Certain words are italicized in the following sentences. In the space provided, identify whether the words are slang (*S*), clichés (*C*), or pretentious words (*PW*). Then replace them with more effective words.

1. Donna *came out of her shell* after she joined a singing group at school.

2. I *flipped out* when my little brother *got busted* for underage drinking.

3. I'm *suffering from a temporary depletion of all cash reserves.*

_____ 4. The coach *went bananas* at halftime and *chewed out* the team for twenty minutes.

_____

_____ 5. I got angry at the park visitors who did not put their *waste materials* in the *trash receptacle*.

_____

_____ 6. Hearing I had passed the accounting final really *took a load off my mind.*

_____

_____ 7. We all thought it was *too good to be true* when the teacher said that most of us would get A's in the course.

_____

_____ 8. Fred *asserted to* the collection agency that he had sent the *remuneration.*

_____

_____ 9. My old Chevy Impala just *bit the dust,* so I'm *checking out* new cars.

_____

_____ 10. That book was written by a millionaire who *didn't have a dime to his name* as a boy.

_____

Review Test 2

Rewrite the following sentences, omitting needless words.

1. At 6 A.M. early this morning, I suddenly heard a loud and noisy banging by someone at the front door of my apartment.

_____

_____

2. The fact of the matter is that I did not remember until, of course, just now that I had an appointment to meet you.

_____

_____

3. We are very pleased to have the opportunity to inform you that your line of credit on your credit card with us has just been increased.

_____

_____

4. At this point in time, the company has no plan of adding to anyone's salary by giving a raise in pay in the near or distant future.

    _____

    _____

5. If you are out on the job market seeking a job, you just might benefit from professional help to assist you in your search for employment.

    _____

    _____

PART TWO

REINFORCEMENT OF THE SKILLS

INTRODUCTION

To reinforce the sentence skills presented in Part One, this part of the book consists of mastery tests, combined mastery tests, proofreading tests, and editing tests. Four *mastery tests* appear for each of the skills where errors occur most frequently; two *mastery tests* are provided for each of the remaining skills. A series of *combined mastery tests* will measure your understanding of important related skills. *Editing* and *proofreading tests* offer practice in finding and correcting one kind of skills error in a brief passage. *Combined editing tests* then offer similar practice—except that the passages contain a variety of skills mistakes. Both the editing and proofreading tests will help you become a skillful editor and proofreader. All too often, students can correct mistakes in practice sentences but are unable to do so in their own writing. They must learn to look carefully for skills errors and to make such close checking a habit.

Appendix C provides progress charts that will help you keep track of your performance on these tests.

Mastery Tests

SUBJECTS AND VERBS

Mastery Test 1

Draw one line under the subjects and two lines under the verbs. Cross out prepositional phrases where needed to help find subjects. (Be sure to underline all the parts of a verb. Also, remember that you may find more than one subject and one verb in a sentence.)

1. The sailboat drifted for hours on the calm sea.
2. Career Day at my high school was a big success.
3. Tall pine trees hid the farmhouse from view.
4. Sandy's revealing suit attracted stares from everyone at the swimming pool.
5. Televisions, radios, and microwave ovens are on sale at greatly reduced prices.
6. All the fish in that lake have become contaminated.
7. Several garbage cans lined the weathered fence behind the old hotel.
8. Gloria often buys secondhand clothes and brightens them up by dyeing or embroidering them.
9. Weapons from police raids are kept under lock and key.
10. The old lady got back on her feet and surprised her attacker with a karate chop.

Score: Number correct _____ × 10 = _____%

SUBJECTS AND VERBS

 ## Mastery Test 2

Draw one line under the subjects and two lines under the verbs. Cross out prepositional phrases where needed to help find subjects. (Be sure to underline all the parts of a verb. Also, remember that you may find more than one subject and one verb in a sentence.)

1. Sharks swim continuously in their search for food.
2. The spider floated down from the ceiling and landed on my arm.
3. Most of the applicants for office jobs type about thirty words per minute.
4. The elderly man sat on the park bench and carefully opened his newspaper.
5. The shrubs are growing too close to the side of the house.
6. Andrew wants to learn to repair watches but does not have enough time on his hands.
7. All my friends, except my boyfriend, like my new hairstyle.
8. Carl washed his sports car every weekend and polished it once a month to protect the finish.
9. With only a day till the wedding, the bride and groom were having second thoughts.
10. Astrologers and astronomers agree on the importance of the stars but disagree on almost everything else.

Score: Number correct _____ × 10 = _____%

SUBJECTS AND VERBS

 **Mastery Test 3**

Draw one line under the subjects and two lines under the verbs. Cross out prepositional phrases where needed to help find subjects. (Be sure to underline all the parts of a verb. Also, remember that you may find more than one subject and one verb in a sentence.)

1. Blue wildflowers fill the empty lot.
2. No quarrel between good friends lasts for very long.
3. We borrowed my uncle's truck to move the refrigerator.
4. A young boy paid with a fistful of pennies for the lollipop.
5. Fewer people have been attending the school games this year.
6. Toward evening, my appetite seems to increase by the minute.
7. The woman in front of me was wearing a straw hat with a large daisy.
8. After a long search, I found my sweater in my sister's closet.
9. Giant lions and camels once roamed the American West.
10. An ancient footbridge formerly spanned the narrow stream but now lies under water.

Score: Number correct _____ × 10 = _____%

SUBJECTS AND VERBS

ⵔ Mastery Test 4

Draw one line under the subjects and two lines under the verbs. Cross out prepositional phrases where needed to help find subjects. (Be sure to underline all the parts of a verb. Also, remember that you may find more than one subject and one verb in a sentence.)

1. The sharp edge of a book page slit my finger.
2. Floyd should have waxed his car in the shade.
3. A maze of gopher tunnels winds under our lawn.
4. I am planning to protest the school's suspension policy.
5. The thick coating on the fried chicken slipped off like a jacket.
6. My sister and I have agreed to share only our everyday clothes.
7. A ghostly image appeared on the instant print and slowly turned into a portrait of Nick and Fran.
8. Canned salmon and tuna contain significant amounts of calcium.
9. A small dog followed me home and waited on my doorstep.
10. Dexter and Gale are taking their vacations at the same time and will rent a cottage on the lake for two weeks.

Score: Number correct _____ × 10 = _____%

SENTENCE FRAGMENTS

⚲ Mastery Test 1

Each word group in the student paragraph below is **numbered**. In the space provided, write *C* if a word group is a **complete sentence**; write *frag* if it is a fragment. You will find ten fragments in the paragraph.

1. _____
2. _____
3. _____
4. _____
5. _____
6. _____
7. _____
8. _____
9. _____
10. _____
11. _____
12. _____
13. _____
14. _____
15. _____
16. _____
17. _____
18. _____
19. _____
20. _____

[1]If an advertisement captures your interest. [2]It may be because it uses some of the proven psychological methods of gaining attention. [3]Such as change. [4]A flashing light, for example, is more noticeable than a continuously lit one. [5]Which is why many signs flash on and off. [6]And change colors and shapes. [7]Another advertising device is repetition. [8]We remember many advertising slogans and jingles because we have heard them so often. [9]In a thirty-second commercial, for instance, a message to use a certain toothpaste might be repeated five or six times. [10]In addition, frequent appearances of such ads. [11]Contrast, too, gains people's interest. [12]An advertiser may make a bright gold bracelet more appealing by placing it on a black velvet background. [13]Creating a dramatic visual effect. [14]Finally, to grab our attention. [15]Advertisers also use novelty. [16]Since people are drawn to the new and different, companies often change their products slightly. [17]Or make new products that are just variations of the old ones. [18]Then they emphasize the newness in their ads with various slogans. [19]Including "new and improved" and "different from anything you've ever tried before." [20]Even if the products are not very new and different.

Score: Number correct _____ × 5 = _____%

SENTENCE FRAGMENTS

Mastery Test 2

Underline the fragment in each selection. Then make whatever changes are needed to turn the fragment into a sentence.

Example   In grade school, I didn't want to wear glasses, ~~A~~nd avoided having to get them by memorizing the Snellen eye chart.

1. Lee went to the beauty parlor. To have her nails done for the vampire party.

2. When the Millers moved away last winter. The entire town was mystified. They had left all their furniture behind.

3. Nobody knew when the next train would arrive. Impatient commuters waited in line. And checked their watches every few minutes.

4. Richard brought a stepladder to the parade. Planning to sell seats on the top rungs. Several police officers vetoed that idea.

5. I don't like to go to the bank. Except on Fridays. That's the day I put money *into* my account.

6. Dawn is almost always early for work. But was late this morning. The boss told her not to worry.

7. Sitting on the boat dock. Eddie was lost in thought. The rising sun climbed slowly in the sky.

8. Nan felt around for the scissors at the back of the crowded drawer. She realized she had found them. When they stabbed her.

9. The battery in Frank's Chevy is five years old. And barely able to start the engine on a cold morning. He is waiting to buy a new battery on sale.

10. We had to wait at the airport for quite a while before leaving. All departing flights were delayed. Because a small private plane had to make an emergency landing.

Score: Number correct _____ × 10 = _____%

SENTENCE FRAGMENTS

Mastery Test 3

Underline the fragment in each selection. Then make whatever changes are needed to turn the fragment into a sentence.

1. The police recruits lined up on the practice range. And loaded their pistols with bullets. Then they began firing at the targets in the distance.

2. Having gone on an all-day hike. We walked into the restaurant with dusty clothes and dirty faces. The hostess led us to a table in back by the kitchen.

3. The sanitation workers made quite a racket this morning. Also bent my new metal trash can. If they continue to be so rough, the can will soon be trash.

4. Sometimes my boss disappoints me. He can be very rude. For example, interrupting me while I'm making excuses.

5. My son wants to buy all the toys advertised on TV. Even if we had the money for it all. We wouldn't have the space.

6. I put off studying for the test until the last minute. As a result, being up all night. During the test the next morning, I was too tired to think clearly.

7. Nancy likes to be a know-it-all. She pretends to identify the stars on camping trips. But consults her map when no one is looking.

8. George and Kate woke up at four this morning. To stand in line at the box office. They wanted front-row seats for the rock concert.

9. The boss gave all the secretaries bonuses at Christmas. Even Ms. Foster, who just joined the company in November. Many people felt he was too generous.

10. The newest ride at the amusement park is the "Elevator." You are hauled to the top of a tall shaft. And then dropped four stories to the ground. Fortunately, the brakes prevent your death.

Score: Number correct _____ × 10 = _____%

SENTENCE FRAGMENTS

 ## Mastery Test 4

Underline and then correct the ten fragments in the following passage.

My cousin Darryl is the worst driver I know. When he picks me up for school in the morning, he screeches to a halt outside my door. And peels away again in a cloud of blue exhaust fumes. Before hitting the highway, we speed through several narrow streets. Doing forty-five in twenty-mile-an-hour zones. On the four-lane road, Darryl weaves from lane to lane, tailgating cars six inches from their rear bumpers. Then passes them with a burst of stomach-flattening acceleration. To pass a car that's moving somewhat slowly in the passing lane. Darryl will get behind it, beep his horn, and even flash his high beams. Nothing infuriates him more than the "idiots," as he calls them. Who ignore these hints to move over. As we approach the jug-handle turn leading to school, Darryl speeds up. He is determined to make the light allowing cars to cross the highway into campus. If the light turns red and a car has already stopped. Darryl tromps on the pedal at the last possible second before impact and curses various things. Such as the red light and the car that stopped for it. Once in the parking lot, he finishes with a flourish. Pulling into a parking space at thirty-five miles an hour. As I reach out a limp hand to open the car door. I usually vow that I soon will buy my own car. Or find another ride to school.

Score: Number correct _____ × 10 = _____%

RUN-ONS

◎ Mastery Test 1

In the space provided, write *R-O* beside run-on sentences. Write *C* beside the one sentence that is punctuated correctly. Some of the run-ons have no punctuation between the two complete thoughts; others have only a comma.

Correct each run-on by using (1) a period and a capital letter, (2) a comma and a joining word, or (3) a semicolon. Do not use the same method of correction for every sentence.

Examples

_____R-O_____ I applied for the job,ᴧ*but* I never got called in for an interview.

_____R-O_____ Carla's toothache is getting worse,✶*S*he should go to a dentist soon.

_____ 1. He enjoys watching a talk show, she prefers watching a late movie.

_____ 2. Elena tried one of those herbal shampoos, her hair smelled just like a meadow.

_____ 3. My last vacation trip was very broadening I gained five pounds.

_____ 4. Some people prefer very loud music their bodies vibrate with the pulsing sound.

_____ 5. Bob is determined to find a new job, for his old one has given him an ulcer.

_____ 6. The rain fell softly outside it was a relaxing day to stay indoors.

_____ 7. A little girl toddled down the street she was attached to her mother by a chest harness and leash.

_____ 8. The school bus stopped at the corner children scattered like leaves in the wind.

_____ 9. The restaurant was closing waiters were already stacking chairs on the tables for the night.

_____ 10. His nose had become very cold, he pressed the warm underside of his forearm against it.

Score: Number correct _____ × 10 = _____%

RUN-ONS

◯ Mastery Test 2

In the space provided, write *R-O* beside run-on sentences. Write *C* beside one sentence that is punctuated correctly. Some of the run-ons have no punctuation between the two complete thoughts; others have only a comma.

Correct each run-on by using (1) a period and capital letter, (2) a comma and a joining word, or (3) a semicolon. Do not use the same method of correction for every sentence.

_____ 1. This semester our teacher gained a lot of weight he opened his belt another notch every two weeks.

_____ 2. First Darlene washes her hair, then she goes to the hairdresser.

_____ 3. The blue whale is an endangered animal, its population has been reduced to near extinction by whaling.

_____ 4. Barbara saw a funeral on television, she thought of her brother's recent death.

_____ 5. I began to get sleepy during the long ride, so I opened all the windows and pinched myself.

_____ 6. A flock of crows settled on a dimly lit tree their silhouettes stood out against the moon.

_____ 7. The average American teenager spends thirty-eight hours a week on schoolwork the average Japanese teenager spends about sixty.

_____ 8. Many complained that the proposed apartment building would obstruct the scenery the water tower was bad enough.

_____ 9. I spoke to the growling dog in a friendly tone, I hoped his owner would show up soon.

_____ 10. At the crack of dawn, our neighbor started his lawnmower our "Saturday morning symphony" had begun.

Score: Number correct _____ × 10 = _____%

RUN-ONS

Mastery Test 3

In the space provided, write *R-O* beside run-on sentences. Write *C* beside the one sentence that is punctuated correctly. Some of the run-ons have no punctuation between the two complete thoughts; others have only a comma.

Correct each run-on by using (1) a period and capital letter, (2) a comma and a joining word, or (3) a semicolon. Do not use the same method of correction for every sentence.

1. The early bird catches the worm, the early worm is not so lucky.

2. A mountain of garbage bags stood on the curb I wondered about the fate of all that plastic.

3. Some cities sponsor odd food festivals one celebrates spring with a dandelion-eating spree.

4. Confinement in bed was the worst part of my illness, for I had to use a bedpan.

5. At first, Ann forgot to serve the dinner rolls the smoke from the oven reminded her.

6. The roadside trees were infested webbed caterpillar nests filled the tree branches.

7. Al slammed the New York City phone book down with disgust it was impossible to find the right John Smith in it.

8. Few trout live in the stream its once-clear waters are cloudy with the runoff from the new subdivision.

9. The dashboard lights flickered on and off there was a short in the electrical system.

10. The children enjoyed seeing the animals at the zoo, but the high points of their visit were the cotton candy and popcorn.

Score: Number correct _____ × 10 = _____%

RUN-ONS

Mastery Test 4

In the space provided, write *R-O* beside run-on sentences. Write *C* beside one sentence that is punctuated correctly. Some of the run-ons have no punctuation between the two complete thoughts; others have only a comma.

Correct each run-on by using (1) a period and a capital letter, (2) a comma and a joining word, or (3) a semicolon. Do not use the same method of correction for every sentence.

_____ 1. The sky in the country seems to have more stars, no city pollution blocks the view.

_____ 2. An old engraving of New York City shows a startling fact pigs once ran loose on Broadway.

_____ 3. Sandy sat quietly in the empty church it was better than any tranquilizer.

_____ 4. On the way home, Linda wanted to get her gas tank filled the stations she passed were all closed.

_____ 5. Numerous trim shrubs lined the driveway they were a pruner's nightmare.

_____ 6. Victor turned to look at the unexpected face in the window it was his own reflection.

_____ 7. An elephant's thin ears cool the animal in two ways they fan the body and cool blood on its way to the heart.

_____ 8. A vigorous wind lashed through the forest trees nodded and bowed toward each other like old men in conversation.

_____ 9. Frank chose a bad time to teach his tardy wife a lesson, for he showed up four hours late for dinner on the night of his surprise birthday party.

_____ 10. Soldiers in the Revolutionary Army had to be at least sixteen they also had to have good teeth in order to tear the paper cartridges filled with gunpowder.

> ***Score:***   Number correct _____ × 10 = _____%

STANDARD ENGLISH VERBS

Mastery Test 1

Underline the correct words in the parentheses.

1. Bert's car (have, has) a horn that (play, plays) six different tunes.
2. When the pile of rags (start, started) to catch on fire, Dave (reach, reached) for the hose.
3. I (don't, doesn't) think my mother (has, have) gone out to a movie in years.
4. When she (is, be) upset, Mimi (tell, tells) her troubles to her houseplants.
5. The play (was, were) ruined when the quarterback (fumble, fumbled) the handoff.
6. My husband (think, thinks) more clearly in the morning than he (do, does) at night.
7. I (want, wanted) to take off my rings, but they (was, were) stuck on my swollen fingers.
8. Dolores (has, have) only three more courses before she (earn, earns) her degree.
9. Sometimes I (think, thinks) the happiest people (be, are) those with the lowest expectations of life.
10. The street musician (count, counted) the coins in his donations basket and (pack, packed) his trumpet in its case.

Score: Number correct _____ × 5 = _____%

STANDARD ENGLISH VERBS

Mastery Test 2

Cross out the nonstandard verb form and write the correct form in the space provided.

seems   **Example**   The job offer ~~seem~~ too good to be true.

_____   1. Billy always clown around in back of the class.

_____   2. When the last guests left our party, we was exhausted but happy.

_____   3. The computer in the library keep saying, "No such file."

_____   4. Today my counselor advise me to drop one of my courses.

_____   5. My sister Louise walk a mile to the bus stop every day.

_____   6. I don't think that Juan have thought enough about his future.

_____   7. The fans all stood up and cheer when the home team made a goal-line stand.

_____   8. Dora's husband don't like to talk about his experiences in Vietnam.

_____   9. After fumbling with his papers, the nervous announcer mispronounce the President's name.

_____   10. Some students heads for the parking lot between classes to sit in their cars and blast their radios.

Score: Number correct _____ × 10 = _____%

STANDARD ENGLISH VERBS

Mastery Test 3

Part 1:   Fill in each blank with the appropriate standard verb form of *be, have,* or *do* in present or past tense.

I _____ this problem called a little brother. Though I
                ₁

_____ always nice to him, he enjoys embarrassing me. The other night,
        ₂

for example, I _____ my boyfriend over to the house. The lights were
                ₃

turned down low, and my boyfriend and I _____ alone on the living-
                                        ₄

room couch. At least I thought so. That Dennis-the-Menace clone who _____
                                                                    ₅

my brother crawled into the living room with a portable cassette recorder. My boyfriend

and I _____ not notice him because we _____ started
        ₆   ₇

getting "friendly." It _____ the next night when I discovered what that
                        ₈

little brat _____ been up to. In front of my parents, he played the tape.
            ₉

His plan _____ a big success, because I felt embarrassed to death.
            ₁₀

Part 2:   Fill in the correct form of the regular verb in parentheses.

Shopping at a convenience store isn't always so convenient. The other night I (stop)

_____ off at the local Seven-Eleven to pick up a two-liter bottle of diet
        ₁

soda and a package of chips. After I had (park) _____ my car and gone
                                                ₂

inside, I was (greet) _____ by the sight of a long line of customers,
                        ₃

which was (back) _____ up down one aisle. Since Seven-Eleven was
                    ₄

the only place still open at that time of night, I (decide) _____ to stay.
                                                            ₅

I (pick) _____ up my soda and potato chips and (walk)
            ₆

_____ to the end of the line. I saw that the delay was (cause)
        ₇

_____ by a woman who had (place) _____ a large
        ₈   ₉

order for lunch meat. And the teenage boy waiting on her (move) _____
                                                                ₁₀

like someone in a slow-motion film.

Score:	Number correct _____ × 5 = _____%

STANDARD ENGLISH VERBS

ℚ Mastery Test 4

Part 1: Fill in each blank with the appropriate standard verb form of *be, have,* or *do* in the present or past tense.

There _____ 1 one thing my mother does better than anybody else in the world—make requests. It seems she _____ 2 to start right in as soon as I wake up. "_____ 3 you make your bed, Arnold?" she always asks me. "_____ 4 you going to wear that nice sport shirt I pressed for you last night? _____ 5 not forget to put out the trash before you leave for school, dear. _____ 6 you still going to paint the basement this weekend? _____ 7 you remember to stop by the grocery on your way home from school?" She _____ 8 an endless supply of such appeals. I think I _____ 9 to get out of here. Maybe it _____ 10 time to get married, which happens to be another thing she wants me to do.

Part 2: Fill in each blank with the appropriate form of the regular verb shown in parentheses. Use present or past tense as needed.

Driving on trips with my three-year-old son has its drawbacks. For one thing, he (find) _____ 1 it difficult to sit still for long. Besides that, when he (eat) _____ 2 in the car, which is frequently, he (scatter) _____ 3 crumbs all over the backseat and floor. And after each time he (snack) _____ 4 on something, he (insist) _____ 5 on touching everything in sight with his dirty hands. My mother (believe) _____ 6 he actually (enjoy) _____ 7 smudging the windows with grease. Last week, driving (affect) _____ 8 his stomach, which (require) _____ 9 an unpleasant stop at the side of the road. The only good thing about traveling with my son is that he still (take) _____ 10 naps a couple of times a day.

> **Score:** Number correct _____ × 5 = _____%

IRREGULAR VERBS

Mastery Test 1

Underline the correct word in the parentheses.

1. (Lying, Laying) in the hot sun is bad for the skin.
2. Last night I (saw, seen) a dead collie on the road.
3. My girlfriend (teached, taught) me how to make curtains for my van.
4. The judge reminded Daniel that he had (sworn, swore) to tell the truth.
5. My boss has (chosen, chose) to treat me the way a baby treats a diaper.
6. Whenever I had an important date, my brother (lended, lent) me his good jacket.
7. Molly has finally (took, taken) aspirin for the headache she's had all day.
8. Five different people had (bringed, brought) huge bowls of potato salad to the barbecue.
9. I scratched the spot where the hornet (stinged, stung) me till I bled.
10. The picture I (drawed, drew) in art class ended up looking like a plate of spaghetti.
11. Taking care of two of the neighbor's children this week has (worn, wore) me out.
12. I left the wine in the freezer to cool, and it (froze, freezed) into wine slush.
13. Our cat (stoled, stole) home in the middle of the night after being gone for a week.
14. Stan's truck (rises, raises) a cloud of dust when it comes down the dirt road.
15. My research paper is due in two weeks, and I haven't even (begun, began) to work on it.
16. Having (slept, sleeped) all day, Dracula looked forward to a bite to eat.
17. I accidentally (throwed, threw) away the parking ticket when I cleaned out my glove compartment.
18. After playing touch football all afternoon, Jake (drunk, drank) a quart of Gatorade.
19. Since Carol left a third of the answer spaces blank, she (knew, knowed) she had failed the psychology exam.
20. After you have (broke, broken) up with a boyfriend or girlfriend, it feels like every day is a cloudy and cold Monday morning.

Score: Number correct _____ × 5 = _____%

IRREGULAR VERBS

Mastery Test 2

Cross out the incorrect verb form. Write the correct form in the space provided.

_____   1. The phone rung once and then stopped.

_____   2. Rosie spended an entire week's salary on a new pair of boots.

_____   3. No one had broke the news to Rich that he had not made the team.

_____   4. The hurricane winds blowed several beach houses off their foundations.

_____   5. I've swam in this lake for years, and I've never seen it so shallow.

_____   6. That trucker has drove over a million accident-free miles.

_____   7. How did the police know where the kidnappers had hid their victim?

_____   8. My cotton sweater shranked so much in the wash that I gave it to my daughter.

_____   9. If I had took more notes in that class, I would have done better on the exam.

_____   10. The second baseman fielded the grounder, stepped on the bag, and then throwed to first for a double play.

Score: Number correct _____ × 10 = _____%

IRREGULAR VERBS

Mastery Test 3

Write in the space provided the correct form of the verb shown in the margin.

grow   1. My nephew must have _____ six inches since last summer.

drive   2. We _____ almost seven hundred miles before pulling over for a break.

fall   3. Frowning, the building inspector stood where the store's sign had _____ .

fight   4. My parents _____ with the IRS for a year before finally paying the additional tax.

break   5. During last night's storm, lightning _____ the clock over the town hall.

write   6. The police found the hit-and-run driver because Aunt Edith had _____ the license number down.

eat   7. Hank's dog climbed onto the kitchen table at night and _____ most of the chocolate chip cookies.

tear   8. After he _____ the cartilage in his knee for the third time, Bubba decided to retire from football.

take   9. The orchestra arrived two hours late for the New Year's Eve party because the bus driver had _____ a wrong turn.

go   10. When his boss caught him sleeping at his desk, Norman wished he had _____ to bed earlier the night before.

Score: Number correct _____ × 10 = _____%

IRREGULAR VERBS

Mastery Test 4

Write in the space provided the correct form of the verb shown in the margin.

see   1. My roommate and I _____ a double feature this weekend.

bring   2. I should have _____ a gift to the office Christmas party.

speak   3. Has the supervisor _____ to Marcia yet about being late for work?

come   4. Just as we were talking about Rob's new pickup truck, he _____ up the driveway.

throw   5. Huey _____ out his back trying to put a new air conditioner in his bedroom window.

sing   6. I could have _____ professionally, but I lacked the determination to pursue a career.

sit   7. When I have company for dinner, I _____ in the middle of the table rather than at one end.

speak   8. Our guest is a former police detective who has _____ all over the country on the subject of teenage drug abuse.

choose   9. I know I should have _____ a different major, but I don't want to start from the beginning now.

give   10. The state trooper _____ Harley a warning for riding his motorcycle on the interstate without a safety helmet.

Score: Number correct _____ × 10 = _____%

SUBJECT-VERB AGREEMENT

Mastery Test 1

Underline the correct verb in the parentheses. Note that you will first have to determine the subject in each sentence. To help find subjects in certain sentences, you may find it helpful to cross out prepositional phrases.

1. Many stories in the *National Enquirer* (seems, seem) hard to believe.
2. Where (has, have) all the pens gone to in this house?
3. One of my sweaters (has, have) moth holes in the sleeves.
4. There (is, are) plenty of reasons for not going to the party tonight.
5. Each of the marathon runners (receives, receive) a special T-shirt.
6. The records in my collection (is, are) arranged alphabetically.
7. Football players who (scores, score) touchdowns get most of the glory.
8. The major story on all the news programs (concerns, concern) the President's operation.
9. Both of the drive-in windows at the bank (closes, close) at three o'clock.
10. Here (is, are) my address and phone number, so you can get in touch.
11. On the front page of the newspaper (was, were) a story about my accident.
12. Someone (keeps, keep) calling me and hanging up when I answer.
13. How (does, do) the weather forecasters determine if it's partly sunny or partly cloudy?
14. Growing in the middle of our flower bed (was, were) a single stalk of wild asparagus.
15. Every one of the boxers (seems, seem) to follow a different training regimen.
16. Each of my little boys (needs, need) a warmer jacket for the winter.
17. The level of water in local reservoirs (has, have) dropped dramatically recently.
18. The figure that intrigues Wayne most in his geometry class (belongs, belong) to the girl sitting next to him.
19. Why (does, do) many appliances stop working as soon as their warranties expire?
20. Orange slices and ginger ale still (needs, need) to be added to the punch.

Score: Number correct _____ × 5 = _____%

SUBJECT-VERB AGREEMENT

◎ Mastery Test 2

In the space provided, write the correct form of the verb shown in the margin.

cares,
care

1. Gina seems like the kind of person who _____ more about style than about substance.

was, were

2. There _____ only two handkerchiefs left in the drawer.

runs, run

3. The portable television and the radio _____ on batteries or house current.

snarls,
snarl

4. Either construction work or accidents _____ expressway traffic every morning.

has, have

5. The professor, along with the two graduate assistants, _____ conducted the experiment hundreds of times.

is, are

6. At least a few of the gray hairs on your poor father's head _____ due to you and that no-good brother of yours.

finds, find

7. Each runner, summoning all the courage and adrenaline he has left, _____ that the ultimate challenger is himself.

is, are

8. Lined up outside the movie theater _____ dozens of impatient children and their angry parents.

seems,
seem

9. Politicians, I have noticed, often _____ to choose words very carefully, as if selecting stones to step on while crossing a stream.

was, were

10. I found it almost impossible to believe that this seventy-year-old man, with his rumpled clothes, _____ a mass murderer.

Score: Number correct _____ × 10 = _____%

SUBJECT-VERB AGREEMENT

Mastery Test 3

Cross out the incorrect form of the verb. In addition, underline the subject that goes with the verb. Then write the correct form of the verb in the space provided. Mark the one sentence that is correct with a *C*.

_____   1. Each of the secretaries work from nine to five.

_____   2. The price of the theater tickets seem much too high.

_____   3. A salad, beverage, and dessert accompanies the meal.

_____   4. There was only three pieces of wood left in the pile.

_____   5. The new tenant and her little boy makes a lot of noise.

_____   6. Corn on the cob, iced tea, and watermelon is symbolic of summer.

_____   7. One of the most regal-looking animals in the zoo are the big-horned sheep.

_____   8. The picture on the cover of that paperback gives the wrong idea of the book's story.

_____   9. Neither Brenda nor her sisters has enough money to go to the movies tonight.

_____   10. The roots of the tree on the beach was exposed by erosion from the surf.

Score: Number correct _____ × 10 = _____%

SUBJECT-VERB AGREEMENT

Mastery Test 4

Cross out the incorrect form of the verb. In addition, underline the subject that goes with the verb. Then write the correct form of the verb in the space provided. Mark the one sentence that is correct with a *C*.

_____   1. When is Kay and her parents going on vacation?

_____   2. One of the patients wander aimlessly down the halls.

_____   3. My sister and her husband takes my father bowling every Thursday night.

_____   4. Each of the fast-food restaurants now have a breakfast special.

_____   5. Next to the newly born chicks were one of the barn rats.

_____   6. Whenever the coach gets angry, both sides of his mouth curls up in a sneer.

_____   7. The clouds part, and the warming rays of the sun shine through, bringing instant heat with them.

_____   8. Anyone who comes in late to Mr. Barker's class have to have a good excuse.

_____   9. Snuggling under the covers feel wonderful on Saturday mornings.

_____   10. A box of shredded wheat last about a year in our house, since the kids call it "shredded steel wool."

Score: Number correct _____ × 10 = _____%

CONSISTENT VERB TENSE

Mastery Test 1

In each selection one verb must be changed so that it agrees in tense with the other verbs. Cross out the inconsistent verb and write the correct form in the space provided.

_____ 1. Susan asked the grouchy cashier for change, and he counts out twenty-five pennies.

_____ 2. After dinner, my parents watched the news while the children clear the table and washed the dishes.

_____ 3. I walked through town yesterday, and a friend from grade school calls to me.

_____ 4. Rose tried to avoid breathing the fumes as she sprays her houseplants with pesticide.

_____ 5. When we arrived at the theater, I suddenly remember that I had left the oven turned on at home.

_____ 6. Annie sighed as her little boy repeatedly guides the spoonful of mashed carrots to his ear.

_____ 7. I drank the ice water too quickly; sharp pains rush to my temple and forced me to stop walking for a minute.

_____ 8. Upon finding a seat on the bus, Victor unfolded his newspaper, turns to the sport section, and began to read.

_____ 9. Polar bear cubs stay with their mothers for two years; then they leave home and faced the Arctic winter alone.

_____ 10. Our family car was in sad shape; the tires were worn, the chrome is pitted, and the paint came off if you rubbed it too hard.

Score: Number correct _____ × 10 = _____%

CONSISTENT VERB TENSE

Mastery Test 2

In each selection one verb must be changed so that it agrees in tense with the other verbs. Cross out the inconsistent verb and write the correct form in the space provided.

_____ 1. Sandy eats a nutritional breakfast, skipped lunch, and then enjoys a big dinner.

_____ 2. The wrestler stepped into the ring, salutes the crowd, and banged on his chest like Tarzan.

_____ 3. Tears streamed down little Heather's face as her father combs her tangled hair.

_____ 4. The restaurant near the wharf opened in May, stays busy all summer, and then closes for the winter.

_____ 5. At the game, Danny hums along with the national anthem when he forgot some of the words.

_____ 6. Terri buys and reads several romance novels every month, for she wanted to escape from her dull daily routine.

_____ 7. When he prepared the omelet, the chef grated fresh cheese, chopped an onion, and slices a crisp green pepper.

_____ 8. To make the dress fit, Inez shortened the shoulder straps, moved a button, and tightens the waist.

_____ 9. Stu got his driver's license after he had an eye exam, took a written quiz, and passes a driving-skills test.

_____ 10. Before she decided to buy the wall calendar, Magda turns its pages and looked at all the pictures.

Score: Number correct _____ × 10 = _____ %

MISPLACED MODIFIERS

🔍 Mastery Test 1

Circle the misplaced modifier in each sentence. Then make the needed correction by moving the misplaced modifier next to the word it describes. In some cases, you may have to rewrite the whole sentence.

Example (Every six hours) the doctor told me to take a pill.

1. Barry decided to quit smoking while jogging.

2. The suburbs nearly had five inches of rain.

3. I decided to send fewer Christmas cards out this year in October.

4. My mother talked about her plans to start a garden while preparing dinner.

5. The car was parked along the side of the road with a flat tire.

6. Olivia stretched out on the lounge chair wearing her bathing suit.

7. Martin is that guy carrying packages with curly brown hair.

8. I bought a diary at the campus bookstore with a silver leather cover.

9. Caryl read an article about starting your own business in the dentist's office.

10. A cake baked by my brother covered with coconut and candies was the prizewinner.

Score: Number correct _____ × 10 = _____%

MISPLACED MODIFIERS

 Mastery Test 2

Circle the misplaced modifier in each sentence. Then make the needed correction by moving the misplaced modifier next to the word it describes. In some cases, you may have to rewrite the whole sentence.

1. I replaced the shingle on the roof that was loose.

2. The teacher explained why cheating was wrong on Friday.

3. Mike ordered a large pizza for his family topped with extra cheese.

4. The helicopter filmed the migrating antelope hovering overhead.

5. We bought a television set at our neighborhood video store that has stereo sound.

6. The passengers on the bus stared at the ceiling or read newspapers with tired faces.

7. The magician almost held his breath for five minutes while escaping from the submerged trunk.

8. Neighborhood children watched the new family move in from the street corner.

9. Newspapers ran the story of the congressman's lies in every part of the country.

10. I threw some jeans with a candy bar in the pocket into the dryer which became melted and sticky.

Score: Number correct _____ × 10 = _____%

DANGLING MODIFIERS

Mastery Test 1

Make the changes needed to correct the dangling modifier in each sentence.

Example   ~~Out~~ *Because she was out* late the night before, Rita's eyes were red and strained.

1. Being on a diet, my pie had no whipped cream.

2. Running as fast as I could, the bus waited for me.

3. After a nap in my room, my mother always gave me a snack.

4. Running to catch the ball at full speed, my cap went flying into the wind.

5. Boring and silly, I turned the TV show off.

6. While looking for bargains at Sears, an exercise bike caught my eye.

7. Having burned the hamburger to cinders, my dinner was scrambled eggs.

8. Filled with sand, Debbie took off her shoes before going into the house.

9. Pedaling as fast as possible, Todd's bike pulled away from the snapping dog.

10. Punctured by a pin, Dexter mended his water bed with a plastic bandage.

Score: Number correct _____ × 10 = _____%

DANGLING MODIFIERS

 ## Mastery Test 2

Make the changes needed to correct the dangling modifier in each sentence.

1. Being hungry as a bear, my dinner was enormous.
2. Feet spread, the police frisked the suspects for weapons.
3. Having had too little sleep, Lena's eyes were bloodshot.
4. Blown over in the hurricane, Jim had to build a new garage.
5. Stolen from the mall parking lot, my girlfriend spotted my sports car the next day.
6. Even before being housebroken, I thought the beagle was lovable.
7. Walking down the weedy path, the old, weathered house loomed larger than I had remembered.
8. Despite having been stored in the refrigerator, I could smell that the milk was sour.
9. While dreaming about the beach, the alarm suddenly woke Lynn up.
10. After spending most of the night outdoors in a tent, the sun rose, and we went into the house.

Score: Number correct _____ × 10 = _____%

PARALLELISM

 **Mastery Test 1**

The unbalanced part of each sentence is italicized. Rewrite this part so that it matches the rest of the sentence.

1. The theater popcorn was greasy, stale, and *had too much salt.*

   _____

2. I would rather have you call me on the phone than *sending me a letter.*

   _____

3. The orchestra leader had slick black hair, a long thin nose, and *eyes that were dark blue.*

   _____

4. Whenever I get home, my dog barks, *is running to get his ball,* and drops it at my feet.

   _____

5. The job applicant—well dressed, well spoken, and *with a good education*—impressed the interviewer.

   _____

6. I stood for two hours in the hot sun in my heavy wool dress, long-sleeved jacket, and *shoes that were tight.*

   _____

7. After his family's weekend visit ended, Enrique was exhausted and relieved but *was feeling lonely.*

   _____

8. Before assembling the casserole, Marty had to sauté the onions and *stirring them into the ground meat.*

   _____

9. As they neared the ocean, they could hear the waves, smell the salt water, and *the dampness was felt by them.*

   _____

10. They spent a relaxing afternoon enjoying the view from their balcony, eating lunch at an old inn, and *window-shopped* in the village square.

   _____

Score: Number correct _____ × 10 = _____%

PARALLELISM

 ## Mastery Test 2

Draw a line under the unbalanced part of each sentence. Then rewrite the unbalanced part so that it matches the other items in the sentence.

1. The movie contains adult language, nudity, and it is violent.

   _____

2. My doctor told me to stop smoking and that I should lose weight.

   _____

3. Holly was frightened, upset, and a nervous wreck; she had three exams in the next two days.

   _____

4. We had a choice of chocolate-flavored coffee or coffee flavored with cinnamon.

   _____

5. After moving the furniture, spreading a drop cloth, and the wall edges were taped, we were ready to paint.

   _____

6. Roy promised his girlfriend he would be more reliable, less moody, and jealous less often.

   _____

7. I've tried several cures for my headaches, including medication, exercise, meditation, and massaging my head.

   _____

8. The astronauts' concerns were landing on the satellite, to take off again, and reentering the earth's atmosphere.

   _____

9. I'm attending college to gain knowledge, to meet people, and preparation for a good job.

   _____

10. My aunt believes that the moon landing was a hoax, in the secret invasion of earth by aliens, and that Hitler is living in South America.

   _____

Score: Number correct _____ × 10 = _____%

PRONOUN REFERENCE, AGREEMENT, AND POINT OF VIEW

◯ Mastery Test 1

Underline the correct word in the parentheses.

1. As Jill argued with her mother, (she, Jill) became more and more upset.
2. One of the female astronauts will take (her, their) first space walk during the flight.
3. If you stay up too late watching television, (one, you) may walk around like a zombie the next day.
4. At the library, (they, the librarian) showed me how to use the microfilm machines.
5. Everyone who works in this company must have (his or her, their) chest x-rayed every two years.
6. The nurse finally penetrated my vein with a large needle, although (it, the vein) had been hard to find.
7. I like living in a large apartment house because (I, you) have more chances to meet people.
8. Jesse's brother called to say that (he, Jesse) had gotten bad news from the doctor.
9. Although I was an announcer on my college radio station, I wouldn't want to make a career of (announcing, it).
10. Anybody who lives to (their, his or her) ninetieth year is eligible to receive a birthday card from the President.

Score: Number correct _____ × 10 = _____%

PRONOUN REFERENCE, AGREEMENT, AND POINT OF VIEW

◯ Mastery Test 2

In the space provided, write *PE* beside sentences that contain pronoun errors. Write *C* beside the two sentences that use pronouns correctly. Then cross out each pronoun error and write the correction above it.

_____PE_____ ***Example***   Each of the boys explained ~~their~~ *his* project.

_____   1. Frank doesn't like visiting his in-laws because you never feel like part of the family.

_____   2. Nadine told her niece that she would be famous someday.

_____   3. I ordered three albums from the record store, but they never sent them.

_____   4. We are treated so horribly at work; they must think we're slaves.

_____   5. Someone on the team shared his complaints with a reporter.

_____   6. Ernie placed the ladder against the wall of the garage and then leaned against it for a moment.

_____   7. Each of these jobs has its advantages: one has good pay, and the other has short hours.

_____   8. I like to watch TV quiz shows because you can learn a lot from their questions.

_____   9. The college teachers made sure that the students understood they were bright and capable.

_____   10. Any salesperson in our office can win a free trip to Hawaii if they sell one house in the next twenty-four hours.

Score: Number correct _____ × 10 = _____%

PRONOUN REFERENCE, AGREEMENT, AND POINT OF VIEW

Mastery Test 3

In the space provided, write *PE* beside sentences that contain pronoun errors. Write *C* beside the two sentences that use pronouns correctly. Then cross out each pronoun error and write the correction above it.

_____ 1. When the car banged into the wall, it was damaged.

_____ 2. One of my friends entered their dog in a Frisbee tournament.

_____ 3. One of the floorboards is warped, and I keep tripping on them.

_____ 4. As I slowed down at the scene of the accident, you could see long black skid marks on the highway.

_____ 5. As we looked out the plane window, we could see roads and buildings get smaller and smaller.

_____ 6. All visitors should stay in their cars while driving through the wild animal park.

_____ 7. My girlfriend and I avoid office parties because one always has to watch out for the office Romeos.

_____ 8. I always shop at that market because they have such a large selection.

_____ 9. A person who likes to criticize others often objects when someone teases them.

_____ 10. If anyone works with an irresponsible lab partner, you will find it difficult to complete experiments successfully.

Score: Number correct _____ × 10 = _____%

PRONOUN REFERENCE, AGREEMENT, AND POINT OF VIEW

◯ Mastery Test 4

In the space provided, write *PE* beside sentences that contain pronoun errors. Write *C* beside the two sentences that use pronouns correctly. Then cross out each pronoun error and write the correction above it.

_____ 1. Bill spent a half hour complaining to Gary about his girlfriend.

_____ 2. As I watched the pro wrestling match, you could tell the violence was faked.

_____ 3. Each gymnast has to develop his or her own floor routine.

_____ 4. I arrived late for the final exam in English, which is why I failed it.

_____ 5. Anybody willing to volunteer their time to work at the shelter for the homeless should sign up here.

_____ 6. My sister and I fought a lot as children, but you learn to get along better as grown-ups.

_____ 7. Sally received an ad in the mail that said she could make six hundred dollars a month addressing envelopes.

_____ 8. One of the players on the women's basketball team scored their thousandth point yesterday.

_____ 9. Mr. Penge invited his students to his home to meet a famous scientist, which made them feel special.

_____ 10. I stayed in a dorm during my first year in college, where they chose a roommate for me.

Score: Number correct _____ × 10 = _____%

PRONOUN TYPES

 ## Mastery Test 1

Underline the correct word in the parentheses.

1. Paul is a much faster typist than (I, me).
2. (That, That there) tree will probably fall over with the next strong wind.
3. Since I'm about to get sick, that last drink is (yours, yours') if you want it.
4. My neighbor asked Eric and (I, me) to help him unload his new living-room furniture.
5. The students raised the money for the class trip (theirselves, themselves).
6. Our neighbors take (they, their) dog with them whenever they go for a ride.
7. My sister and (I, me) have both gotten part-time jobs at the same store.
8. I feel certain that Steven will speak for (hisself, himself) at the meeting tonight.
9. Before I dated Don, I dated a number of friends of (his, him).
10. It was up to Kelly and (I, me) to fix the loose handrail on the back porch.
11. (Them, Those) strawberries we picked should taste delicious on our homemade ice cream.
12. After the riot, the members of the rock group (theirselves, themselves) decided to go on with the concert.
13. My father always said to remember to give each man the respect due to (he, him).
14. Julie is the one student (who, whom) is doing well in that class.
15. The audience laughed when Mario and (he, him) walked onstage in the carrot costumes.
16. Terry left some old books of (her, hers) when she moved out of the apartment.
17. The encyclopedia salesman insisted on talking to my wife and (I, me) at the same time.
18. If any of you want tickets to the play-offs, you will have to pick them up (yourselfs, yourselves).
19. I couldn't decide to (who, whom) I should tell the secret.
20. If we don't get overtime pay for working on Veterans' Day, (we, us) employees are going to file a complaint.

Score: Number correct _____ × 5 = _____%

PRONOUN TYPES

Mastery Test 2

Cross out the incorrect pronoun in each sentence and write the correct form in the space provided.

_____   1. That there house across the street has been vacant for two years now.

_____   2. The wallet that was stolen from the health club is hers'.

_____   3. Give Chet and I a few hours, and we'll have that washing machine running again.

_____   4. Jim convinced hisself he would win the bowling match, and he did.

_____   5. If I have to be marooned on a desert island with someone, I hope it is him.

_____   6. Carla has put everything of yours' in the front-hall closet.

_____   7. Just between you and I, the mayor is a horrible womanizer.

_____   8. The coaches themself took full blame for the loss of the football game.

_____   9. You two have a better attitude about school than them.

_____   10. Please clear your books off the table, so I can set these here dishes down.

_____   11. At the meeting, the store buyers told we salespeople about the new fall line.

_____   12. The tornado destroyed everything in its' path.

_____   13. If you were as nervous as him, your forehead would be sweating too.

_____   14. When our whispering started to annoy her, the librarian asked Paula and I to leave.

_____   15. You can tell them plants haven't been watered in ages because their leaves are turning brown.

_____   16. After the police released us from the station, Father read my brother and I the riot act.

_____   17. Margo did not recognize the man whom stood at her apartment door.

_____   18. Our students seem to have less school spirit than theirs'.

_____   19. We asked ourself why such a young girl would try to take her own life.

_____   20. Although we got a late start, Herbie and me collected enough aluminum cans along the highway to fill three plastic trash bags.

Score: Number correct _____ × 5 = _____%

ADJECTIVES AND ADVERBS

Mastery Test 1

Part 1:   Cross out the incorrect adjectival or adverbial form in each sentence. Then write the correct form in the space provided.

_____   1. I did my work silent, but I was seething inside.

_____   2. The children's smiles were so sweetly that I knew they were up to something.

_____   3. Rita was proud that she had stuck to her diet faithful for two weeks.

_____   4. The students gazed longing at the clock as the teacher's voice droned on.

_____   5. The water was coming out too slow, so I increased the pressure.

Part 2:   Cross out the error in comparison in each sentence. Then write the correct form in the space provided.

_____   6. Roy can't pitch, but he catches good.

_____   7. You gave me a more smaller slice of pizza than you gave to Bud.

_____   8. A king-size bed is much comfortabler than a single bed.

_____   9. Mrs. Partridge owns several banks, but she's the most stingiest person I know.

_____   10. My coach said I had the most good chance of any person on the team of becoming a professional ballplayer.

_____

Score: Number correct _____ × 10 = _____%

ADJECTIVES AND ADVERBS

Mastery Test 2

Part 1: Cross out the incorrect adjectival or adverbial form in each sentence. Then write the correct form in the space provided.

_____ 1. Too many children complain that their parents don't take them serious.

_____ 2. The President's spouse greeted all the guests at the reception warm.

_____ 3. He is the most fiendishly culprit the police have ever encountered.

_____ 4. Fran polished the dull chrome tabletop until she could see her face clear in it.

_____ 5. The doctor said I wasn't good enough to travel, but I stubbornly refused to listen to him.

Part 2: Add to each sentence the correct form of the word in the margin.

good   6. Of the two hundred applicants, Olivia was easily the _____.

few   7. _____ people live in Los Angeles than in New York.

boring   8. Of all the new television shows I have watched this year, that comedy is the

_____.

high   9. Since my car is twelve years old, it requires a _____ octane gasoline than yours.

scary   10. *The Night of the Living Dead* is the _____ movie I have ever seen.

Score: Number correct _____ × 10 = _____%

CAPITAL LETTERS

Mastery Test 1

Cross out the two capitalization errors in each of the following sentences. Then write the corrections in the spaces provided.

_____
_____
1. One of our thanksgiving traditions is sending a check to an organization dedicated to relieving World hunger.

_____
_____
2. Vince couldn't understand why the U.S. Naval academy would want to have a goat for a Mascot.

_____
_____
3. Until he actually walked on the boardwalk in Atlantic City, my Brother thought it was just a blue stripe on the monopoly game board.

_____
_____
4. I spent my vacation visiting grandmom and grandpop in New York City.

_____
_____
5. To get to the Lake, go West for five miles until you see a Honda billboard.

_____
_____
6. There are only a few people in Louisiana who still speak cajun, a language similar to french.

_____
_____
7. In uncle Charlie's last letter, he wrote he was thinking of retiring and moving to the south.

_____
_____
8. Vern's old chevy finally broke down outside a wendy's a few blocks from his home.

_____
_____
9. Count dracula asked doctor Frankenstein to make a donation to the annual blood drive.

_____
_____
10. When the red cross arrived, many of the flood victims were wandering the muddy streets in a daze.

Score: Number correct _____ × 5 = _____%

CAPITAL LETTERS

Mastery Test 2

Cross out the two capitalization errors in each of the following sentences. Then write the corrections in the spaces provided.

_____
_____

1. A sign on a closed office door at the Kennedy Space center read, "out to launch."

_____
_____

2. While I was driving my toyota to canada, the state police stopped me for speeding.

_____
_____

3. Dr. quinn told me that if I didn't lose twenty pounds, I'd be risking a Heart attack.

_____
_____

4. Laura was happy that Mr. Armstrong would be teaching technical writing II this semester.

_____
_____

5. It was *Star Trek*'s mr. Spock who said, "live long and prosper."

_____
_____

6. Lena and I wrote to the National Park service for information on camping sites out west.

_____
_____

7. My brother james benefits from my poor business judgment whenever we play monopoly.

_____
_____

8. Carlos, an exchange student from latin America, spent last Summer living with our family.

_____
_____

9. Each Christmas, big motion picture studios such as MGM and paramount release new films aimed at attracting huge Holiday audiences.

_____
_____

10. The makers of Cigarettes such as eve and Virginia Slims try to lure women consumers by using pastel colors and slender shapes.

Score: Number correct _____ × 5 = _____%

CAPITAL LETTERS

Mastery Test 3

Cross out the two capitalization errors in each of the following sentences. Then write the corrections in the spaces provided.

_____ 1. Is it possible to order a Steak sandwich at a chinese restaurant?

_____ 2. Many romances that blossom in Spring wilt by september.

_____ 3. Doctor jekyll seemed to do better with the women when he turned into mr.
_____   Hyde.

_____ 4. Nicole feels sentimental every time the beatles' song ''yesterday'' is played
_____   on the radio.

_____ 5. At Bloomingdales there is a Sale on Calvin Klein jeans until tuesday.

_____ 6. My Brother's idea of a balanced meal is pizza followed by a snickers bar.
_____

_____ 7. I've been thinking of converting to Hinduism, because hindus believe in
_____   Reincarnation.

_____ 8. My father died in Vietnam, so we recently visited washington, D.C., to see
_____   his name carved on the Vietnam memorial.

_____ 9. The teacher explained, ''by the end of the course, you should be very
_____   comfortable writing on a Computer.''

_____ 10. i never could understand how every time Clark Kent decides to become
_____   superman, he can find an empty phone booth.

Score: Number correct _____ × 5 = _____%

CAPITAL LETTERS

Mastery Test 4

Cross out the two capitalization errors in each of the following sentences. Then write the corrections in the spaces provided.

_____   1. Do you think february is too early to start planning a Summer vacation?

_____

_____   2. After i heard about John Lennon's death, I cried for Weeks.

_____

_____   3. Before she could stop Herself, Maggie had bought three boxes of girl Scout
cookies.

_____   4. Since I did so well in introduction to Sociology, my adviser suggested I take
an Advanced course.

_____   5. "I can never win at scrabble," Nellie complained, "Because I'm always at
a loss for words."

_____   6. It seems the minute I turn on the television to watch the News, my Telephone
rings.

_____   7. Many Walt Disney Films, such as *cinderella,* are timeless.

_____

_____   8. The Video store on Baltimore avenue will let us rent as many as four
cassettes at a time.

_____

_____   9. The Knights of Columbus convention was the reason all the motels along
the beach in ocean city, Maryland, were so crowded last weekend.

_____   10. My little brother's favorite Bible story is the one about Adam and eve; He
loves hearing about other people who get into trouble.

_____

Score: Number correct _____ × 5 = _____%

NUMBERS AND ABBREVIATIONS

☉ Mastery Test 1

Cross out the mistake in numbers or abbreviations in each sentence and correct it in the space provided.

_____ 1. Roberta was arrested for doing 80 miles an hour on Skyline Drive.

_____ 2. Our tel. bill listed three long-distance calls to someone in Australia.

_____ 3. When I retire, I want to sleep until ten-thirty every morning.

_____ 4. Convicted speeders will lose their driver's lic. in this state.

_____ 5. The corn crop was cut in half this year due to 2 months of hot, dry weather.

_____ 6. Three different classmates called Marty and urged him to attend the ten-year reunion of his h.s. class.

_____ 7. I never seem to be able to find a gas sta. open before six o'clock in the morning.

_____ 8. Billy has about 250 baseball cards and almost one thousand clippings from *Sports Illustrated.*

_____ 9. Dr. Goldsmith's secretary called to confirm my Wed. dental appointment.

_____ 10. I won twenty-five dollars and fifty cents in the lottery after spending at least five times that much to buy tickets.

Score: Number correct _____ × 10 = _____%

NUMBERS AND ABBREVIATIONS

Mastery Test 2

Cross out the mistake in numbers or abbreviations in each sentence and correct it in the space provided. Mark the one sentence that is correct with a *C*.

_____	1. My dr. told me the best way to lose weight is little by little.
_____	2. The third baseman struck out ten of his last eleven times at bat.
_____	3. My aunt has a patriotic address: seventeen seventy six North Street.
_____	4. My car performs very well if I don't go over thirty miles an hr.
_____	5. I enjoy watching shows on the 3 major networks, but I prefer the shows on PBS.
_____	6. Grandma Belle jokingly gives her birth date as nineteen hundred and one B.C.
_____	7. I started working as a part-time salesperson at Sears in nineteen eighty-six.
_____	8. At about 1:30 last night I woke up and made myself a ham sand. on rye.
_____	9. The teacher said our class is bankrupt when it comes to Chapter Eleven in our economics text.
_____	10. My little bro. wants to join the FBI so he can snoop into other people's business.

Score: Number correct _____ × 10 = _____%

END MARKS

◯ Mastery Test 1

Add a period, question mark, or exclamation point, as needed, to each of the following sentences.

Note: End marks always go *inside* the quotation marks that appear in some sentences.

1. Sometimes I wonder why I always seem to learn lessons the hard way
2. Look out or you'll smash the car
3. When you finish with the dishes, please put them neatly in the cupboards
4. Do you always find time to read the Sunday newspaper
5. I asked Heather where her club's party is being held
6. Claudio had to cut one of his sneakers to make room for his swollen toe
7. All the game show contestant could do was yell, ''I won, I won ''
8. People often buy through a mixture of rational and irrational motives
9. Jerry looked up from the stack of bills and asked, ''Whose idea was it to have teenagers ''
10. Carla shouted, ''If that's the way you feel, you can take back your ring ''
11. There's a woman at the door asking if we want to save our souls
12. Will you still need me, and will you still feed me, when I'm sixty-four
13. If it's noon here, what time is it in Tokyo
14. The patriot Tom Paine wrote: ''These are the times that try men's souls ''
15. Barbara always gets terrific bargains the day after Christmas
16. The larger pieces of farm equipment stood next to the empty barn, waiting for the auction to begin
17. ''But Mr. Wilson,'' Margie said to the bank manager, ''how can I be overdrawn when I still have four checks left ''
18. In the early part of the next century, half the population of the United States will be senior citizens
19. For the convenience of our customers, employees will no longer park in the spaces near the front entrance of the store
20. As the members of the cast took their final bows, a woman called from the back of the audience, ''That's my Bernie up there ''

Score: Number correct _____ × 5 = _____%

END MARKS

 ## Mastery Test 2

Add a period, question mark, or exclamation point, as needed, to each of the following sentences.

Note: End marks always go *inside* the quotation marks that appear in some sentences.

1. That dog's bite is worse than its bark
2. Please run down to the store and buy a loaf of rye bread
3. Hurry, Alan, the movie will be starting any minute
4. I wonder what Beethoven would think of the Beatles
5. What do you think about before you fall asleep
6. The young apprentice was inspired by the skill of the master carpenter
7. Judging by all the television ads, Americans are in great need of pain relief
8. Which is better, one long vacation a year or several shorter ones
9. Erica cried out in her sleep, "Please—somebody help me "
10. Mark keeps a mug full of pencils on his desk, but every one of them has a broken point
11. Why do I always pick the slowest checkout line in the supermarket
12. If I catch you kids in my yard again, I'm calling the police
13. Due to a printing error, all the months in the calendars had thirty-five days
14. The sign in front of Buckingham Palace seemed to scream, "Don't even think of parking here "
15. "Dear Abby," wrote Lana, "do you think you can love someone too much "
16. The first time I saw your car, I thought you must have strayed into the wrong neighborhood
17. Richard sat for over an hour watching a pair of robins building a nest in the tree outside his bedroom window
18. The player won the championship game with a half-court basket, and the sportscaster shouted, "What a shot "
19. Because of the increase of sexually transmitted diseases, monogamous relationships are becoming more popular
20. Dried grapes are raisins, and dried plums are prunes, but dried apricots are always called "dried apricots"

> ***Score:*** Number correct _____ × 5 = _____%

APOSTROPHE

Mastery Test 1

Cross out the word in each sentence that needs an apostrophe. Then write the word correctly in the space provided.

_____ 1. That department stores prices are too high.

_____ 2. Christines aunt has a very deep voice for such a small woman.

_____ 3. The black rhino will eventually become extinct, because it wont breed in captivity.

_____ 4. As the snow fell harder, the children began to plan for tomorrows holiday from school.

_____ 5. When lost on the road, Carl will never ask questions or admit that he doesnt know the way.

_____ 6. The TV program dealt with a mothers concern about drugs and alcohol.

_____ 7. Matt stood silently in the darkened hallway and tried to remember why hed come there.

_____ 8. "If you pull that cats tail one more time," Rhona told her little daughter, "you will be very sorry."

_____ 9. Spectators were thrilled by the stunt pilots ability to put the biplane through breathtaking loops and rolls.

_____ 10. The district attorneys address to the jury was so convincing that Perry Mason resigned from the case on the spot.

Score: Number correct _____ × 10 = _____ %

APOSTROPHE

Mastery Test 2

In each sentence two apostrophes are missing or are used incorrectly. Cross out the two errors and write the corrections in the spaces provided.

_____   1. Its not unusual for students ideas to change during their college years.
_____

_____   2. Every time Dave park's his car downtown, he worries that someones going
_____   to steal it.

_____   3. If you dont know where youre going, how will you know when you get
_____   there?

_____   4. Marie always watches music videos at Terrys house, since she isnt allowed
_____   to see them at home.

_____   5. Garys mother woke his sisters' and him in the middle of the night to watch
_____   the meteor shower.

_____   6. People have been buying lottery ticket's for centuries, always hoping theyll
_____   win the grand prize.

_____   7. Sallys grades in math might improve if shed only stop wearing sunglasses
_____   and headphones in class.

_____   8. In the United States', farmers get more production out of their' land because
_____   of the heavy use of chemical fertilizers.

_____   9. The announcer told the fans that theyd seen baseball at its best in the Yankees
_____   victory over the Orioles.

_____ 10. My grandfathers old canoe sprang a leak before wed made it halfway across
_____   the lake.

Score: Number correct _____ × 5 = _____%

APOSTROPHE

◎ Mastery Test 3

In each sentence two apostrophes are missing or are used incorrectly. Cross out the two errors and write the corrections in the spaces provided.

_____   1. The invitation's to the wedding arent being mailed until the couple start
_____   speaking to each other again.

_____   2. On Wednesday morning, youre supposed to report to the boys gym for your
_____   physical.

_____   3. Tobys parents gave him a new leather briefcase on the morning he started
_____   his' new job at the insurance agency.

_____   4. Looking through the classified ads only reminded Roger of the many thing's
_____   he didnt know how to do.

_____   5. My cousins, Sharon and Ben, work for Meals on Wheels, a volunteer
_____   organization that provide's hot food to many of the towns senior citizens.

_____   6. The sight of Lolas tanned body in a black bikini was enough to make young
_____   mens heads spin around as if they were on ball bearings.

_____   7. With each new scandal in the athletic department, the universitys reputation
_____   for integrity slips' another notch.

_____   8. Grandmothers eye's were misty as she remembered the nights Grandfather
_____   called for her in a Model T Ford.

_____   9. A blue whales tongue weighs' as much as forty men.

_____   10. Ricks decision to begin attending classes so close to the semesters end is
_____   like turning off the faucets on the sinking _Titanic_.

> **_Score:_**   Number correct _____ × 5 = _____%

APOSTROPHE

Mastery Test 4

In each sentence two apostrophes are missing or are used incorrectly. Cross out the two errors and write the corrections in the spaces provided.

_____   1. Whats mine is your's, darling, including the bills.

_____

_____   2. "Stay away from my brothers stuff if you dont want your face removed,"
_____   said Gladys.

_____   3. Slivers from the glass Id broken glistened like diamond's on the kitchen tile.

_____

_____   4. The young mans hands were shaking as he dialed Colleens number on the
_____   phone.

_____   5. Craigs medical exam revealed that he has high blood pressure and that hes
_____   twenty pounds overweight.

_____   6. The pitcher whod given up the home run doffed his cap to the jeering
_____   spectator's as he exited.

_____   7. In considering new admissions, most colleges look at each applicants grades,
_____   extracurricular activities, test score's, and personal recommendations.

_____   8. If this weekends forecast for heavy rain and flash floods comes true, many
_____   peoples houses are in danger.

_____   9. Nick and Ellen havent seen their friends much since having the baby; they
_____   say shes more work than a full-time job.

_____   10. We wouldve won the sardine race after stuffing fifteen people into Annemaries
_____   Volkswagen, but she couldn't budge the gearshift to drive the car.

> *Score:*   Number correct _____ × 5 = _____%

QUOTATION MARKS

◉ Mastery Test 1

Place quotation marks or underlines where needed.

1. A sign in a cluttered hardware store read, We've got it if we can find it.
2. Go ahead, make my day! snarled Dirty Harry.
3. I can't do the dishes, Tyrone said, because the cat is sitting on my lap.
4. This machine will do half your work for you, the salesclerk promised.
5. That's terrific, I replied. I'll take two of them.
6. Robert Frost's poem The Road Not Taken influenced Gordon's decision to be an architect.
7. When someone asked Willie Sutton why he kept robbing banks, he replied, Because that's where the money is.
8. I'd never date him, Celia said. He switches girlfriends at the blink of an eyelid.
9. One of Murphy's laws states: An optimist believes we live in the best of all possible worlds; a pessimist fears this is true.
10. The bittersweet song At the Ballet is one of several showstoppers in A Chorus Line, the longest-running musical in Broadway history.

Score: Number correct _____ × 10 = _____%

QUOTATION MARKS

Mastery Test 2

Place quotation marks or underlines where needed.

1. Get back behind the railing! the zookeeper yelled to the little boy.
2. A New York subway sign showing little confidence in the public reads, No spitting.
3. The job is yours, Ms. Washburn said, as long as you're willing to work a fifty-hour week.
4. Mae West once said, It's better to be looked over than overlooked.
5. The only part of the income-tax form I like to read is the one called How to Claim Your Refund.
6. Why don't you watch where you're going? the drunk mumbled to the lamppost.
7. In a special section of Harper's magazine called Tools for Living, I saw an ad for a gadget that triples the life of a light bulb.
8. Turning to his father during the ball game, Joey mimicked the nearby vendor and said, Hot dogs! Hot dogs! Get your son a hot dog right here.
9. One letter to Abigail Van Buren from a man named Henry read, Dear Abby: Between you and me, the people who write to you are either morons or just plain stupid.
10. Abby's response was, Dear Henry: Which are you?

Score: Number correct _____ × 10 = _____%

QUOTATION MARKS

◯ Mastery Test 3

Place quotation marks or underlines where needed.

1. If life's a bowl of cherries, sighed Reggie, mine are canned.
2. My friends are mistaken when they say I'm afraid of flying, said my aunt.
3. Then she added, It's crashing I'm afraid of.
4. Stephen King's short story The Body was the basis for the successful movie Stand By Me.
5. The comedian said, I took a cab to the drive-in; the movie cost me ninety-five dollars.
6. If a tree falls in the forest and nobody is there to hear it, asked the philosophy teacher, is there a noise?
7. The late Spencer Tracy's advice on acting was, To be a good actor, just remember your lines and don't bump into the furniture.
8. Here's some sound financial advice, Mr. Green said to his son, who was dressing for a date. Take her to a place that has a cook, not a chef.
9. Many music critics consider the Beatles' song Sgt. Pepper's Lonely Hearts Club Band to be a turning point in the history of rock music.
10. The difference between that weatherman and us, my father said as he watched the news, is that when it comes to telling the weather he has to stick his neck out, but we only have to stick our heads out.

Score: Number correct _____ × 10 = _____%

QUOTATION MARKS

 Mastery Test 4

Place quotation marks or underlines where needed.

1. On our way to the doctor's office, Dad said, Dr. Frank has been practicing medicine for forty years.
2. Hasn't he learned how to do it yet? my little brother asked.
3. No onions on that sandwich, please, Sharon told the deli clerk. I'm on my way to an interview.
4. Ever since my sixth-grade teacher made me memorize Carl Sandburg's poem The Grass, I've hated it.
5. A judge asked Oscar Wilde during Wilde's trial, Are you trying to show contempt for this court?
6. On the contrary—I'm trying to conceal it, Wilde replied.
7. Either that painting is crooked or our house is leaning, Teresa said to her husband. Please fix one of them.
8. The lion may be king of the beasts, but the majestic elegance of the giraffe certainly makes it part of the royal court, asserted the zoo tour guide.
9. Of course, I saw the play under unfortunate conditions, wrote the drama critic in the morning paper. The curtain was up.
10. I'm determined to grow roses this summer, my Aunt Freda said. So I bought a copy of McCall's Garden Book and began reading the first chapter, How to Cultivate Your Green Thumb.

Score: Number correct _____ × 10 = _____%

COMMA

 ## Mastery Test 1

Add commas where needed. Then refer to the box below to write, in the space provided, the letter of the one comma rule that applies in each sentence.

---

a. Between items in a series	d. Between complete thoughts
b. After introductory material	e. With direct quotations
c. Around interrupters	

_____ 1. The witness swore to tell the truth the whole truth and nothing but the truth.

_____ 2. When Mona loses her temper she speaks in a very subdued voice.

_____ 3. The coach told me it was his way or the highway so I hit the road.

_____ 4. The undertaker's sign stated ''We're the last ones in the world to let you down.''

_____ 5. Three sets of twins a hospital record were born on the same day.

_____ 6. ''Park your car over there'' the attendant said ''and leave the keys in the ignition.''

_____ 7. Entering the crystal blue ocean like a pin the cliff diver caused hardly a ripple on the surface.

_____ 8. Helen's new food processor slices dices chops and makes mounds of julienne fries.

_____ 9. The next time you dare use language like that in my presence young man will be your last day in this school.

_____ 10. Rob is forty-one years old and runs his own business but his mother still wants to know when he's going to settle down.

Score: Number correct _____ × 10 = _____%

COMMA

 ## Mastery Test 2

Add commas where needed. Then refer to the box below to write, in the space provided, the letter of the one comma rule that applies in each sentence.

<table>
<tr><td>a. Between items in a series</td><td>d. Between complete thoughts</td></tr>
<tr><td>b. After introductory material</td><td>e. With direct quotations</td></tr>
<tr><td>c. Around interrupters</td><td></td></tr>
</table>

_____ 1. As I opened the car door a wave of hot air spilled out of the baking interior.

_____ 2. Cindy bought two lamps a beach chair and plastic salt and pepper shakers at a yard sale.

_____ 3. Hal's instructions to the prospective models were "Don't just do something, stand there."

_____ 4. Mark realized checkmate was inevitable so he conveniently knocked over the four pawns closest to him.

_____ 5. Cary Grant a symbol of sophisticated charm for many moviegoers never won an Oscar the film industry's highest honor.

_____ 6. After the wild dog had devoured my pet rabbits it disappeared into the woods behind our house.

_____ 7. "This is the worst coffee I've ever had" protested Rose.

_____ 8. The wrestler's face fleshy and pockmarked and dominated by big green eyes seemed too small for such a colossal body.

_____ 9. Mrs. Evans scooped Tommy up as he headed for the mouthwash display but her unattended shopping cart smashed into a mountain of cereal boxes.

_____ 10. The lifeguard had white-blond hair piercing blue eyes a deep bronze tan and a scraggly beard that the teenage girl mistook for a sign of maturity.

Score: Number correct _____ × 10 = _____%

COMMA

 Mastery Test 3

Add commas where needed. Then refer to the box below to write, in the space provided, the letter of the one comma rule that applies in each sentence.

a. Between items in a series	d. Between complete thoughts
b. After introductory material	e. With direct quotations
c. Around interrupters	

_____ 1. The dean of the law school I am told was arrested for fraud and embezzlement.

_____ 2. The accident outside the mall destroyed both cars but no one was killed.

_____ 3. After I flunked out of school I realized that studying might have been a good idea.

_____ 4. The thirsty sore and exhausted marathon runner collapsed as she staggered across the finish line.

_____ 5. The professor's stare so disconcertingly frank that it caused me to blush made me forget my question.

_____ 6. Mother tried to probe my eyes for the truth but I avoided her penetrating gaze.

_____ 7. "He's greyhound lean and wolf-pack mean" the sportscaster said in describing the middleweight boxing contender.

_____ 8. Ted Kelly one of my high school friends was nicknamed "Gingersnap" for the large freckles on his face.

_____ 9. Because the convict showed no remorse for his brutal crime the judge imposed the maximum sentence allowed under law.

_____ 10. The construction workers had already torn down the fence uprooted the trees and dug a trench across the front yard before they realized they were at the wrong address.

Score: Number correct _____ × 10 = _____%

COMMA

 Mastery Test 4

Add commas where needed. Then refer to the box below to write, in the space provided, the letter of the one comma rule that applies in each sentence.

a. Between items in a series	d. Between complete thoughts
b. After introductory material	e. With direct quotations
c. Around interrupters	

_____ 1. I sat there open-mouthed and embarrassed listening to the class laugh at my answer.

_____ 2. Calvin couldn't sleep because the baby upstairs was crying a neighborhood dog was barking and someone nearby kept racing his car engine.

_____ 3. Joe has taken trumpet lessons for five years but most people agree they have been in vain.

_____ 4. The defendant had to be extremely careful of his testimony for the prosecutor was clever and determined.

_____ 5. "Stay tuned" said the announcer "for an important message for everyone who would like to become a millionaire."

_____ 6. My father shut his eyes put his hands in his lap and said a quiet prayer as he waited for the news from the doctor.

_____ 7. With the utmost care little Jenny placed the kitten in her coat pocket and headed for the school playground.

_____ 8. Tom Xydakis became tired of spelling his name over the telephone so he now orders all his pizzas for "Smith."

_____ 9. Irving Berlin composed "White Christmas" one of the most popular Christmas songs of all time while sitting by his swimming pool.

_____ 10. Realizing that every one of the six lottery numbers matched her ticket Roxanne could hear a surge of blood to her temples.

Score: Number correct _____ × 10 = _____ %

OTHER PUNCTUATION MARKS

Mastery Test 1

At the appropriate spot (or spots), place the punctuation mark shown in the margin.

—
1. He's so rich he doesn't count his money he weighs it.

;
2. Mary's savings have dwindled to nothing she's been borrowing from me to pay her rent.

-
3. The quick witted little boy called the rescue squad for help.

:
4. Martha likes only two kinds of books cookbooks and bankbooks.

( )
5. The size of the lot two acres was just what Bob had been looking for.

-
6. The anti nuclear activitists staged a rally to protest the opening of the new power plant.

—
7. I think as a matter of fact, I'm positive I returned your power drill last week.

:
8. The novelist Jessamyn West once defined irony as follows "Irony is when you buy a suit with two pairs of pants and then burn a hole in the coat."

( )
9. If you're running out of storage space, there are only two solutions: 1 store your possessions more efficiently or 2 get rid of some of the junk you never use.

;
10. An old Chinese proverb says, "If you are planting for a year, sow rice if you are planting for a decade, plant trees and if you are planting for a lifetime, educate a person."

Score: Number correct _____ × 10 = _____%

OTHER PUNCTUATION MARKS

 ## Mastery Test 2

Each sentence below needs one of the following punctuation marks:

colon :	hyphen -	semicolon ;
dash —	parentheses ( )	

Insert the correct mark (or pair of marks) as needed.

1. Call the toll free number for quick service from our catalogue.
2. My sister is allergic to cats and dogs therefore, we never could have any pets when we were little.
3. The counseling center's hours 9:00 A.M. to 5:00 P.M. are inconvenient since all my classes are at night.
4. My distinguished opponent is a highly qualified person if you ignore his long prison record.
5. There are two basic rules for travelers take half as many clothes and take twice as much money.
6. A sixty year old woman is entered in the marathon.
7. The crippled airliner landed safely the passengers and crew walked away unharmed.
8. Lola said, "My first boyfriend I'll never forget him proposed to me fifteen minutes after we met."
9. Before the party, Alicia had to stop at the cleaner's, where her dress was ready at the bakery, where she had ordered a decorated cake and at the convenience store for ice, so they'd have plenty for punch.
10. In his book *On Writing Well*, William Zinsser wrote about wordiness "If you give me an article that runs to eight pages and I tell you to cut it to four, you'll howl and say it can't be done. Then you will go home and do it, and it will be infinitely better. After that comes the hard part: cutting it to three."

Score: Number correct _____ × 10 = _____%

DICTIONARY USE

Mastery Test 1

Use your dictionary to answer the following questions.

1. How many syllables are in the word *inconsequential?* _____

2. Where is the primary accent in the word *contemplation?* _____

3. In the word *frivolity*, the first *i* is pronounced like
   a. long *e*
   b. long *i*
   c. schwa
   d. short *i*

4. In the word *rudiment*, the *u* is pronounced like
   a. short *u*
   b. long *u*
   c. short *a*
   d. schwa

5. In the word *inhalation*, the first *a* is pronounced like
   a. schwa
   b. short *i*
   c. short *a*
   d. long *a*

Items 6–10:   There are five misspelled words in the following sentence. Cross out each misspelled word and write in the correct spelling in the spaces provided.

I had a chance to work thirty hours a week at a restarant this semestir, but my parants told me that it was more importent to have sufficent time for studying.

6. _____   9. _____

7. _____   10. _____

8. _____

Score: Number correct _____ × 10 = _____%

DICTIONARY USE

Mastery Test 2

Use your dictionary to answer the following questions.

1. How many syllables are in the word *subsequently?* _____

2. Where is the primary accent in the word *fastidious?* _____

3. In the word *cantankerous,* the *e* is pronounced like
    a. short *i*
    b. short *e*
    c. long *e*
    d. schwa

4. In the word *demoniac,* the *o* is pronounced like
    a. short *a*
    b. short *i*
    c. short *o*
    d. long *o*

5. In the word *malleable,* the first *a* is pronounced like
    a. schwa
    b. short *a*
    c. long *a*
    d. short *e*

Items 6–10:   There are five misspelled words in the following sentences. Cross out each misspelled word and write the correct spelling in the space provided.

My dauhter Judy wants to legaly change her name to ''Violet'' because she thinks ''Judy'' is too commen and ''Violet'' has a sence of mystery and glamer to it.

6. _____   9. _____

7. _____   10. _____

8. _____

Score: Number correct _____ × 10 = _____%

SPELLING IMPROVEMENT

 Mastery Test 1

Use the three spelling rules to spell the following words.

1. inflate + able = _____   5. trim   + er   = _____

2. ban   + ing   = _____   6. plenty   + ful = _____

3. thrifty + est   = _____   7. concern + ed   = _____

4. refer   + ed   = _____   8. derive   + ing = _____

Circle the correctly spelled plural in each pair.

9. sheafs	sheaves	12. quarrys	quarries
10. pitches	pitchs	13. echos	echoes
11. pastries	pastrys	14. relays	relais

Circle the correctly spelled word (from the basic word list) in each pair.

15. direction	direcion	18. awkwerd	awkward
16. wellcome	welcome	19. believe	beleive
17. generel	general	20. comfortible	comfortable

Score: Number correct _____ × 5 = _____ %

SPELLING IMPROVEMENT

Mastery Test 2

Use the three spelling rules to spell the following words.

1. grip   + ed   = _____   5. date   + ing   = _____

2. fancy + ful = _____   6. employ + er   = _____

3. imply + ed   = _____   7. spine   + less = _____

4. curve + ing = _____   8. duty   + ful   = _____

Circle the correctly spelled plural in each pair.

9. embargoes   embargos   12. hobbys   hobbies
10. wolves   wolfs   13. guards   guardes
11. attorney-at-laws attorneys-at-law 14. reflexs   reflexes

Circle the correctly spelled word (from the basic word list) in each pair.

15. atempt   attempt   18. several   severel
16. attenshun   attention   19. alot   a lot
17. personal   perssonal   20. diferent   different

| Score: | Number correct _____ × 5 = _____% |

OMITTED WORDS AND LETTERS

Mastery Test 1

Part 1:   In the spaces provided, write in the two small connecting words needed in each sentence. Use carets (∧) within the sentences to show where these words belong.

_____

1. A carton milk leaked all over floor of my car.

_____

2. I'd like introduce you to man I'm going to marry.

_____

3. The supermarket was full shoppers who heard about big sale.

_____

4. When spring is the air, most people seem feel especially happy.

_____

5. After the torrents rain turned to ice, condition of the streets was treacherous.

Part 2:   Add the two -*s* endings needed in each sentence.

_____

6. Between you and me, raisin make a better pie than apple do.

_____

7. Darien spent forty-five minute balancing his checkbook and found four error.

_____

8. The member of the sixth grade collected Christmas toy for needy children.

_____

9. Together, both of my daughter and my husband have twenty-seven mateless sock.

_____

10. There is little doubt remaining that many student cheated on several final examination.

> *Score:*   Number correct _____ × 5 = _____%

OMITTED WORDS AND LETTERS

Mastery Test 2

Part 1:   In the spaces provided, write in the two small connecting words needed in each sentence. Use carets (ʌ) within the sentences to show where these words belong.

_____
_____   1. I noticed number of anthills our backyard while I was mowing the lawn.

_____
_____   2. Please put timer on so you remember take the cookies out of the oven.

_____
_____   3. Without a doubt, Jenny's drawing was best all the students' art projects today.

_____
_____   4. My brother couldn't remember the name of book on which he had to write book report.

_____
_____   5. At first, the mountains looked like a foggy dream off the distance; then, as we approached, they seemed be almost too real.

Part 2:   Add the two -s endings needed in each sentence.

_____
_____   6. All the houseplant on my sun porch have aphid.

_____
_____   7. In our basic math course, the final exam covers statistic and graph.

_____
_____   8. At the beginning of the football season, most of the defensive player got Mohawk haircut.

_____
_____   9. Your children left their coat on the sidewalk about two block away from here.

_____
_____   10. Too many cook may spoil the broth, but I still want as many helper in the kitchen as possible.

Score: Number correct _____ × 5 = _____%

COMMONLY CONFUSED WORDS

Mastery Test 1

Choose the correct words in each sentence and write them in the spaces provided.

_____ 1. If you want my (advice, advise), the (right, write) thing to do is apologize.

_____

_____ 2. (Being that, Because) Leon had (all ready, already) dropped off his last assignment, he prepared to leave campus for spring vacation.

_____

_____ 3. I wish I (knew, new) (whose, who's) dog is responsible for the mess in my front yard.

_____ 4. You (to, too, two) troublemakers are (threw, through) with this team as of right this minute.

_____ 5. The reason I signed up for an accounting (coarse, course) is that I want to know the basic (principals, principles) of bookkeeping.

_____ 6. If you intend to continue living (hear, here), young man, (your, you're) going to have to follow my rules.

_____ 7. Ann and George's friendship developed into love as the years (passed, past), and now, in midlife, (their, there, they're) newlyweds.

_____ 8. (Beside, Besides) the fact that this car runs like a dream, (its, it's) trade-in value remains quite high.

_____ 9. Randy, you must have a (hole, whole) in your head if you really believe you can (right, write) a term paper in one night.

_____ 10. (Their, There, They're) was so much alcohol served with dinner that the noise at our table became (quite, quiet) loud.

_____

Score: Number correct _____ × 5 = _____%

COMMONLY CONFUSED WORDS

Mastery Test 2

Choose the correct words in each sentence and write them in the spaces provided.

_____
_____

1. When my son's stereo broke, (their, there, they're) was finally some (peace, piece) around the house.

_____
_____

2. By using pieces of her children's old (clothes, cloths), Lois gave her quilt a wonderfully colorful (affect, effect).

_____
_____

3. The hosts of the New Year's Eve party (passed, past) glasses of champagne (among, between) the guests just after midnight.

_____
_____

4. If you (knew, new) you weren't feeling well this morning, you (should have, should of) called in sick and stayed home.

_____
_____

5. An easy way to eat (fewer, less) calories is to simply eliminate all (deserts, desserts) from your diet.

_____
_____

6. Is it important (weather, whether) I use up all my vacation this year, or (can, may) I apply this year's leftover days to next year?

_____
_____

7. I think I (would have, would of) collapsed any minute if the coach hadn't given us a (brake, break) from those wind sprints when he did.

_____
_____

8. I don't (know, no) a nicer couple than the Wenofs, who are just (plain, plane) folks despite their wealth.

_____
_____

9. You (can't hardly, can hardly) blame people for avoiding you when you (loose, lose) your temper all the time.

_____
_____

10. Our English professor is a tough grader, but students like her because she can (learn, teach) better (than, then) anyone else in that school.

Score: Number correct _____ × 5 = _____%

COMMONLY CONFUSED WORDS

Mastery Test 3

Cross out the two mistakes in usage in each sentence. Then write the correct words in the spaces provided.

_____ 1. If you're family is starving, is it better to become a beggar then a thief?

_____

_____ 2. If you ate less snacks between meals, you probably would loose some weight.

_____

_____ 3. We're already for our vacation, accept for the usual last-minute packing.

_____

_____ 4. Who's job was it to give the dog it's bath?

_____

_____ 5. In the dessert, plant life has learned too survive with very little rainfall.

_____

_____ 6. Write from the beginning, we could tell the knew professor was going to be a pushover.

_____

_____ 7. The fog was so thick that Ed couldn't hardly see the break lights of the car ahead of him.

_____

_____ 8. Denzel would of learned his brother to play the drums, but their mother hid the drumsticks.

_____

_____ 9. The acting principle of the new high school addressed the hole student body on the first day of school.

_____

_____ 10. As Wilma paddled along the quite stream, the only sounds she heard were the calls of a pear of mourning doves.

_____

Score: Number correct _____ × 5 = _____%

COMMONLY CONFUSED WORDS

Mastery Test 4

Cross out the two mistakes in usage in each sentence. Then write the correct words in the spaces provided.

_____   1. Charlotte has never learned to except an compliment without blushing.
_____

_____   2. I'd have less worries if I didn't let the opinions of others effect me so much.
_____

_____   3. Vern holds to the principal that true wisdom comes only threw experience.
_____

_____   4. I should of mowed the lawn as soon as I heard their was going to be a
_____   thunderstorm tonight.

_____   5. Chuck's car would of passed inspection accept for the hole in its muffler.
_____

_____   6. Being that the airport bus was late, we missed our flight and had to wait too
_____   hours for the next one.

_____   7. I new there was something questionable about the magazine when it arrived
_____   in a plane brown wrapper.

_____   8. Some guys think its a lot easier to break up with a girlfriend when they all
_____   ready have a replacement lined up.

_____   9. We must of past ten service stations, but Lennie wouldn't stop until he found
_____   one that gave out trading stamps.

_____   10. A California man once rode a skateboard down a mountainside coarse at
_____   speeds greater then seventy miles an hour.

Score: Number correct _____ × 5 = _____%

EFFECTIVE WORD CHOICE

Mastery Test 1

Certain words are italicized in the following sentences. In the space at the left, identify whether the words are slang (*S*), clichés (*C*), or pretentious words (*PW*). Then replace the words with more effective diction.

_____   1. I *get off* on horror *flicks*.

_____

_____   2. You should file all office *memorandums* after *perusing* them.

_____

_____   3. Building your own house *is easier said than done*.

_____

_____   4. Because Ted realized he had *had one too many,* he decided to take a taxi home.

_____

_____   5. My little brother's *demeanor* always *ameliorates* just before Christmas.

_____

_____   6. Often when I am called on in school, *my brain is out to lunch.*

_____

_____   7. When Flora tried *to bum* a *cancer stick* from me, I told her I quit smoking a week ago.

_____

_____   8. The committee's *mission* is to *alleviate* scheduling problems.

_____

_____   9. Because Nadia kept forgetting to clean her room, our mother decided to *put her foot down.*

_____

_____   10. The students *manifested* delight with the *communication* that classes would be canceled Tuesday morning.

_____

Score: Number correct _____ × 10 = _____%

EFFECTIVE WORD CHOICE

◯ Mastery Test 2

Certain words are italicized in the following sentences. In the space at the left, identify whether the words are slang (*S*), clichés (*C*), or pretentious words (*PW*). Then replace the words with more effective diction.

_____   1. Receiving an A on my final was *as sweet as pie.*

_____   2. If you don't *get off my case,* I'll *punch your lights out.*

_____   3. The school board's decision to drop football *had many parents up in arms.*

_____   4. The interviewer *inquired as to the location of my permanent residence.*

_____   5. Too many people *get hung up on* the way teenagers look, instead of trying to understand *where they're coming from.*

_____   6. Our *refuse* cans were bent up by the *sanitation personnel.*

_____   7. John, your mother and I *have had it up to here* with your careless attitude.

_____   8. The teacher *raked him over the coals* for missing class, but Jed *kept his cool.*

_____   9. *An excess of precipitation* has caused crop failure.

_____   10. I *let out a sigh of relief* when I saw my grade for the paper.

Score: Number correct _____ × 10 = _____%

EFFECTIVE WORD CHOICE

◎ Mastery Test 3

The following sentences include examples of wordiness. Rewrite the sentences in the space provided, omitting needless words.

1. A total of eight students in our class were given failing grades for the exam we took.

    _____

    _____

2. During the time that the Millers were off on vacation somewhere, their home was burglarized by unknown persons.

    _____

    _____

3. Holly took three hundred dollars from her bank account for the purpose of buying a television in the near future.

    _____

    _____

4. At this point in time, I have not as yet fully and completely made my decision concerning just what it is that I should do.

    _____

    _____

5. If you want to make sure that the answer you have come up with is correct, you should refer to the answer key that you will find by turning to the back of the book.

    _____

    _____

Score: Number correct _____ × 20 = _____%

EFFECTIVE WORD CHOICE

○ Mastery Test 4

The following sentences include examples of wordiness. Rewrite the sentences in the space provided, omitting needless words.

1. Owing to the fact that I was half an hour late, I did not do very well on the test and failed it.

   _____

   _____

2. The actual true reason I don't watch much television is that there are too many television commercials to look at.

   _____

   _____

3. After a great deal of driving practice that she had with the family car, my sister said she felt she was finally ready to take and pass her driver's test.

   _____

   _____

4. In this day and age, the majority of people seem more than ever to want to get something of value in return for the money they pay out.

   _____

   _____

5. Because of the fact that the amount of my salary is less than the total sum of my expenses, it has been necessary for me to find a second job in addition to my present one.

   _____

   _____

Score: Number correct _____ × 20 = _____%

Combined Mastery Tests

SENTENCE FRAGMENTS AND RUN-ONS

Combined Mastery Test 1

Each of the word groups below is numbered. In the space provided, write *C* if a word group is a complete sentence, write *F* if it is a fragment, and write *R-O* if it is a run-on. Then correct the errors.

1. _____
2. _____
3. _____
4. _____
5. _____
6. _____
7. _____
8. _____
9. _____
10. _____
11. _____
12. _____
13. _____
14. _____
15. _____
16. _____
17. _____
18. _____
19. _____
20. _____

¹Richard was an angry young man a few years ago. ²And still has some scars to prove it. ³He once became so furious. ⁴That he broke a window with his fist and cut his hand on the glass. ⁵Another time, he threw a plate of spaghetti across a room through the years, his temper got him into many arguments. ⁶And even fistfights. ⁷Richard finally realized he had to bring his anger under control, or it would defeat him. ⁸Making him the biggest victim of his own fury. ⁹To get some perspective on the problem. ¹⁰He asked his Uncle Jay for help, Jay pointed out that Richard's explosions only made bad situations worse. ¹¹When a person has lot of rage inside, Jay said. ¹²His explosions often have little to do with the incidents that seem to cause the anger. ¹³Jay suggested that Richard might get some insight into the problem. ¹⁴By keeping a diary of his feelings and of his temper tantrums. ¹⁵Jay also advised Richard to ask himself a question whenever he began to feel angry. ¹⁶The question was, "Is this really important enough to get upset about?" ¹⁷Richard took his uncle's advice, he began to seek new responses to situations that frustrated and angered him. ¹⁸Although it hasn't been easy. ¹⁹He has gradually learned how to control his temper even more important is that by examining his feelings, Richard has changed his outlook on life. ²⁰Which has resulted in less temper to control.

> **Score:** Number correct _____ × 5 = _____%

SENTENCE FRAGMENTS AND RUN-ONS

Combined Mastery Test 2

In the space provided, indicate whether each item below contains a fragment (*F*) or a run-on (*R-O*). Then correct the error.

_____ 1. A pungent odor filled the house cabbage was simmering on the stove. I suddenly felt hungry.

_____ 2. Stella clips out many recipes. That she finds in the newspaper. However, she rarely tries them out.

_____ 3. Hummingbirds eat half their weight every day. They are tiny, colorful creatures. Weighing no more than a dime.

_____ 4. The impatient driver could hardly wait for the green light. He kept edging his car into the intersection, then he started driving when the light turned yellow.

_____ 5. Using Tupperware containers as molds. The children built an elaborate sand castle on the beach. A helpful wave filled in their moat.

_____ 6. Pauline has taught in many elementary classes she finds first-graders the most rewarding to teach. Most of them still think school is fun.

_____ 7. Some feel we should bring our own bags to the supermarket. We could save millions of trees. Instead of throwing away usable paper.

_____ 8. When I got home. I stuffed my wet shoes with newspaper. I didn't want the toes to curl up as they dried.

_____ 9. On my way to class, I spied a dollar bill on the ground, of course, I stooped to pick it up. But as I bent over, I dropped and broke my twelve-dollar thermos.

_____ 10. Andrea decorated her home with purchases from the novelty store where she worked. She put a red satin pillow shaped like a pair of lips on the couch. And a pink and green rug with a watermelon design on the floor.

> ***Score:*** Number correct _____ × 10 = _____%

VERBS

Combined Mastery Test 1

Each sentence contains a mistake involving (1) standard English or irregular verb forms, (2) subject-verb agreement, or (3) consistent verb tense. Cross out the incorrect verb and write the correct form in the space provided.

_____ 1. Only two pieces of lemon meringue pie remains on the plate.

_____ 2. Every morning, he starts the car, tuned in the radio, and adjusts the heat.

_____ 3. The basketball team's center growed almost five inches between his freshman and sophomore seasons.

_____ 4. Uncle Edwin became frightened as we approached the airport, for he had never flew before.

_____ 5. Each of the cupcakes for Jenny's birthday were decorated with blue roses.

_____ 6. I came home, settled down for a short nap, and sleep for three hours.

_____ 7. On my way home, an oncoming car's headlights were so bright I have to slow down till it passed.

_____ 8. When the accident victim complained of dizziness, the paramedics told him to lay on the stretcher.

_____ 9. After I checked my bank balance, I realize I did not have enough money for a new stereo.

_____ 10. The full moon covered the beach with a cool blue light, and the water shimmers as a soft breeze blows off the lake.

Score: Number correct _____ × 10 = _____%

VERBS

Combined Mastery Test 2

Each sentence contains a mistake involving (1) standard English or irregular verb forms, (2) subject-verb agreement, or (3) consistent verb tense. Cross out the incorrect verb and write the correct form in the space provided.

_____ 1. Jim chopped the wood from the dead maple tree and stack it against the shed.

_____ 2. School closings because of bad weather is announced on the radio.

_____ 3. By the time we reached our seats in the upper deck, the game had already began.

_____ 4. Pam took down some books, thumbed through their indexes, and then returns them to the library shelf.

_____ 5. Every morning, several people on the bus smokes cigarettes.

_____ 6. He makes me so angry I can feel my blood pressure raise every time he's nearby.

_____ 7. There is two fat pigeons strutting back and forth on my windowsill.

_____ 8. An elderly, poorly dressed man came up to us on the sidewalk and asks if we had any spare change.

_____ 9. Bernice had not took the hamburger out of the freezer, so we're having peanut butter sandwiches tonight.

_____ 10. Members of the rescue team climbed down the cliff, grabbed the frightened boy, and haul him to safety.

Score: Number correct _____ × 10 = _____%	

FAULTY MODIFIERS
AND PARALLELISM

Combined Mastery Test 1

In the space provided, indicate whether each sentence contains a misplaced modifier (*MM*), a dangling modifier (*DM*), or faulty parallelism (*FP*). Then make the changes needed to correct the error.

_____   1. Being frightened, the skunk's odor filled the air.

_____   2. We watched the traffic pile up bumper to bumper from the window.

_____   3. A police officer needs an open mind, sharp eyes, and to be cool-headed.

_____   4. Wondering if my hair is naturally blonde, I told Jim the truth.

_____   5. The biology students saw one-celled animals squirming through their microscopes.

_____   6. Snuggling under the warm comforter, the cold room didn't bother me.

_____   7. After sitting through a long class, my foot was asleep.

_____   8. My lasagna recipe includes chopped spinach, grated cheese, and onions that have been sliced.

_____   9. Learning to shift gears, the Volkswagen lurched into the garage door when I started it.

_____   10. The new employee is not only intelligent but also friendly, dedicated, and can be counted on.

Score: Number correct _____ × 10 = _____%

FAULTY MODIFIERS AND PARALLELISM

Combined Mastery Test 2

In the space provided, indicate whether each sentence contains a misplaced modifier (*MM*), a dangling modifier (*DM*), or faulty parallelism (*FP*). Then make the changes needed to correct the error.

_____   1. The guests were hungry, noisy, and they messed up the room.

_____   2. The last of a set, I used the old cup as a pencil holder.

_____   3. Leroy and Ella watched the stars lying on their backs in the grass at dusk.

_____   4. Waiting in the icy rain for twenty minutes, the bus finally arrived.

_____   5. After bragging so much, Lester's friends became impatient with him.

_____   6. The receptionist opens the mail, sorts it, and it is piled neatly on her boss's desk.

_____   7. At the zoo, Hazel watched a hippopotamus that sat near a stone wall and ate a sandwich.

_____   8. Mrs. Sanchez has lived in the area for most of her life, and she almost knows everyone by name.

_____   9. Grateful for the relief from the heat, the air-conditioned library made it easier for Ruth to study.

_____   10. We couldn't decide whether taking a ride in the country, barbecuing in the backyard, or to go to the park to play basketball was how we should spend the afternoon.

Score: Number correct _____ × 10 = _____%

PRONOUNS

Combined Mastery Test 1

Choose the sentence in each pair that uses pronouns correctly and write the letter of that sentence in the space provided at the left. Then, in the space provided below, explain why the pronoun is used incorrectly in the other sentence.

_____ 1. a. The five students in our lab group developed a closeness that you could feel grow as the semester progressed.
b. The five students in our lab group developed a closeness that we could feel grow as the semester progressed.

_____

_____ 2. a. Carrie and he have a surprise for everyone at the dance tonight.
b. Carrie and him have a surprise for everyone at the dance tonight.

_____

_____ 3. a. This here fudge is the creamiest I've ever tasted.
b. This fudge is the creamiest I've ever tasted.

_____

_____ 4. a. Though we started our diets at the same time, Hal has lost twice as much weight as me.
b. Though we started our diets at the same time, Hal has lost twice as much weight as I.

_____

_____ 5. a. The teacher told the children that everyone could choose his or her partner for the class trip to the zoo.
b. The teacher told the children that everyone could choose their partner for the class trip to the zoo.

_____

_____
| **Score:** Number correct _____ × 20 = _____% |
_____

PRONOUNS

◌ Combined Mastery Test 2

In the space provided, write *PE* beside each of the nine sentences that contain pronoun errors. Write *C* beside the sentence that uses pronouns correctly. Then cross out each pronoun error and write the correction above it.

_____   1. Kathy doesn't like them jelly-filled doughnuts.

_____   2. Neither of the candidates writes their own speeches.

_____   3. Mary asked her friend why she wasn't invited to the party.

_____   4. Most people who know my brother and me think I am more shy than him.

_____   5. What I don't like about eating a heavy lunch is that you always feel sleepy afterward.

_____   6. People who work with young children must have his or her share of patience.

_____   7. I want to get a part-time restaurant job, but they just won't give me a chance.

_____   8. Carl decided to add a porch on the house by hisself.

_____   9. Last Halloween, him and Anita went to the neighborhood-center party dressed as Mr. Ed, the talking horse.

_____   10. If you want to get along with others, you have to know how to be a good listener.

Score: Number correct _____ × 10 = _____%

CAPITAL LETTERS AND PUNCTUATION

 Combined Mastery Test 1

Each of the following sentences contains an error in capitalization or punctuation. Refer to the box below to write, in the space provided, the letter identifying the error. Then correct the error.

a.	missing capital	c.	missing quotation marks
b.	missing apostrophe	d.	missing comma

_____ 1. The Texas flight attendant asked "Is everyone tied down to a seat?"

_____ 2. Todays paper had a story about a councilman who was arrested for drunk driving.

_____ 3. I had to write two papers during my first college english class.

_____ 4. "My cellar is so damp," the comedian said, that when I set a mousetrap there, I caught a herring."

_____ 5. You may not believe this, but I havent watched television in a week.

_____ 6. My little brothers worst trick was to hide a dead fish in my closet.

_____ 7. "One of the most important things a writer can do, the speaker told his audience, "is to satisfy the reader's curiosity."

_____ 8. Because of the noise of the dishwasher Emma didn't hear the doorbell ring.

_____ 9. Martin hates winter so much that he wishes he could go to sleep every november and not wake up until spring.

_____ 10. The little girl, her eyes filled with desperation believed the shadow on the wall of her bedroom was a monster.

Score: Number correct _____ × 10 = _____ %

CAPITAL LETTERS AND PUNCTUATION

ℒ Combined Mastery Test 2

Each of the following sentences contains an error in capitalization or punctuation. Refer to the box below to write, in the space provided, the letter identifying the error. Then correct the error.

a. missing capital	c. missing quotation marks
b. missing apostrophe	d. missing comma

_____ 1. Its often not what you do but how you do it that counts.

_____ 2. Dolores enjoys reading books of all kinds but she probably spends more time with nonfiction than with fiction.

_____ 3. An instant polaroid camera will not provide the same sharp pictures as a 35-millimeter camera.

_____ 4. ''The trouble with this office, Darryl confided, ''is that the only ones who are sharp are the pencils.''

_____ 5. Coffee tea, colas, and chocolate all contain caffeine.

_____ 6. My father always told me, ''when you drive, watch out for the other guy.''

_____ 7. In many rural areas of the west, mail deliveries are made at odd hours.

_____ 8. My daughters purse is full of jelly beans and dandelions.

_____ 9. Peter was amazed at his compact cars trunk space when he fit all the camping gear into it with room to spare.

_____ 10. ''It's not my fault that I'm having trouble with spelling, my little brother insisted. ''The teacher keeps changing the words.''

Score: Number correct _____ × 10 = _____%

WORD USE

 ## Combined Mastery Test 1

Each of the following sentences contains a mistake identified in the left-hand margin. Underline the mistake and then correct it in the space provided.

Slang

1. Gene trained to the max for the school marathon.

_____

Wordiness

2. At this point in time, I haven't decided which courses I'll take next semester.

_____

Cliché

3. I am so sick and tired of television commercials that I watch only cable shows.

_____

Pretentious language

4. After a year on the job, the foreman received an increase in remuneration.

_____

Adverb error

5. Balancing several plates on my arm careful, I turned and bumped into a customer.

_____

Error in comparison

6. That last game was the most bad one I ever bowled.

_____

Confusing word

7. For those who want help with the final exam, their will be a review on Thursday.

_____

Confusing word

8. We must have past ten service stations, but Lennie wouldn't stop until he found one that gives out trading stamps.

_____

Confusing word

9. San Francisco's Golden Gate Bridge is constructed out of more then eighty thousand miles of wire.

_____

Confusing word

10. The mayor's remarks aggravated the all ready bad feelings that existed among the city's rival street gangs.

_____

> ***Score:*** Number correct _____ × 10 = _____%

WORD USE

Combined Mastery Test 2

Each of the following sentences contains a mistake identified in the left-hand margin. Underline the mistake and then correct it in the space provided.

Slang

1. The boss has been on my case for leaving half an hour before quitting time.

_____

Wordiness

2. Violence seems to be increasing more and more every day in our cities.

_____

Cliché

3. The championship game slipped through our fingers when our best receiver dropped the ball in the end zone.

_____

Pretentious language

4. My husband and I have lost weight as a result of our reducing regimen.

_____

Adverb error

5. The water was coming out of the hose too slow, so I increased the pressure.

_____

Error in comparison

6. Accounting has been the usefulest course that I have ever taken.

_____

Confusing word

7. Irregardless of my beliefs, I am willing to listen to your views with an open mind.

_____

Confusing word

8. It's plane to see that nobody in this class studied for the exam.

_____

Confusing word

9. I asked my doctor what the side affects might be from the medicine he prescribed.

_____

Confusing word

10. In the passed few years, it seems that adults have become as interested in dressing up for Halloween as their children.

_____

| **Score:** Number correct _____ × 10 = _____% |

Editing and Proofreading Tests

The passages in this section can be used in either of two ways:

1 *As Editing Tests:* Each passage contains a number of mistakes involving a single sentence skill. For example, the first passage (on page 341) contains five sentence fragments. Your instructor may ask you to proofread the passage to locate the five fragment errors. Spaces are provided at the bottom of the page for you to indicate which word groups are fragments. Your instructor may also have you correct the errors, either in the text itself or on separate paper. Depending on how you do, you may also be asked to edit the second and third passages for fragments.

There are three passages for each skill area, and there are twelve skills covered in all. Here is a list of the skill areas:

Test 1 Sentence fragments

Test 2 Run-ons (fused sentences)

Test 3 Run-ons (comma splices)

Test 4 Standard English verbs

Test 5 Irregular verbs

Test 6 Misplaced and dangling modifiers

Test 7 Faulty parallelism

Test 8 Capital letters

Test 9 Apostrophes

Test 10 Quotation marks

Test 11 Commas

Test 12 Commonly confused words

2 _As Guided Composition Activities:_ To give practice in proofreading as well, your instructor may ask you to do more than correct the skill mistakes in each passage. You may be asked to rewrite the passage, correcting it for skill mistakes _and also_ copying perfectly the rest of the passage. Should you miss one skill mistake or make even one copying mistake (for example, omitting a word, dropping a verb ending, misspelling a word, or misplacing an apostrophe), you may be asked to rewrite a different passage that deals with the same skill.

Here is how you would proceed. You would start with sentence fragments, rewriting the first passage, proofreading your paper carefully, and then showing it to your instructor. He or she will check it quickly to see that all the fragments have been corrected and that no copying mistakes have been made. If the passage is error-free, the instructor will mark and initial the appropriate box in the progress chart on pages 475–476 and you can move on to run-ons.

If even a single mistake is made, the instructor may question you briefly to see if you recognize and understand it. (Perhaps he or she will put a check beside the line in which the mistake appears, and then ask if you can correct it.) You may then be asked to write the second passage under a particular skill. If necessary, you will remain on that skill and rewrite the third passage (and even perhaps go on to repeat the first and second passages) as well. You will complete the program in guided composition when you successfully work through all twelve skills. Completing the twelve skills will strengthen your understanding of the skills, increase your chances of transferring the skills to actual writing situations, and markedly improve your proofreading ability.

In doing the passages, note the following points:

a For each skill you will be told the number of mistakes that appear in the passages. If you have trouble finding the mistakes, turn back and review the pages in this book that explain the skill in question.

b Here is an effective way to go about correcting a passage. First, read it over quickly. Look for and mark off mistakes in the skill area involved. For example, in your first reading of a passage that has five fragments, you may locate and mark only three fragments. Next, reread the passage carefully so you can find the remaining errors in the skill in question. Finally, make notes in the margin about how to correct each mistake. Only at this point should you begin to rewrite the passage.

c Be sure to proofread with care after you finish a passage. Go over your writing word for word, looking for careless errors. Remember that you may be asked to do another passage involving the same skill if you make even one mistake.

Test 1: Sentence Fragments

Mistakes in each passage: 5

Passage A

¹I can't remember a time when my sister didn't love to write. ²In school, when teachers assigned a composition or essay. ³Her classmates often groaned. ⁴She would join them in their protests. ⁵Because she didn't want to seem different. ⁶Secretly, though, her spirit would dance. ⁷Words were special to her. ⁸I remember an incident when she was in third grade. ⁹She wrote a funny story. ¹⁰About the time my dog made a mess out of our kitchen. ¹¹The teacher made my sister stand in front of the class and read it aloud. ¹²By the time she finished. ¹³The classroom was bedlam. ¹⁴Even the teacher wiped away tears of laughter. ¹⁵It was a magic moment. ¹⁶Which made my sister more in love with writing than ever.

Word groups with fragments: _____ _____ _____ _____ _____

Passage B

¹Too little attention is paid to the common household problem of single socks. ²Although it seems missing socks must have fallen behind the washer or stuck to other clothing. ³Careful searches always end in failure. ⁴Some sock wearers react by buying only one type and color of socks. ⁵So that they can deny ever losing any. ⁶Accepting the inevitability of single socks is braver. ⁷Also, finding uses for them is a creative challenge. ⁸They are often transformed into containers for small items in drawers and suitcases. ⁹Or used to shine shoes. ¹⁰Many people even wear single socks that are only slightly mismatched. ¹¹Deluding themselves into thinking the mismatch will go unnoticed. ¹²A better strategy is to be bold and wear pairs that do not match at all. ¹³Such as a bright red sock and a gray one. ¹⁴This establishes the wearer as a trendsetter and turns the appearance of a single sock into a welcome event.

Word groups with fragments: _____ _____ _____ _____ _____

Passage C

¹If you have ever been to a flea market. ²You know that Americans love to collect things. ³In fact, shopping at flea markets has become a social event. ⁴As activities at county fairs once were. ⁵At these markets there are long rows of tables on which sellers display toy trains, glassware, jewelry, old magazines, and records. ⁶And anything else that can be collected. ⁷While people shop, they can buy hot dogs, sodas, ice cream, and local food favorites. ⁸Business begins early in the morning and lasts till late afternoon. ⁹In the morning, prices are high. ¹⁰However, they usually get lower later on. ¹¹As closing time approaches. ¹²The really smart shopper does a lot of browsing. ¹³But doesn't buy anything until the end and goes home with real bargains.

Word groups with fragments: _____ _____ _____ _____ _____

Test 2: Run-Ons (Fused Sentences)

Mistakes in each passage: 5

Passage A

[1]When Mark began his first full-time job, he immediately got a credit card a used sports car was his first purchase. [2]Then he began to buy expensive clothes that he could not afford while still in school he also bought impressive gifts for his parents and his girlfriend. [3]Several months passed before Mark realized that he owed an enormous amount of money. [4]To make matters worse, his car broke down a stack of bills suddenly seemed to be due at once. [5]Mark tried to cut back on his purchases then he realized he had to cut up his credit card to prevent himself from using it. [6]He also began keeping a careful record of his spending he had no idea where his money had gone up till then. [7]He hated to admit to his family and friends that he had to get his budget under control. [8]However, his girlfriend said she did not mind inexpensive dates, and his parents were proud of his growing maturity.

Sentences with run-ons: _____ _____ _____ _____ _____

Passage B

[1]A young girl looks at a fashion magazine she sees clothes modeled by women who weigh 115 pounds although they are nearly six feet tall. [2]She receives a ''teen doll'' as a present and studies its proportions. [3]The doll has legs nearly two-thirds the length of its body it also has a tiny waist and nonexistent hips and thighs. [4]She goes to the movies the screen heroines resemble adolescent boys more than mature women. [5]Her favorite television shows are filled with commercials showing attractive men and women. [6]The commercials are for weight-loss programs these programs insist that a person must be slender to be desirable. [7]By the time the girl reaches her teens, she has been thoroughly brainwashed. [8]The media have given her the same messages over and over they all say that to be thin is the only acceptable option.

Sentences with run-ons: _____ _____ _____ _____ _____

Passage C

¹Before there were Hindus, Christians, or Jews, there were Jains. ²In all of its history, this religious group has avoided violence in fact, it has never fought a war. ³Today ten million Jains live in India of these millions, not one has a criminal record. ⁴Jains restrict themselves to occupations that do not destroy the environment or other living creatures they work as computer operators, teachers, and doctors. ⁵In spite of these limitations, the Jains are India's most successful people. ⁶They contribute more to charity than any other group they have built schools, hospitals, and shelters for the poor all over India. ⁷Their kindness even extends to animals the Jains eat no meat and wear no skins or furs. ⁸What is the secret of this remarkable people? ⁹They not only teach nonviolence; they also live it.

Sentences with run-ons: _____   _____   _____   _____   _____

Test 3: Run-Ons (Comma Splices)

Mistakes in each passage: 5

Passage A

¹Mickey Mouse is extremely popular in Japan, in fact, some children there probably believe Mickey is as Japanese as they are. ²Disney merchandising—Mickey can be seen on lunch pails, T-shirts, sandals, and so on—has obviously paid off, Tokyo has even had its very own Disneyland for the last three years. ³With a few slight changes, it's an exact copy of the Disney parks in California and Florida, everything there, except for signs and a few ride sound tracks, is in English. ⁴The long lines, too, are familiar to Americans who have endured two-hour waits for a three-minute ride in the United States. ⁵It's not uncommon at this park to see a Japanese woman in a robe with Mickey Mouse ears on her head, she will probably also be carrying a bag full of Disney souvenirs. ⁶Just as in the States, Japanese visitors eat fried chicken and hamburgers, a small picnic area is available for those who bring traditional Japanese food along.

Sentences with run-ons: _____ _____ _____ _____ _____

Passage B

¹In any high school, three subcultures exist within the larger school environment. ²The three groups are quite different, almost every student can be identified with one of them. ³The first one is the delinquent subculture, this one is the least popular of the three groups. ⁴Members of the delinquent group despise school, they hate the faculty, the staff, and any other symbols of authority. ⁵The next step up the social ladder is the academic subculture, it is composed of hardworking students who value their education. ⁶The third major student group is the fun subculture. ⁷These students care most about looks, clothes, cars, and dates, for this group, social status is the most important thing in the world. ⁸Needless to say, the fun subculture is the most popular of the three groups.

Sentences with run-ons: _____ _____ _____ _____ _____

Passage C

[1]A trip to the supermarket can be quite frustrating, especially if you need only a few items. [2]When you arrive, you look for a parking space close to the store, you can't find one and have to walk half the distance of the parking lot. [3]Then you must find an empty cart, those which don't bounce or squeak are in short supply. [4]When you finally start shopping, you discover that the items you want are "out of stock until Tuesday" or that their prices have gone up since your last visit. [5]Eventually, you approach the so-called express lane. [6]You're supposed to have ten items or less for this lane, the person in front of you usually has many more. [7]It also seems that the store's slowest checkout person is assigned to that register. [8]But, eventually, it is your turn, and you pay for your order and leave. [9]Then, with a bag in each hand, you make the long walk back to your car, you are understandably frazzled at this point. [10]Struggling to unlock the car without dropping your bags, you decide to try the local mini-market next time, it's closer to home anyway.

Sentences with run-ons: _____ _____ _____ _____ _____

Test 4: Standard English Verbs

Mistakes in each passage: 5

Passage A

[1]Few issues generate more heated debate than gun control. [2]Most of the controversy has center on the sale of handguns, which, because they can be concealed easily, are usually the weapons use in armed robberies and murders. [3]For that reason, while it is often easy to buy a rifle, many localities ban private ownership of handguns or require owners to get licenses from the police. [4]Advocates of gun control argue that these restrictions do not go far enough. [5]They feel, for example, that selling handguns through the mail should be abolish. [6]Their opponents maintain that further restrictions would prevent law-abiding citizens from buying guns for protection or recreation. [7]Such debates have continue for years, with both sides frequently appealing to emotion rather than reason. [8]Opponents of gun-control laws, for example, shout, ''Guns don't kill people— people do,'' which is true enough but has little to do with the issue. [9]And advocates of tougher laws accuse the other side of wanting guns in order to live out childish or macho fantasies. [10]Neither side attempt to understand the other, which has made it difficult to reach a rational public consensus.

Sentences with nonstandard verbs (write down the number of a sentence twice if it has two nonstandard verbs): ＿＿＿ ＿＿＿ ＿＿＿ ＿＿＿ ＿＿＿

Passage B

[1]The Race Across America, an annual bicycle race, starts in Huntington Beach, California, and end 3,107 miles later in Atlantic City, New Jersey. [2]One man always train for this race by peddling a stationary bike five hours at a time in a totally dark basement. [3]Once the race begins, there are no time-outs. [4]The cyclists go for days without sleeping. [5]Eventually, they grab sixty- or ninety-minute catnaps every day or so. [6]But it is a time test, and each biker knows that every moment of sleep give someone the chance to get ahead of him. [7]In one of these races, the leader rode for fifty-four hours and 940 miles without sleep. [8]When he got off his bike, his muscles were so cramp that the flesh on his thighs hopped as if Mexican jumping beans were under his skin. [9]The winner of a recent race cross the continent in eight days, nine hours, and forty-seven minutes.

Sentences with nonstandard verbs: ＿＿＿ ＿＿＿ ＿＿＿ ＿＿＿ ＿＿＿

Passage C

[1]When I was a part-time library assistant at our public high school, I work the Friday afternoon shift. [2]In the middle of an unusually hectic and complicated Friday morning of errand running, I realize that I would never make it to work by 12:30. [3]I tried several times to telephone the high school but kept getting busy signals. [4]So I decided to just keep going and explain later, since I had never been late before. [5]When I finally arrive at the library at 1:10, the librarian shot a glance at me and then look up at the wall clock. [6]"I was in the neighborhood, so I thought I'd drop in," I quipped. [7]We both laughed, and I went right to work. [8]The librarian never ask me to explain, but I made a point of getting to work the following Monday forty minutes early.

Sentences with nonstandard verbs (write down the number of a sentence twice if it has two nonstandard verbs): _____   _____   _____   _____   _____

Test 5: Irregular Verbs

Mistakes in each passage: 10

Passage A

¹Although Margo Carbone has hiked and skied in frigid weather, her greatest risk from cold was when her car breaked down in a rural area during a winter storm. ²The temperature had fell below zero. ³At first she stayed in her car and waited for help, but she was so cold she shaked. ⁴She hoped that moving would warm her up, so she begun to walk briskly toward the nearest town. ⁵Walking did warm her at first, but it also drained her energy reserves. ⁶She knowed that her body was losing heat fast. ⁷As she struggled against the wind, she started to feel disoriented. ⁸She was afraid her low body temperature had begun to affect her brain. ⁹If she did not get help soon, she could become too tired and confused to save herself. ¹⁰Luckily, a car soon come plodding through the snow, and the driver insisted that Margo get in and then taked her to a nearby diner. ¹¹Once she drunk some hot tea, warmed up, and rested, she felt better. ¹²However, she knew that she had been lucky. ¹³She could have froze to death. ¹⁴Her experience taught her a lesson. ¹⁵Now she carries a blanket and candy bars in her car during the winter and never takes cold weather for granted.

Sentences with mistakes in irregular verbs (write down the number of a sentence twice if it contains two mistakes):

_____ _____ _____ _____ _____

_____ _____ _____ _____ _____

Passage B

¹Harvey was chose the most valuable player in the championship game by the Mudville Mudhawks softball team. ²Everybody agreed that he deserved it. ³In the first inning, Harvey catched a ground ball and threw it over the first baseman's head and into the stands. ⁴Later the same inning, he losed a fly ball in the sun. ⁵It bounced off the top of his head, and the runner come home. ⁶At bat in the fourth inning, Harvey smacked a long fly ball off the centerfield fence, but he falled over first base and was throwed out at second. ⁷But his best performance took place in the ninth inning. ⁸With two outs and the Mudhawks ahead by one run, Harvey stepped to the plate and hitted another

ball off the fence. ⁹This time he flied past first base and then around second and third. ¹⁰When he crossed the plate, he was smiling—but his teammates were not. ¹¹In his determination to avoid tripping on first base, he had forgot to tag it. ¹²The umpire shouted, ''Yer out!'' ¹³The game was over, and Harvey become the first member of the Hadleyville Hooters to be named M.V.P. of the opposing team.

Sentences with mistakes in irregular verbs (write down the number of a sentence twice if it contains two mistakes):

_____   _____   _____   _____   _____

_____   _____   _____   _____   _____

Passage C

¹It was delightful to visit a day care center and watch children at play. ²In the playground, some throwed colorful balls to one another while others swinged on the play equipment. ³Inside, some of the children had took coloring books off a shelf. ⁴They were laying on the floor and giving serious attention to their artwork. ⁵Two others had began to build a castle with blocks, but it falled down when a little girl runned into it. ⁶Then there was the little girl who played nurse to her doll. ⁷She pretended that it had been bit by a dog and put a bandage on its finger. ⁸I loved seeing all the children having such a good time while learning to play together. ⁹After a while, the bell ringed, and all the children wented to take a nap.

Sentences with mistakes in irregular verbs (write down the number of a sentence twice or more if it contains two or more mistakes):

_____   _____   _____   _____   _____

_____   _____   _____   _____   _____

Test 6: Misplaced and Dangling Modifiers

Mistakes in each passage: 5

Passage A

¹Your friend's new restaurant is a big success. ²Attracting large numbers of customers, you are thrilled for her. ³Or do you in fact feel depressed when you think of her? ⁴Maybe you were secretly hoping the restaurant would be a flop in the back of your mind. ⁵It's not unusual for people to have negative feelings about other people they like occasionally. ⁶Many people are secretly pleased when their friends fail at something and are tortured when they succeed with envy. ⁷Psychologists say that such feelings have a lot to do with people's self-image. ⁸Thinking very little of themselves, a friend's success threatens them. ⁹Their friend's good fortune makes them feel less important by comparison.

Sentences with misplaced modifiers: _____ _____ _____

Sentences with dangling modifiers: _____ _____

Passage B

¹If carelessly used, consumers can be harmed as much by prescription medications as by illegal drugs. ²Patients should always be aware of the possible side effects of a prescription drug. ³Unexpected side effects can frighten a patient, such as nausea or dizziness. ⁴To protect themselves, patients would be wise to ask their doctors about prescribed drugs. ⁵Especially if taking several medications already, the doctor should explain how the new medication will react with the others. ⁶Some drug combinations can be deadly. ⁷Also, medications should be stored only in their own labeled bottles, not moved to other containers. ⁸Mixing up drugs accidentally, the results can be tragic. ⁹Finally, drugs should be taken exactly as prescribed. ¹⁰More is not always better. ¹¹One patient became violently ill after almost taking all the pills in a bottle.

Sentences with misplaced modifiers: _____ _____

Sentences with dangling modifiers: _____ _____ _____

Passage C

[1]Much has been written about fear of heights, fear of open places, and fear of closed spaces in newspapers and magazines. [2]But there is another phobia, less known but just as disabling—fear of bridges. [3]Frightened they will get dizzy, this phobia causes motorists to go very slowly. [4]Expecting they will faint, the protective railing seems like a magnet. [5]They fear they will be pulled through the railing into the water below. [6]One help for such drivers is provided by the Chesapeake Bay Bridge police force, our nation's longest span bridge. [7]The Chesapeake police will drive cars across the bridge for motorists. [8]A welcome service, the police perform it many times each day.

Sentences with misplaced modifiers: _____ _____

Sentences with dangling modifiers: _____ _____ _____

Test 7: Faulty Parallelism

Mistakes in each passage: 5

Passage A

[1]For many athletes, life after a sports career is a letdown. [2]While they are in the limelight, sports pages praise them for the records they break and winning games. [3]The public cheers them on and is seeking their autographs. [4]But what happens when a sports figure is no longer able to play? [5]Most athletes, because of the physical demands of the game or injuring themselves, are unable to play into their thirties. [6]While a few former athletes move on to success in other fields, most are not prepared for nonathletic careers and lives that are private. [7]Sadly, a large percentage of former players are unable to find a second career. [8]Many suffer from depression, and with some there are suicide attempts. [9]Players' associations, having become aware of the problem, are investigating ways to prepare their members for life after athletics.

Sentences with faulty parallelism:

_____   _____   _____   _____   _____

Passage B

[1]When a few people in one community decided to form a homeowners' association, many of their neighbors were skeptical. [2]Some objected to stirring things up, and others were feeling the dues were too high. [3]But many neighbors joined, and their first big success was a garage sale. [4]They scheduled a day for everybody in the neighborhood to bring unwanted items to a community center. [5]Big appliances and other items that are heavy were picked up by volunteers with trucks. [6]The association promoted the sale by placing ads in newspapers and with the distribution of fliers at local shopping centers. [7]Dozens of families took part. [8]After that, the association helped plant trees, start a Crime Watch Program, and in repairing the cracked sidewalks. [9]Members now receive discounts from local merchants and theater owners. [10]This association's success has inspired many more neighbors to join and people in other neighborhoods, who are starting their own organizations.

Sentences with faulty parallelism:

_____   _____   _____   _____   _____

Passage C

¹Humanity's longtime dream of flying remained just a dream until two brothers, Joseph and Etienne Montgolfier, built the first hot-air balloon. ²Joseph had experimented with parachutes and mechanical devices. ³Then Etienne decided to leave an architectural career and was working with his brother. ⁴They came to believe that if one made a sufficiently light container and would fill it with a gas that was lighter than air, the container must rise. ⁵Joseph proved this theory by building small paper balloons and filling them with air that was hot. ⁶When they rose, the brothers made larger and larger paper balloons, and then the building of a paper balloon seven hundred cubic feet in size. ⁷Eventually, they constructed a silk balloon, which they kept aloft for ten minutes. ⁸It carried the first air passengers—a rooster, a duck, and a sheep. ⁹The animals were placed in a basket that dangled below the balloon, arousing great interest, and it attracted crowds. ¹⁰That balloon was launched September 19, 1783, and the rest, as they say, was history.

Sentences with faulty parallelism:

_____ _____ _____ _____ _____

✐ Test 8: Capital Letters

Mistakes in each passage: 10

Passage A

¹Orlando, an area in florida that used to be known primarily for citrus groves, has become one of the most popular vacation spots in the world. ²It all began with Disney World, a wildly successful theme park far bigger and more lavish than even disneyland in california. ³Disney World's success has drawn other tourist attractions to the orlando area. ⁴Sea World, featuring shamu, the killer whale, is the most successful of these, drawing over one million visitors a year. ⁵The Elvis Presley Museum, Flea World (a huge flea market), Reptile World, and the tupperware Museum, which exhibits food containers used through the ages, are other nearby attractions. ⁶But perhaps the most striking is Faith world, billed as "god's tourist attraction in central Florida." ⁷This church is in a huge red and white airline hangar that was formerly an air museum. ⁸In addition, hundreds of hotels, restaurants, and nightclubs have grown up in the area to accommodate an annual eight million visitors. ⁹Still, the center of attention remains Disney World itself, bringing millions to America's south to meet such international stars as Donald duck and Goofy.

Sentences with missing capitals (write the number of a sentence as many times as it contains capitalization mistakes):

_____ _____ _____ _____ _____

_____ _____ _____ _____ _____

Passage B

¹The morning I visited the lincoln Memorial, it was raining. ²I had never seen it before, although I had been to Washington, D.C., twice before. ³The first time I came with a friend, and we went to see the veterans administration. ⁴The second visit was a two-hour business stop at the smithsonian institution. ⁵This day, I promised myself there would be time enough for one more stop. ⁶The air was cold—even for october. ⁷It was quiet at the site, and I heard my feet scrape the granite steps as I climbed them. ⁸On my left I saw the potomac river. ⁹I walked between the columns and stopped. ¹⁰Lincoln's massive statue dwarfed everything around it—just as the man had done in life. ¹¹I read

a plaque with the gettysburg address and remained there for a time in silence, touched again by the simple eloquence of that speech. [12]There were no other visitors there that morning. [13]Only the guards watched as another tourist brushed away a tear and went down the granite steps in the rain.

Sentences with missing capitals (write the number of a sentence as many times as it contains capitalization mistakes):

_____ _____ _____ _____ _____

_____ _____ _____ _____ _____

Passage C

[1]Most immigrants who came to the United States by ship at the beginning of the century were thrilled at the sight of the statue of liberty. [2]But none were delighted with ellis island. [3]This drab little island off the southern tip of manhattan was the primary immigration center from january 1, 1902, until late in 1943. [4]The majority of immigrants came to this island from Europe. [5]On arrival, their first task was to prove they were physically and morally fit. [6]Herded into a big hall with all their possessions, these people were given medical and legal examinations. [7]Doctors had to certify they were not carrying or suffering from serious diseases; legal inspectors, asking questions in english, had to determine that the immigrants had a place to go, money, and potential employment. [8]Immigrants were asked questions such as, ''are you an anarchist?'' and ''do you have a criminal record?'' [9]For most people, this investigation took three to five hours. [10]The immigrants were then free to join their waiting relatives and begin their new life in america.

Sentences with missing capitals (write the number of a sentence as many times as it contains capitalization mistakes):

_____ _____ _____ _____ _____

_____ _____ _____ _____ _____

Test 9: Apostrophes

Mistakes in each passage: 10

Passage A

¹Sharon has worked at a convenience store long enough to spot three types of customers. ²She recognizes the first type by their haggard faces and bewildered expressions. ³Such people may buy soft drinks or candy bars, but their main purpose for coming in is to ask directions. ⁴Unfortunately, they dont know north from south or any of the areas landmarks. ⁵Although Sharons city has a population of forty thousand, they ask such questions as, ''Do you know where Bill Hendersons house is?'' ⁶The second type buys more, but people in this category are never satisfied. ⁷They complain that the dairy products arent fresh enough or act astonished that the store doesnt stock a product such as plum catsup. ⁸''Im an expert in these matters'' seems to be this types attitude. ⁹Luckily, Sharon sees many of her favorite customers, the friendly type, who often buy the same things each visit. ¹⁰By the time one of her favorites, Mr. Clauser, reaches her counter each morning, she has gotten his coffee and roll and has begun to ring them up. ¹¹Mr. Clausers purchases are bagged so quickly that he has time to chat for a moment. ¹²Without this type of customer, Sharon is sure she wouldve quit her job by now.

Sentences with missing apostrophes (write down the number of a sentence twice if it contains two missing apostrophes):

_____   _____   _____   _____   _____

_____   _____   _____   _____   _____

Passage B

¹Did anyone ever throw a surprise party for you? ²Its supposed to be fun, but Im not so sure about that anymore. ³I had one at my girlfriends house last week. ⁴When I walked into Ellens living room, people hiding behind doors rushed out in such a frenzy that her dogs leash got caught in a wire and pulled down a lamp, which crashed to the floor. ⁵All that noise plus the guests screams made me so nervous, I fell over a chair. ⁶I couldnt believe this was happening to me. ⁷When everyone calmed down, I noticed how dressed up they all were. ⁸My girlfriend had told me we were going to plant

vegetables in her mothers garden, so I was wearing old messy clothes. [9]Everyone elses clothes were at least clean and nice. [10]I suppose it didnt really matter, but somehow I felt something was wrong about the guest of honor being dressed like a slob. [11]On my next birthday, I want to go to a nice quiet horror show.

Sentences with missing apostrophes (write down the number of a sentence twice if it contains two missing apostrophes):

_____   _____   _____   _____   _____

_____   _____   _____   _____   _____

Passage C

[1]I love all kinds of food, but Ive a special fondness for fresh fruit. [2]There are many reasons for this. [3]The apples chewy skin covers a crispy treat. [4]The oranges rind is bitter, but the fruit beneath is sweet and juicy. [5]Peeling a bananas smooth skin reveals a mushy delight inside. [6]Other fruits offer more of a challenge and more of a reward. [7]It can be almost dangerous to remove the pineapples prickly exterior or the coconuts tough shell, but it is worth the effort to get to the delicious contents. [8]Another reason for eating fresh fruits is that theyre usually a good source of vitamins and fiber. [9]And theyre naturally sweet—an ideal substitute for foods with refined sugar. [10]Youll probably find that cake and candy are more popular, but you cant choose anything better for you than fresh fruit.

Sentences with missing apostrophes (write down the number of a sentence twice if it contains two missing apostrophes):

_____   _____   _____   _____   _____

_____   _____   _____   _____   _____

◯ Test 10: Quotation Marks

Quotation marks needed in each passage: 10 pairs

Passage A

¹Tony and Lola were driving down the interstate highway at about sixty-five miles an hour. ²You should slow down, Lola, Tony said. ³We can't afford another ticket.

⁴Oh, don't worry, Lola replied. ⁵I haven't seen a police car all morning. ⁶Besides, everyone else is driving just as fast.

⁷Suddenly, a police car driving in the opposite direction made a quick U-turn, turned on its lights and siren, and came up behind their car.

⁸I knew it! Tony moaned. ⁹Half a week's paycheck down the drain.

¹⁰Now, this just isn't fair, Lola said to the officer as he walked toward the car. ¹¹It's not fair to stop us when everyone else is driving just as fast.

¹²You may be right, the policeman answered. ¹³But what's really unfair is that there's just one of me and so many speeders. ¹⁴I can stop only one car at a time.

Sentences or sentence groups with missing quotation marks:

_____ _____ _____ _____ _____

_____ _____ _____ _____ _____

Passage B

¹The phone rang as the Parkers ate dinner. ²I'll bet that's another nuisance call, said Mr. Parker, groaning as he got up to answer it.

³Hello, my name is Marge. ⁴May I speak to Mr. or Mrs. Parker?

⁵This is Mr. Parker. ⁶He rolled his eyes toward the ceiling.

⁷Mr. Parker, you are probably aware of changes in the tax laws, inflated prices, and . . .

⁸Yes, but I'm really not interested in buying anything, said Mr. Parker, trying to be patient.

⁹Marge stumbled over a few words, cleared her throat, and said, I represent a service that will . . .

¹⁰Perhaps you didn't understand me, said Mr. Parker, beginning to get angry. ¹¹I do not want to buy anything from you. ¹²Now please hang up, because that's what I'm going to do.

[13]But Mr. Parker . . .

[14]The receiver slammed onto its base. [15]Mr. Parker returned to his dinner, sighed, and said, I hope I wasn't too rough on her. I know she's just trying to earn a living, but I hate being interrupted at dinnertime.

Sentences or sentence groups with missing quotation marks:

_____ _____ _____ _____ _____

_____ _____ _____ _____ _____

Passage C

[1]Harry and his friend Susan got stuck on an elevator. [2]Another man was stuck with them. [3]Harry turned to Susan and asked, Has this ever happened to you before?

[4]Once, she said [5]About ten years ago in a department store. [6]We weren't stuck long.

[7]Harry took a deep breath. [8]It's lucky only three of us are here. [9]I don't like being closed up in small spaces.

[10]Then the other man asked, Is there an intercom here so we can talk to somebody?

[11]I think it might be behind the panel underneath the buttons, said Susan.

[12]The man opened the panel, found a telephone, and dialed the security number written nearby. [13]Can anyone hear me? he asked.

[14]A voice on the phone said, Yes, and we know you're stuck. [15]Just wait a few minutes.

[16]When Harry heard that people knew about their problem, he let out a sigh. [17]I sure hope they can fix this quickly, he said softly, wringing his hands.

[18]Susan put her arm around him and smiled. [19]Don't worry. [20]We'll be out of here in no time.

Sentences or sentence groups with missing quotation marks:

_____ _____ _____ _____ _____

_____ _____ _____ _____ _____

Test 11: Commas

Mistakes in each passage: 10

Passage A

¹How many homeless people live in the United States? ²Estimates range as high as 3000000. ³Today's homeless include not only single people but also families with small children. ⁴Run-down boardinghouses and hotels the places where the poor once lived have been replaced by expensive houses and condominiums. ⁵Although some of the homeless have jobs they do not make enough money to pay for food rent and other necessities. ⁶Others are unable to find work. ⁷Many of them have been released from mental hospitals but are still ill. ⁸A few of the homeless refuse to live in shelters but most of them live on the street because they have nowhere else to go. ⁹They are often seen sleeping in boxes or huddled in doorways. ¹⁰To find enough food they search through garbage cans or accept handouts. ¹¹Life on the street is dangerous and short. ¹²Our society is slow in realizing that these dirty poorly dressed people have not brought their problems upon themselves. ¹³They cannot solve their problems without help.

Sentences with missing commas (write down the number of a sentence as many times as it contains comma mistakes):

_____   _____   _____   _____   _____

_____   _____   _____   _____   _____

Passage B

¹There are many who believe that people who watch a lot of television are addicted but I think they're wrong. ²Some people turn on their sets the moment they get up. ³I don't do that. ⁴I turn on my set when my first regular show comes on and that's at least a half hour after I wake up. ⁵I don't need to watch game shows soap operas and situation comedies to get through the day. ⁶I watch all these programs simply because I enjoy them. ⁷I also keep the television turned on all evening because thanks to cable there is always something decent to watch. ⁸If I did not have good viewing choices I would flick the set off without hesitation. ⁹Lots of people switch channels rapidly to preview what is on. ¹⁰I on the other hand turn immediately to the channel I know I want. ¹¹In other

words I am not addicted; I am a selective viewer who just happens to select a lot of shows.

Sentences with missing commas (write down the number of a sentence as many times as it contains comma mistakes):

_____   _____   _____   _____   _____

_____   _____   _____   _____   _____

Passage C

[1]On one bitterly cold day a week ago I experienced one of the nicest features of rural life—old-fashioned neighborliness. [2]I had gotten a flat tire while driving to work on a back road so I walked to the nearest house and knocked at the door. [3]An elderly kind-eyed woman answered. [4]I quickly explained my problem and asked to use her telephone to call my boss and a gas station. [5]The woman graciously led me inside and then said her son might be willing to change the tire. [6]As I started to protest she left the room. [7]She soon returned to inform me that her son would change it. [8]Then she explained that she had to take her husband to a doctor. [9]She insisted however that I sit by the wood stove and have some coffee while I waited. [10]Too astonished and grateful to protest again I thanked her profusely as she left. [11]About twenty minutes later I saw from the window that her son was finishing with my tire. [12]I went out to my car. [13]"Thanks so much. Please accept this for your kindness" I said as I offered him a bill from my wallet. [14]He waved it away. [15]"Hope your day gets better" he said as he headed back to his house.

Sentences with missing commas (write down the number of a sentence as many times as it contains comma mistakes):

_____   _____   _____   _____   _____

_____   _____   _____   _____   _____

Test 12: Commonly Confused Words

Mistakes in each passage: 10

Passage A

[1]How does a magician saw a woman in half? [2]Thought this illusion usually makes a strong impression on an audience, its an easy one for magicians, irregardless of experience. [3]In fact, it requires more skill on the part of a pear of female assistants than the magician. [4]The trick begins when a table holding the coffinlike box is rolled onstage. [5]One assistant is hiding inside that table. [6]When the magician displays the box to the audience, it is, of coarse, empty. [7]Than the magician asks an assistant on stage to climb into the box. [8]As she dose this, the hidden woman enters the box through a trapdoor in the table, sticks her feet out one end, and curls up with her head between her knees. [9]The other woman, drawing her knees up to her chin, puts her head out the other end. [10]Now the box appears to be holding one hole woman, and the magician can saw write through. [11]To complete the affect, the woman at the foot end slides back into the table as the magician reopens the box.

Sentences with commonly confused words (write down the number of a sentence more than once if it contains more than one commonly confused word):

_____ _____ _____ _____ _____

_____ _____ _____ _____ _____

Passage B

[1]In my neighborhood, their is an old mansion that is widely believed to be haunted. [2]The house, enormous and dark, stands at the top of a steep hill overlooking a desserted railroad depot. [3]Boarded-up windows, peeling paint, and an badly damaged roof add to the bleakness of the place. [4]Accept for the packs of large rats that occasionally scurry across the property, the hole area seems frozen in a strange, silent world of its own. [5]It seems that all other living things no better then to come too near this unnatural-looking spot. [6]Though no one is quiet sure why, many agree that some undefinable sense of evil lurks there. [7]The overall affect of the place is to make the heart beat fast and the blood run cold in all who pass by. [8]Weather there is some wicked spirit or unholy monster

walking the halls of the house, I'm not sure. [9]I am sure, however, that if there is something living there, it walks the halls without human company.

Sentences with commonly confused words (write down the number of a sentence twice if it contains two commonly confused words):

_____   _____   _____   _____   _____

_____   _____   _____   _____   _____

Passage C

[1]Increasing social pressure is encouraging many smokers to try to quit their habit. [2]Many restaurants allow smoking only in special sections, and smoking has been banned in some other public places. [3]When asked weather they would mind if a smoker lights up, people are more likely to object then they once were. [4]At parties, smokers may be forced too sneak outside for a cigarette while their friends enjoy themselves inside. [5]Less employers tolerate smoking, and family members also complain about smoke that reaches them threw the air. [6]Its no wonder that many smokers are trying to quit. [7]Succeeding is easy for a few people, but many find it almost impossible to brake the habit. [8]Quitting is like ending a dozen habits, being that people smoke in so many different situations. [9]They may light up when they wake up, when they have coffee or snacks, and when they drive there cars. [10]In any such familiar situation, a person whose quit smoking is at risk of starting again. [11]Luckily, the more times a person tries, the greater his or her chances are of quitting for good the next time.

Sentences with commonly confused words (write down the number of a sentence twice if it contains two commonly confused words):

_____   _____   _____   _____   _____

_____   _____   _____   _____   _____

Combined Editing Tests

EDITING FOR
SENTENCE-SKILLS MISTAKES

The ten editing tests in this section will give you practice in finding a variety of sentence-skills mistakes. People often find it hard to edit a paper carefully. They have put so much work into their writing, or so little, that it's almost painful for them to look at the paper one more time. You may have to simply *force* yourself to edit. Remember that eliminating sentence-skills mistakes will improve an average paper and help ensure a strong grade on a good paper. Further, as you get into the habit of editing your papers, you will get into the habit of using the sentence skills consistently. They are a basic part of clear and effective writing.

In the first six tests, the spots where errors occur have been underlined; your job is to identify each error. In the last four tests, you must locate as well as identify the errors. Use the progress chart on page 477 to keep track of your performance on these tests.

Combined Editing Test 1

Identify the sentence-skills mistakes at the underlined spots in the selection that follows. From the box below, choose the letter that describes each mistake and write it in the space provided. The same mistake may appear more than once.

a. sentence fragment	d. missing quotation marks
b. run-on	e. missing comma
c. missing apostrophe	

      I never drink at parties anymore. <u>Which seems to upset people.</u> Even my best friend

                                     1

feels that by not drinking I'm <u>saying "Look</u> at me. I'm better than <u>you.</u> Well, I guess

                                  2   **3**

<u>its</u> <u>true, I</u> don't feel that I'm your average type of guy. But there are several good

4 **5**

reasons I don't drink at <u>parties one</u> is that I like to have control over myself. I've seen

                                       6

people at parties say and do ugly <u>things, they</u> would not behave that way if sober. Also,

                                                    7

I have never enjoyed splitting <u>headaches hangovers,</u> and <u>being nauseated.</u> In addition,

                                          8   **9**

by not drinking, I'll never end up with a long-term alcohol problem. Finally, I don't

like to spend my hard-earned money for the privilege of feeling terrible. <u>When I wake</u>

                                                                              10

<u>up the next morning.</u>

1. _____   3. _____   5. _____   7. _____   9. _____

2. _____   4. _____   6. _____   8. _____   10. _____

◎ Combined Editing Test 2

Identify the sentence-skills mistakes at the underlined spots in the selection that follows. From the box below, choose the letter that describes each mistake and write it in the space provided. The same mistake may appear more than once.

a. sentence fragment
b. run-on
c. mistake in subject-verb agreement
d. mistake in parallelism
e. missing apostrophe
f. missing comma

In "What a Deal!" (*Newsweek,* February 9, 1987), Harry F. Water describes why game shows attract millions of viewers. Such shows appeal to <u>Americas</u> preoccupation
1
with <u>money consumerism,</u> and sensationalism. The most popular show is *Wheel of*
2
Fortune. <u>Drawing about forty-three million viewers daily.</u> Winners shop for prizes on
3
this <u>program, the</u> show appeals to both our love of money and our love <u>to shop.</u> <u>Which</u>
4   5
<u>distinguishes it from previous spinning-wheel shows and accounts for its popularity.</u>
6
Vanna White, who does nothing much more than turn letters and look beautiful on this show, has become a national star. Other game shows draw viewers by fueling the strike-it-rich <u>dream one</u> such show is *The $1,000,000 Chance of a Lifetime,* which features a
7
million dollars surrounded by guards. And game programs like *The Dating Game* and *The Newlywed Game* <u>appeals</u> to our interest in other <u>peoples</u> love lives. The chance to
8   9
win fame and fortune on game shows has led some people to attend a school for would-be contestants and even <u>offering bribes</u> to get on the show.
10

1. _____   3. _____   5. _____   7. _____   9. _____

2. _____   4. _____   6. _____   8. _____   10. _____

Combined Editing Test 3

Identify the sentence-skills mistakes at the underlined spots in the selection that follows. From the box below, choose the letter that describes each mistake and write it in the space provided. The same mistake may appear more than once.

a.	sentence fragment	d.	missing capital letter
b.	run-on	e.	missing comma
c.	dropped verb ending	f.	homonym mistake

The best advice I ever got was from a minister. I went to see him. After an episode in which I betrayed my wife. I had been married for a little over a year and felt closed

<u>1</u>

in by my marriage. Somehow, seeing my unmarried friends play the field made me feel left out, I loved my wife but want freedom to have an affair on the side. I thought I

<u>2</u>   <u>3</u>

found it with the owner of a beauty parlor. Whom I met in my job selling supplies to

<u>4</u>

beauty shops. One day, we arrange to meet at her shop after hours, when I supposedly

<u>5</u>

was to drop off supplies. But we both knew the real purpose of that meeting. I spent an hour with her that afternoon. When I left, feeling guilty and dirty. I went home and

<u>6</u>

took a shower but I still felt like a traitor. I decided I could cleanse myself only by

<u>7</u>

confessing to my wife. But first I went to talk to my minister the next day. "don't tell

<u>8</u>

your wife," he said. "Their's no reason to give her the pain. You must carry it alone

<u>9</u>

and learn from it." I never did tell my wife, I have never betrayed her again either.

<u>10</u>

1. _____ 3. _____ 5. _____ 7. _____ 9. _____

2. _____ 4. _____ 6. _____ 8. _____ 10. _____

Combined Editing Test 4

Identify the sentence-skills mistakes at the underlined spots in the selection that follows. From the box below, choose the letter that describes each mistake and write it in the space provided. The same mistake may appear more than once.

a. sentence fragment	d. faulty parallelism
b. run-on	e. mistake in pronoun agreement
c. mistake in subject-verb agreement	f. apostrophe mistake
	g. missing comma

<u>Although living alone can sometimes be lonely.</u> It is very convenient. No one ever
1
gives you a hard time for being a slob when you live by yourself. You can do <u>Mondays</u>
2
breakfast dishes on Tuesday afternoon. <u>Or even wait until Friday if you have enough</u>
3
<u>spare dishes.</u> The same is true with the vacuuming and dusting. If you choose to wait
until things start growing out of the carpet or the knickknacks are knee deep in dust
before <u>cleaning nobody</u> will care in the least. Also, you get to watch whichever television
4
shows you want at any time that you wish. The same is true for the radio and the <u>stereo,</u>
5
<u>you</u> can play whatever music you wish at any volume and never have to listen to
<u>complaints'.</u> Another nice thing about living alone is there <u>are</u> never an argument about
6   7
money. You always know exactly who made every phone call, ate everything in the
refrigerator, and <u>was running</u> up the electric bill. And when you do get lonely, you can
8
always call someone up and invite <u>them</u> over without being stuck with company for too
9
long. <u>Its</u> a lot harder to get rid of somebody who lives with you.
10

1. _____   3. _____   5. _____   7. _____   9. _____

2. _____   4. _____   6. _____   8. _____   10. _____

Combined Editing Test 5

Identify the sentence-skills mistakes at the underlined spots in the selection that follows. From the box below, choose the letter that describes each mistake and write it in the space provided. The same mistake may appear more than once.

a. sentence fragment	d. mistake in pronoun agreement
b. run-on	e. missing comma
c. dangling modifier	f. cliché

When I worked behind a soda fountain during my high-school days. I loved to make
<u>　　　　　　　　　　　　　　　　　　　　　　　　　　　　　</u>
　　　　　　　　　　　　　　　　1

ice cream sodas. Whenever someone ordered <u>one I'd</u> grab a tall, heavy soda glass by
　　　　　　　　　　　　　　　　　　　2

its base. <u>Then move over to where the syrups were kept.</u> <u>Poising my left hand above</u>
　　　　　　3　　　　　　　　　　　　　　　　　　4

<u>the syrup dispenser,</u> two inches of thick chocolate or vanilla flavoring would squirt into

the bottom of the glass. Next, I'd scoop two neat round balls of ice cream and drop <u>it</u>
　　　　　　　　　　　　　　　　　　　　　　　　　　　　　　　　5

into the glass over the syrup. As the ice cream sank slowly into the syrup, causing curls

of color to swirl <u>around I</u> would insert a long-handled spoon with a small ladle. I'd
　　　　　　6

briefly stir this mixture with the <u>spoon, then</u> I would squirt seltzer into the glass. <u>Taking</u>
　　　　　　　　　　　　　　　7

<u>care to aim directly onto the ice cream.</u> <u>Last but by no means least,</u> I'd add a scarlet
　　　8　　　　　　　　　　　　　　　9

cherry and serve the soda on a paper place mat. Often, the customer would <u>smile, I'd</u>
　　　　　　　　　　　　　　　　　　　　　　　　　　　　　10

be given a good tip for my creation.

1. _____ 3. _____ 5. _____ 7. _____ 9. _____

2. _____ 4. _____ 6. _____ 8. _____ 10. _____

Combined Editing Test 6

Identify the sentence-skills mistakes at the underlined spots in the selection that follows. From the box below, choose the letter that describes each mistake and write it in the space provided. The same mistake may appear more than once.

a. sentence fragment	d. mistake in pronoun reference
b. run-on	e. apostrophe mistake
c. inconsistent verb tense	f. missing comma

Children of the Night, founded and directed by Lois Lee, is helping many young runaways in Hollywood California. According to a recent segment on *Sixty Minutes* presented by Ed Bradley. Lee, a sociologist, has a twofold job. First, she spent time on the crime-ridden streets of Hollywood. She looks for missing girls between the ages of twelve and seventeen. And passes out a twenty-four-hour hot line number. The girls who seek her assistance are helped back into mainstream society, Lee said that 80 percent of first-time runaways who get help do not return to the streets'. The second aspect of Lees work is fund-raising. Since she refuses government funds because of the restrictions they make Lee solicits money from various civic groups her goal is to establish a shelter for girls who cannot or will not go home to their families.

1. _____   3. _____   5. _____   7. _____   9. _____

2. _____   4. _____   6. _____   8. _____   10. _____

Combined Editing Test 7

See if you can locate and correct the twenty sentence-skills mistakes in the following passage. The mistakes are listed in the box below. As you locate mistakes, place checks in the spaces provided.

---

4 sentence fragments ____

____ ____ ____

3 run-ons ____ ____

____

2 dropped verb endings

____ ____

1 dangling modifier ____

2 mistakes in parallelism

____ ____

2 missing quotation marks

____ ____

1 missing comma in a series

____

2 missing commas around an
interrupter ____ ____

3 homonym mistakes ____

____ ____

The world seem to be divided up into two kinds of people: the patient and the impatient. People reveal which they are by their behavior in certain situations. Such as waiting in line, for example. Patient people do constructive activities while waiting in line, they read their paperbacks balance their checkbooks, or are doing stomach exercises. Impatient people treat waiting in line as torture. Glaring at the helpless cashier, their   5
fists are clenched. They tap their feet and loud sighs. The way people drive also show who are the patient and impatient. Patient people drive at a reasonable speed. Passing other cars only when necessary. While waiting at stoplights, they hum along with the radio and relax. Impatient people on the other hand install radar detectors, so they can drive as fast as possible without getting caught. They pass other cars at every opportunity.   10
And rev their engines while waiting at stoplights. These two types can be spotted quickly in restaurants, the patient wait politely for the hostess to seat them and for the waitress to arrive. Than, while waiting for they're food, they converse. Impatient people, however, are outraged if they aren't seated immediately. And mumble such remarks as, ''Never coming hear again,'' and, If I had known it would be this crowded. . . . They eat   15
quickly and want the check immediately, a good meal for them is a fast one.

◯ Combined Editing Test 8

See if you can locate and correct the twenty sentence-skills mistakes in the following passage. The mistakes are listed in the box below. As you locate mistakes, place checks in the spaces provided.

---

4 sentence fragments

____ ____ ____ ____

2 run-ons ____ ____

3 dropped verb endings

____ ____ ____

2 irregular verb mistakes

____ ____

1 dangling modifier ____

1 missing capital letter ____

2 apostrophe mistakes

____ ____

2 missing quotation marks

____ ____

1 missing comma between

complete thoughts ____

2 missing commas around an

interrupter ____ ____

I haven't taken a math class in years but I just registered for one. The prospect I guess of attending that class has stirred up my old fear of math. Because I had a dream the other night that can be considered nothing less than a nightmare. I was in a math class where the teacher was explaining a complicated theorem. For all I understood, he could have been speaking greek. But the other students hung on his every word and ⁵ taked notes like crazy, they couldn't have been more interested if he had been lecturing on the great secrets of life. Then he told us to get out our theorem projects. And asked for volunteers to put their work on the board. All the other thirty or so students in that class demonstrate their desire for that privilege by waving their hands wildly. As for me, I hadnt the foggiest notion of what the assignment was about. I slithered down ¹⁰ in my seat. Hoping the teacher would forget I was even in class. He call on three other students, and then I heard my name—You too, Mr. Oliver. Feeling like a kindergartener, my weak legs somehow brang me to the board. I began to doodle on it, and the room suddenly became silent I turn around to discover every pair of eye's in that room staring at me. As if I was insane. Then the school bell rang, but no one budged—until I reached ¹⁵ over to turn off my alarm.

Combined Editing Test 9

See if you can locate and correct the twenty sentence-skills mistakes in the following passage. The mistakes are listed in the box below. As you locate mistakes, place checks in the spaces provided.

<table>
<tr><td>3 sentence fragments

____   ____   ____</td><td>2 missing capital letters

____   ____</td></tr>
<tr><td>3 run-ons

____   ____   ____</td><td rowspan="2">3 missing commas after introductory words ____   ____

____</td></tr>
<tr><td>2 mistakes in subject-verb
agreement ____   ____</td></tr>
<tr><td>1 dangling modifier ____
1 mistake in pronoun agreement

____</td><td>4 missing commas around interrupters ____   ____

____   ____

1 mistake in comparison ____</td></tr>
</table>

The numerous ads for cat and dog products shows that Americans are concerned about the well-being of its pets. The relationship between people and animals however is of as much value to humans as it is to animals. By discovering that pets have feelings, animals help create in us a respect for living creatures. Pets are also important as companions. According to one study they can be especially helpful at special times in   5
people's lives. Including periods of depression and illness and during childhood. They can also revitalize people. When pets are brought into nursing homes depressed and bored elderly patients gain a new optimism. Pets can even reduce anxiety, one study demonstrated for example that gazing at a fish tank can reduce fear among patients about to undergo medical or dental surgery. In a recent magazine article a new york therapist   10
explained that pets can make people more relaxed and more happier about their lives, he told of a bachelor who found that caring for his cat helped him stop getting very upset. When life did not go his way. Yet another of the benefits of animals are that they provide important special services for humans. Seeing-eye dogs offer mobility—and companionship—to many blind people, trained monkeys do chores for the paralyzed.   15
Dogs and horses are used in police work, and cats are valued. For their ability to limit the mouse population. Clearly, animals do as much for people as people do for them.

◐ Combined Editing Test 10

See if you can locate and correct the twenty sentence-skills mistakes in the following passage. The mistakes are listed in the box below. As you locate mistakes, place checks in the spaces provided.

---

2 sentence fragments ____ ____   4 apostrophe mistakes ____

3 run-ons ____ ____   ____ ____ ____

____   2 missing commas after intro-

2 irregular-verb mistakes   ductory words ____ ____

____ ____   2 missing commas around an

3 mistakes in subject-verb   interrupter ____ ____

agreement ____ ____ ____   1 missing comma between

1 parallelism mistake ____   complete thoughts ____

More young people are living with their parents than ever before and there appears to be several reasons for this situation. According to the United States Census Bureau, about 50 percent of people aged eighteen to twenty-four lived either at home or in college dorms in 1985. Thats an increase of almost half since 1980. Several factors are thought to have caused this situation, in the past, children frequently left home when 5 they got married. Today however people tend to get married at an older age than they once did, even getting married doesnt guarantee that the young have flyed the coop for good. The high divorce rate among Americans have brought many of them back home to their parents. Also, the high cost of getting an education today keeps many students from moving to their own apartments. According to the Census Bureau more children 10 who live at home attend school than those who live on their own. However, graduating from school and to enter the job market do not guarantee that young people will finally leave their parents' home. Because many simply do not earn incomes' that allow them to become self-supporting. In addition children from more affluent families are more likely to stay at their parents' home longer. Waiting to be able to support themselves in 15 the life-style they growed up in. Of course, most eventually do leave home, the Census Bureaus statistics for 1985 shows that only 9 percent of men and 5 percent of women aged thirty to thirty-four were still living with their parents.

PART THREE

SENTENCE VARIETY THROUGH COMBINING ACTIVITIES

INTRODUCTION

Part One of this book gives you practice in skills needed to write clear sentences. Part Two helps you work on reinforcing those skills. The purpose of this part of the book is to provide you with methods for writing varied and interesting sentences. Through the technique of sentence combining, you will learn about the many different options open to you for expressing a given idea. At the same time, you will develop a natural instinct and "ear" for choosing the option that sounds best in a particular situation. By the end of Part Three, you will be able to compose sentences that bring to your writing style a greater variety and ease. You will also be able to write sentences that express more complex thoughts.

How Sentence Combining Works: The combining technique used to help you practice various sentence patterns is a simple one. Two or more short sentences are given and then combined in a particular way. You are then asked to combine other short sentences in the same way. Here is an example:

- The diesel truck chugged up the hill.
- It spewed out black smoke.
  Spewing out black smoke, the diesel truck chugged up the hill.

The content of most sentences is given to you, so that instead of focusing on *what* you will say, you can concentrate on *how* to say it.

The sentence-combining activities are presented in a three-section sequence. The first section describes the four traditional sentence patterns in English and explains the important techniques of coordination and subordination central to these patterns. The second section presents other patterns that can be used to add variety to writing. And the last section provides a number of practice units in which you can apply the combining patterns you have learned as well as compose patterns of your own.

Four Traditional Sentence Patterns

Sentences have been traditionally described in English as being simple, compound, complex, or compound-complex. This section explains and offers practice in all four sentence types. The section also describes coordination and subordination—the two central techniques you can use to achieve different kinds of emphasis in your writing.

THE SIMPLE SENTENCE

A simple sentence has a single <u>subject-verb</u> combination.

> <u>Children</u> <u>play</u>.
> The <u>game</u> <u>ended</u> early.
> My <u>car</u> <u>stalled</u> three times last week.
> The <u>lake</u> <u>has been polluted</u> by several neighboring streams.

A simple sentence may have more than one subject:

> <u>Lola</u> and <u>Tony</u> <u>drove</u> home.
> The <u>wind</u> and <u>water</u> <u>dried</u> my hair.

or more than one verb:

> The <u>children</u> <u>smiled</u> and <u>waved</u> at us.
> The <u>lawn mower</u> <u>smoked</u> and <u>sputtered</u>.

or several subjects and verbs:

> <u>Manny</u>, <u>Moe</u>, and <u>Jack</u> <u>lubricated</u> my car, <u>replaced</u> the oil filter, and <u>cleaned</u> the spark plugs.

Activity

On separate paper, write:

Three sentences, each with a single subject and verb
Three sentences, each with a single subject and a double verb
Three sentences, each with a double subject and a single verb

In each case, underline the subject once and the verb twice. (See page 10 if necessary for more information on subjects and verbs.)

THE COMPOUND SENTENCE

A compound, or "double," sentence is made up of two (or more) simple sentences. The two complete statements in a compound sentence are usually connected by a comma plus a joining word (*and, but, for, or, nor, so, yet*).

A compound sentence is used when you want to give equal weight to two closely related ideas. The technique of showing that ideas have equal importance is called *coordination*.

Following are some compound sentences. Each sentence contains two ideas that the writer considers equal in importance.

The rain increased, so the officials canceled the game.

Martha wanted to go shopping, but Fred refused to drive her.

Tom was watching television in the family room, and Marie was upstairs on the phone.

I had to give up wood carving, for my arthritis had become very painful.

Activity 1

Combine the following pairs of simple sentences into compound sentences. Use a comma and a logical joining word (*and, but, for, so*) to connect each pair.

Note: If you are not sure what *and, but, for,* and *so* mean, review pages 41–42.

Example • We hung up the print.
• The wall still looked bare.
We hung up the print, but the wall still looked bare.

1. • Cass tied the turkey carcass to a tree.
   • She watched the birds pick at bits of meat and skin.

   _____

2. • I ran the hot water faucet for two minutes.
   • Only cold water came out.

   _____

3. • Bruno orders all his Christmas gifts from mail-order catalogues.
   • He dislikes shopping in crowded stores.

   _____

4. • I need to buy a new set of tires.
   • I will read *Consumer Reports* to learn about various brands.

   _____

5. • I asked Cecilia to go out with me on Saturday night.
   • She told me she'd rather stay home and watch TV.

   _____

Activity 2

On separate paper, write five compound sentences of your own. Use a different joining word (*and, but, for, or, nor, so, yet*) to connect the two complete ideas in each sentence.

THE COMPLEX SENTENCE

A complex sentence is made up of a simple sentence (a complete statement) and a statement that begins with a dependent word.* Here is a list of common dependent words:

after	if, even if	when, whenever
although, though	in order that	where, wherever
as	since	whether
because	that, so that	which, whichever
before	unless	while
even though	until	who
how	what, whatever	whose

A complex sentence is used when you want to emphasize one idea over another in a sentence. Look at the following complex sentence:

Because I forgot the time, I missed the final exam.

The idea that the writer wishes to emphasize here—*I missed the final exam*—is expressed as a complete thought. The less important idea—*Because I forgot the time*—is subordinated to the complete thought. The technique of giving one idea less emphasis than another is called *subordination*.

Following are other examples of complex sentences. In each case, the part starting with the dependent word is the less emphasized part of the sentence.

While Sue was eating breakfast, she began to feel sick.
I checked my money *before* I invited Tom for lunch.
When Jerry lost his temper, he also lost his job.
Although I practiced for three months, I failed my driving test.

---

* The two parts of a complex sentence are sometimes called an independent clause and a dependent clause. A *clause* is simply a word group that contains a subject and a verb. An *independent clause* expresses a complete thought and can stand alone. A *dependent clause* does not express a complete thought in itself and ''depends on'' the independent clause to complete its meaning. Dependent clauses always begin with a dependent or subordinating word.

Activity 1

Use logical dependent words to combine the following pairs of simple sentences into complex sentences. Place a comma after a dependent statement when it starts the sentence.

Examples I obtained a credit card.
I began spending money recklessly.

When I obtained a credit card, I began spending money

recklessly.

Alan dressed the turkey.
His brother greased the roasting pan.

Alan dressed the turkey while his brother greased the

roasting pan.

1. Cindy opened the cutlery drawer.
   A bee flew out.

   _____

2. I washed the windows thoroughly.
   They still looked dirty.

   _____

3. I never opened a book all semester.
   I guess I deserved to flunk.

   _____

4. Manny gets up in the morning.
   He does stretching exercises for five minutes.

   _____

5. My son spilled the pickle jar at dinner.
   I had to wash the kitchen floor.

   _____

Activity 2

Rewrite the following sentences, using subordination rather than coordination. Include a comma when a dependent statement starts a sentence.

Example   The hair dryer was not working right, so I returned it to the store.

Because the hair dryer was not working right, I returned it to the store.

1. Dan set the table, and his wife finished cooking dinner.

_____

2. Maggie could have gotten good grades, but she did not study enough.

_____

3. I watered my drooping African violets, and they perked right up.

_____

4. The little boy kept pushing the down button, but the elevator didn't come any more quickly.

_____

5. I never really knew what pain is, and then I had four impacted wisdom teeth pulled at once.

_____

Activity 3

Combine the simple sentences on the opposite page into complex sentences. Omit repeated words. Use the dependent words *who, which,* or *that.*

Notes

a   The word *who* refers to persons.
b   The word *which* refers to things.
c   The word *that* refers to persons or things.

Use commas around the dependent statement only if it seems to interrupt the flow of thought in the sentence. (See also pages 181–182.)

Examples
- Clyde picked up a hitchhiker.
- The hitchhiker was traveling around the world.

  Clyde picked up a hitchhiker who was traveling around the *world.*

- Larry is a sleepwalker.
- Larry is my brother.

  Larry, who is my brother, is a sleepwalker.

1.
   - Karen just gave birth to twins.
   - Karen is an old friend of mine.

   _____

2.
   - The tea burned the roof of my mouth.
   - The tea was hotter than I expected.

   _____

3.
   - I dropped the camera on the sidewalk.
   - My sister bought the camera last week.

   _____

4.
   - Ernie brought us some enormous oranges.
   - Ernie is visiting from California.

   _____

5.
   - Liz used a steam cleaner to shampoo her rugs.
   - The rugs were dirtier than she realized.

   _____

Activity 4

On separate paper, write eight complex sentences, using, in turn, the dependent words *unless, if, after, because, when, who, which,* and *that.*

THE COMPOUND-COMPLEX SENTENCE

The compound-complex sentence is made up of two (or more) simple sentences and one (or more) dependent statements. In the following examples, a solid line is under the simple sentences and a dotted line is under the dependent statements.

> When the power line snapped, Jack was listening to the stereo, and Linda was reading in bed.
>
> After I returned to school following a long illness, the math teacher gave me make-up work, but the history teacher made me drop her course.

Activity 1

Read through each sentence to get a sense of its overall meaning. Then insert a logical joining word (*and, or, but, for,* or *so*) and a logical dependent word (*because, since, when,* or *although*).

1. _____ you paint the closet, remember to open the bedroom window, _____ you might get a headache from the smell.

2. _____ I get into bed at night, I try to read a book, _____ I always fall asleep within minutes.

3. Jim ate less butter _____ he learned that his cholesterol level was a little too high, _____ he also included some bran in his diet.

4. _____ she made the honor roll, Molly received a library pass from the principal, _____ she didn't have to sit in study hall the whole semester.

5. We planned to go to a rock concert tonight, _____ it was canceled _____ the lead singer was arrested.

Activity 2

On separate paper, write five compound-complex sentences.

REVIEW OF COORDINATION AND SUBORDINATION

Remember that coordination and subordination are ways of showing the exact relationship of ideas within a sentence. Through coordination we show that ideas are of equal importance. When we coordinate, we use the words *and, but, for, or, nor, so, yet*. Through subordination we show that one idea is less important than another. When we subordinate, we use dependent words like *when, although, since, while, because*, and *after*. A list of common dependent words is given on page 382.

Activity

Use coordination or subordination to combine the groups of simple sentences on the next pages into one or more longer sentences. Omit repeated words. Since a variety of combinations is possible, you might want to jot several combinations on separate paper. Then read them aloud to find the combination that sounds best.

Keep in mind that, very often, the relationship among ideas in a sentence will be clearer when subordination rather than coordination is used.

Example • My car is not starting on cold mornings.
  • I think the battery needs to be replaced.
  • I already had it recharged once.
  • I don't think it would help to charge it again.

Because my car is not starting on cold mornings, I think the battery needs to be replaced. I already had it recharged once, so I don't think it would help to charge it again.

Comma Hints

a Use a comma at the end of a word group that starts with a dependent word (as in "Because my car is not starting on cold mornings, . . .").

b Use a comma between independent word groups connected by *and, but, for, or, nor, so, yet* (as in "I already had it recharged once, so . . .").

1. ● Sidney likes loud music.
   ● His parents can't stand it.
   ● He wears earphones.

   _____

   _____

   _____

2. ● The volcano erupted.
   ● The sky turned black with smoke.
   ● Nearby villagers were frightened.
   ● They clogged the roads leading to safety.

   _____

   _____

   _____

   _____

3. ● Sally had a haircut today.
   ● She came home and looked in the mirror.
   ● She decided to wear a hat for a few days.
   ● She thought she looked like a bald eagle.

   _____

   _____

   _____

   _____

4. ● I ran out of gas on the way to work.
   ● I discovered how helpful strangers can be.
   ● A passing driver saw I was stuck.
   ● He drove me to the gas station and back to my car.

   _____

   _____

   _____

   _____

5. ● Our dog often rests on the floor in the sunshine.
   ● He waits for the children to get home from school.
   ● The sunlight moves along the floor.
   ● He moves with it.

_____

_____

_____

_____

6. ● My father was going to be late from work.
   ● We planned to have a late dinner.
   ● I was hungry before dinner.
   ● I ate a salami and cheese sandwich.
   ● I did this secretly.

_____

_____

_____

_____

7. ● A baseball game was scheduled for early afternoon.
   ● It looked like rain.
   ● A crew rolled huge tarps to cover the field.
   ● Then the sun reappeared.

_____

_____

_____

_____

8. • Cassy worries about the sprays used on fruit.
   • She washes apples, pears, and plums in soap and water.
   • She doesn't rinse them well.
   • They have a soapy flavor.

   _____

   _____

   _____

   _____

9. • Charlene needed to buy stamps.
   • She went to the post office during her lunch hour.
   • The line was long.
   • She waited there for half an hour.
   • She had to go back to work without stamps.

   _____

   _____

   _____

   _____

10. • The weather suddenly became frigid.
    • Almost everyone at work caught a cold.
    • Someone brought a big batch of chicken soup.
    • She poured it in one of the office coffeepots.
    • The pot was empty by noon.

    _____

    _____

    _____

    _____

Other Patterns That Add Variety to Writing

This section gives you practice in other patterns or methods that can add variety and interest to your sentences. The patterns can be used with any of the four sentence types already explained. Note that you will not have to remember the grammar terms that are often used to describe the patterns. What is important is that you practice the various patterns extensively, so that you increase your sense of the many ways available to you for expressing your ideas.

-ING WORD GROUPS

Use an *-ing* word group at some point in a sentence. Here are examples:

> The doctor, *hoping* for the best, examined the x-rays.
> *Jogging* every day, I soon raised my energy level.

More information about *-ing* words, also known as *present participles,* appears on page 85.

Activity 1

Combine each pair of sentences below into one sentence by using an *-ing* word and omitting repeated words. Use a comma or commas to set off the *-ing* word group from the rest of the sentence.

Example   ● The diesel truck chugged up the hill.

● It spewed out smoke.

Spewing out smoke, the diesel truck chugged up the hill

or *The diesel truck, spewing out smoke, chugged up the hill.*

1. ● The tourists began to leave the bus.
   ● They picked up their cameras.

   _____

   _____

2. ● I was almost hit by a car.
   ● I was jogging on the street.

   _____

   _____

3. ● Barbara untangled her snarled hair from the brush.
   ● She winced with pain.

   _____

   _____

4. ● The singer ran to the front of the stage.
   ● She waved her arms to the excited crowd.

   _____

   _____

5. ● The team braced itself for a last-ditch effort.
   ● It was losing by one point with thirty seconds left to play.

   _____

   _____

Activity 2

On separate paper, write five sentences of your own that contain *-ing* word groups.

- *ED* WORD GROUPS

Use an *-ed* word group at some point in a sentence. Here are examples:

Tired of studying, I took a short break.
Mary, *amused* by the joke, told it to a friend.
I opened my eyes wide, *shocked* by the red ''F'' on my paper.

More information about *-ed* words, also known as *past participles*, appears on page 85.

Activity

Combine each of the following pairs of sentences into one sentence by using an *-ed* word and omitting repeated words. Use a comma or commas to set off the *-ed* word group from the rest of the sentence.

Example ● Tim woke up with a start.

       ● He was troubled by a dream.

       Troubled by a dream, Tim woke up with a start.

    or *Tim, troubled by a dream, woke up with a start.*

1. ● Mary sat up suddenly in bed.

    ● She was startled by a sudden thunderclap.

_____

2. ● My parents decided to have a second wedding.

    ● They have been married for fifty years.

_____

_____

3. ● Ellen wouldn't leave her car.

    ● She was frightened by the large dog near the curb.

_____

_____

4. ● The old orange felt like a marshmallow.

    ● It was dotted with mold.

_____

_____

5.   ●   Ernie made a huge sandwich and popped popcorn.

       ●   He was determined to have plenty to eat during the movie.

_____

_____

APPOSITIVES

Use appositives. An *appositive* is a word group that renames a noun (any person, place, or thing). Here is an example:

Rita, a good friend of mine, works as a police officer.

The word group *a good friend of mine* is an appositive that renames the word *Rita*.

Combine each of the following pairs of sentences into one sentence by using an appositive and omitting repeated words. Most appositives are set off by commas.

Example   ●   Alan Thorn got lost during the hiking trip.

            ●   He is a former Eagle Scout.

               Alan Thorn, a former Eagle Scout, got lost during the hiking

               trip.

1.   ●   Hank Sullivan lost his right arm in a drunk-driving accident.

       ●   Hank Sullivan is a well-known painter.

_____

_____

2.   ●   *The Frugal Gourmet* is a simple approach to good cooking.

       ●   *The Frugal Gourmet* is a best-selling cookbook by Jeff Smith.

_____

_____

3. ● Our bird feeder is a big hit with the birds.
   ● Our bird feeder is a pinecone covered with peanut butter.

   _____

   _____

4. ● My grandmother rides a bicycle to the corner grocery.
   ● The bicycle is a three-wheeler with a large basket in back.

   _____

   _____

5. ● The chef's sculpture looks like something out of a fairy tale.
   ● The chef's sculpture is a garden of sugar flowers and chocolate statues.

   _____

   _____

Activity 2

On separate paper, write five sentences of your own that contain appositives. Use commas as necessary to set the appositives off.

- LY OPENERS

Use an -ly word to open a sentence. Here are examples:

Gently, he mixed the chemicals together.
Anxiously, the contestant looked at the game clock.
Skillfully, the quarterback rifled a pass to his receiver.

More information about -ly words, which are also known as *adverbs,* appears on page 132.

Activity 1

Combine each of the following pairs of sentences into one sentence by starting with an *-ly* word and omitting repeated words. Place a comma after the opening *-ly* word.

Example ● I gave several yanks to the starting cord of the lawn mower.
        ● I was angry.

         Angrily, I gave several yanks to the starting cord of the
         lawn mower.

1. ● We ate raw carrots and celery sticks.
   ● We were noisy.

     _____

2. ● Cliff spoke to his sobbing little brother.
   ● He was gentle.

     _____

3. ● The newspaper boy threw our paper in a thornbush.
   ● He was careless.

     _____

4. ● I paced up and down the hospital corridor.
   ● I was anxious.

     _____

5. ● Anita repeatedly dived into the pool to find her engagement ring.
   ● She was frantic.

     _____

Activity 2

On separate paper, write five sentences of your own that begin with *-ly* words.

TO OPENERS

Use a *to* word group to open a sentence. Here are examples:

To succeed in that course, you must attend every class.
To help me sleep better, I learned to quiet my mind through meditation.
To get good seats, we went to the game early.

The *to* in such a group is also known as an *infinitive*, as explained on page 85.

Activity 1

Combine each of the following pairs of sentences into one sentence by starting with a *to* word group and omitting repeated words. Use a comma after the opening *to* word group.

Example   I fertilize the grass every spring.

             I want to make it greener.

             To make the grass greener, I fertilize it every spring.

1.   Sally put a thick towel on the bottom of the tub.
     She did this to make the tub less slippery.

   _____

   _____

2.   We now keep our garbage in the garage.
     We do this to keep raccoons away.

   _____

   _____

3.   Bill pressed two fingers against the large vein in his neck.
     He did this to count his pulse.

   _____

   _____

4.   My aunt opens her dishwasher when it begins drying.
     She does this to steam her face.

   _____

   _____

5. ● We looked through our closets for unused clothing.
   ● We did this to help out the homeless.

   _____

   _____

Activity 2

On separate paper, write five sentences of your own that begin with *to* word groups.

PREPOSITIONAL PHRASE OPENERS

Use prepositional phrase openers. Here are examples:

> *From* the beginning, I disliked my boss.
> *In spite of* her work, she failed the course.
> *After* the game, we went to a movie.

Prepositional phrases include words like *in, from, of, at, by,* and *with*. A full list is on page 13.

Activity 1

Combine each of the following groups of sentences into one sentence by omitting repeated words. Start each sentence with a suitable prepositional phrase and place the other prepositional phrases in places that sound right. Generally you should use a comma after the opening prepositional phrase.

Example ● A fire started.
   ● It did this at 5 A.M.
   ● It did this inside the garage.

   At 5 A.M., a fire started inside the garage.
   _____

1. ● We have dinner with my parents.
   ● We do this about once a week.
   ● We do this at a restaurant.

   _____

   _____

2. ● I put the dirty cups away.

     ● I did this before company came.

     ● I put them in the cupboard.

_____

_____

3. ● My eyes roamed.

     ● They did this during my English exam.

     ● They did this around the room.

     ● They did this until they met the teacher's eyes.

_____

_____

4. ● The little boy drew intently.

     ● He did this in a comic book.

     ● He did this for twenty minutes.

     ● He did this without stopping once.

_____

_____

5. ● A playful young orangutan wriggled.

     ● He did this at the zoo.

     ● He did this in a corner.

     ● He did this under a paper sack.

_____

_____

Activity 2

On separate paper, write five sentences of your own that begin with prepositional phrases and that contain at least one other prepositional phrase.

SERIES OF ITEMS

Use a series of items. Following are two of the many items that can be used in a series: adjectives and verbs.

Adjectives in Series

Adjectives are descriptive words. Here are examples:

The *husky young* man sanded the *chipped, weather-worn* paint off the fence.

Husky and *young* are adjectives that describe *man; chipped* and *weather-worn* are adjectives that describe *paint.* More information about adjectives appears on page 130.

Activity 1

Combine each of the following groups of sentences into one sentence by using adjectives in a series and omitting repeated words. Use commas between adjectives only when *and* inserted between them sounds natural.

Example ● I sewed a set of buttons onto my coat.
　　　　　● The buttons were shiny.
　　　　　● The buttons were black.
　　　　　● The coat was old.
　　　　　● The coat was green.

I sewed a set of shiny black buttons onto my old green coat.

1. ● The shingles blew off the roof during the storm.
　● The shingles were old.
　● The shingles were peeling.
　● The storm was blustery.

_____

_____

2.   ● The dancer whirled across the stage with his partner.
     ● The dancer was lean.
     ● The dancer was powerful.
     ● The partner was graceful.
     ● The partner was elegant.

     _____

     _____

3.   ● The model in the bleach ad wore high heels in the laundry room.
     ● The model was well dressed.
     ● The model was glamorous.
     ● The high heels were three-inch.

     _____

     _____

4.   ● The moon lit up the sky like a street lamp.
     ● The moon was full.
     ● The moon was golden.
     ● The sky was cloudy.
     ● The street lamp was huge.
     ● The street lamp was floating.

     _____

     _____

5.   ● The doorbell of the house played a tune.
     ● The doorbell was oval.
     ● The doorbell was plastic.
     ● The house was large.
     ● The house was ornate.
     ● The tune was loud.
     ● The tune was rock 'n' roll.

     _____

     _____

Activity 2

On separate paper, write five sentences of your own that contain a series of adjectives.

Verbs in Series

Verbs are words that express action. Here are examples:

In my job as a cook's helper, I *prepared* salads, *sliced* meat and cheese, and *made* all kinds of sandwiches.

Basic information about verbs appears on page 11.

Activity 1

Combine each group of sentences below into one sentence by using verbs in a series and omitting repeated words. Use a comma between verbs in a series.

Example
- In the dingy bar Sam shelled peanuts.
- He sipped a beer.
- He talked up a storm with friends.

In the dingy bar Sam shelled peanuts, sipped a beer, and talked up a storm with friends.

1.
- I put my homework on the table.
- I made a cup of coffee.
- I turned the radio up full blast.

_____

_____

2.
- The flea-ridden dog rubbed itself against the fence.
- It bit its tail.
- It scratched its neck with its paws.

_____

_____

3.
- The driver stopped the school bus.
- He walked to the back.
- He separated two children.

_____

_____

4. ● I rolled up my sleeve.

   ● I glanced at the nurse nervously.

   ● I shut my eyes.

   ● I waited for the worst to be over.

   _____

   _____

5. ● The parents applauded politely at the program's end.

   ● They looked at their watches.

   ● They exchanged looks of relief.

   ● They reached for their coats.

   _____

   _____

Activity 2

On separate paper, write five sentences of your own that use verbs in a series.

Note: The section on parallelism (pages 99–104) gives you practice in some of the other kinds of items that can be used in a series.

Sentence-Combining Exercises

This section provides a series of combining exercises. The exercises are made up of a number of short sentence units, each of which can be combined into one sentence. (Occasionally, you may decide that certain sentences are more effective if they are not combined.) The patterns you have already practiced will suggest combining ideas for the units that you work on. However, do not feel limited to previous patterns. Use your own natural instinct to explore and compose a variety of sentence combinations. It will help if you write out possible combinations and then read them aloud. Choose the one that sounds best. You will gradually develop an ear for hearing the option that reads most smoothly and clearly and that sounds most appropriate in the context of surrounding sentences. As you continue to practice, you will increase your ability to write more varied, interesting, and sophisticated sentences.

Here is an example of a short sentence unit and some possible combinations:

- Martha moved in the desk chair.
- Her moving was uneasy.
- The chair was hard.
- She worked at her assignment.
- The assignment was for her English class.

Martha moved uneasily in the hard desk chair, working at the assignment for her English class.

Moving uneasily in the hard desk chair, Martha worked at the assignment for her English class.

Martha moved uneasily in the hard desk chair as she worked at the assignment for her English class.

While she worked at the assignment for her English class, Martha moved uneasily in the hard desk chair.

Note: In combining short sentence clusters into one sentence, omit repeated words where necessary. Use separate paper.

1 Helpful Advice

- People repeat common sayings.
- People do this often.
- People do this without thinking about them.

- These sayings are old proverbs.
- They are based on a lot of experience.
- They can be good advice.

- My mother told me a proverb.
- My mother told it to me many years ago.
- My mother lived by this proverb.

- This old saying still rings in my ears.
- The ringing is often.
- The saying is, "Don't sweat the small stuff."

- My mother realized she worried about problems.
- My mother realized she worried for too long.
- The problems were trivial.
- The problems were soon forgotten.

- She kept this saying in mind.
- The saying reminded her not to fret about little things.
- The fretting was needless.

- I lie in bed sleepless.
- I do this sometimes.
- I worry about the dent in my car.
- I worry about money I owe.
- I worry about a remark someone made.

- I do something then.
- I put things in perspective.
- I do this by remembering my mother's words.
- I decide not to "sweat the small stuff."

- My mother's advice is like a pill.
- The pill is for sleeping.
- The pill allows me to rest.
- I am able to save my worrying.
- My worrying will be for important matters.

2 The Snake and the Frog

- An unusual thing happened.
- It happened in my backyard.
- It happened while I was mowing the grass.

- There is an old wall in the yard.
- It is a stone wall.
- It is bordered by high weeds.

- I approached the wall with the mower.
- I thought I saw something move.
- I thought I saw it move in the weeds.

- I stopped the mower.
- I parted the weeds.
- I saw a snake.
- It was yellow and black.

- I thought the snake had been crushed.
- I thought this at first.
- The snake's "neck" was widened and bulging.

- I decided to lift up the snake.
- I decided to toss it over the wall into the field.
- I ran to get a hoe.

- I slid the metal hoe under the snake.
- I began to lift up the snake.
- I did this gingerly.

- The snake shuddered.
- The snake opened its mouth wide.
- The snake began to regurgitate something.

- I watched in horror.
- The snake coughed up a frog.
- The frog was large.
- The frog was green.

- I had interrupted the snake.
- He had been digesting a fresh meal.
- I did this unknowingly.

- The snake crawled away.
- The snake was suddenly slim.
- The snake slithered into a cranny in the stone wall.

- I was amazed.
- I was shocked.
- I stood staring at the frog.
- The frog was dead.

3 A Remedy for Shyness

- "I'm tired of being shy," Patty Nelson said.
- Patty said it to her cousin Vonda.

- Too often Patty felt herself blushing.
- She felt herself perspiring.
- This happened when she tried to speak to someone.
- She did not know the person well.

- She felt she was on the spot.
- Her heart pounded.
- Her stomach churned.

- Often she avoided speaking.
- She did not want to take a risk.
- The risk was embarrassing herself.

- Luckily, Patty got some advice.
- The advice was good.
- She got the advice from Vonda.

- Vonda said this.
- "Don't blame yourself for being shy."
- "It makes you seem attractive."
- "It makes you seem modest."

- Vonda also helped Patty accept herself.
- She helped her plan ways to build her self-confidence.
- She helped her plan ways to practice her social skills.

- Patty followed her cousin's advice.
- Patty tried joining conversations.
- The conversations were at school.
- The conversations were at work.

- Gradually, she learned something.
- She could start conversations.
- She could start them herself.

- In addition, she did something else.
- She practiced giving compliments.
- She practiced accepting compliments gracefully.

- Patty still feels uncomfortable sometimes.
- She is learning to do new social things.
- She once thought these things were impossible.

- She surprised herself.
- She did this recently.
- She joined a bowling league.
- Some of her new friends invited her to join.
- The friends were from work.

- She is not the best bowler on her team.
- She is winning a victory over shyness.
- She is winning thanks to her cousin's help.
- She is winning thanks to her own determination.

4   Shopping Malls

- America's main streets are losing customers.
- They are losing them to shopping malls.

- The malls are unlike city streets.
- The malls offer free parking.
- They offer a special selection of stores.
- They offer climate-controlled walkways.

- The layout of the mall is intended to encourage browsing.
- It is intended to encourage buying.

- Many kinds of stores are located in malls.
- Supermarkets are rarely included in malls.
- Grocery buyers do not like to linger in malls.

- Large department stores are located in the malls.
- They are located at the corners of the malls.
- The location is deliberate.

- Shoppers must do something in order to reach the department stores.
- They must walk by specialty stores.
- The specialty stores sell products such as clothing.
- They sell products such as shoes.
- They sell products such as jewelry.

- Bad weather need not discourage mall shoppers.
- The temperature in malls is predictable all year round.
- The temperature is sixty-eight degrees.

- When shopping malls first opened, shows were presented.
- The shows featured movie stars.
- They featured acrobats.
- The shows were to attract people to the malls.

- People came to the malls primarily to shop.
- These events proved to be unnecessary.

- Today, less elaborate entertainment is provided.
- Crafts fairs are included.
- Free movies are included.

- Shopping continues to be the favorite entertainment.
- It is the favorite of most of the people who gather in the mall.

- Old and young alike enjoy strolling from store to store.
- They enjoy window-shopping.
- They enjoy meeting friends.
- They enjoy spending their money.

5 To Build a Fire

- I just rented a town house.
- It has a fireplace.
- The fireplace is in the living room.
- The fireplace is built of brick.

- I knew it would be simplest to burn artificial logs.
- Artificial logs are made of sawdust.
- The sawdust is pressed.

- These logs look a little like long fruitcakes.
- They burn cleanly.
- They are very easy to ignite.

- But fires can be made with real logs.
- These logs crackle.
- They crackle when they burn.
- These logs give off a pleasant smell.

- I soon discovered something.
- Wood has a drawback.
- The drawback is real.
- It is very difficult to set ablaze.

- First I put newspapers under the wood.
- The newspapers ignited quickly.
- They roared with flame.

- Then the flames subsided.
- The wood was not burning.

- Next, I collected kindling.
- The kindling was from the woods.
- The woods were behind the house.

- The kindling burned.
- The firewood didn't catch fire.

- So I did something else.
- I used an artificial log.
- I put it in with the real wood.
- I lit it.

- It burned nicely.
- It burned for three hours.
- It only charred the real logs.

- I finally decided something.
- I decided the house might burn.
- It might burn to the ground.
- If it did, I might salvage only one thing.
- I might salvage my firewood.

6 Doctor's Waiting Room

- People visit the doctor.
- Their ordeal begins.
- It begins upon their arrival.
- Their arrival is in the waiting room.

- A patient has an appointment.
- The appointment is for 2:00.
- He arrives at 1:45.
- He is told something.
- He will have to wait.
- The wait will be at least one hour.

- Another patient arrives.
- She has three small children.
- The children are hanging on to her coat.
- The children are crying.
- The children are begging to go home.

- Other people arrive.
- Everyone takes a seat.
- Soon the room becomes crowded.

- People do many things.
- The things are different.
- The things are to help pass the time.

- Some people stare at the ceiling.
- Others count the stripes.
- The stripes are in the wallpaper.
- Some people try to sleep.

- Still others look at magazines.
- The magazines are on the table.
- The magazines are in piles.
- The magazines have torn covers.
- The magazines are old.

- Other people look at each other.
- The looking is shy.
- No one talks to anyone else.

- Everyone listens to the music.
- The music is in the background.
- The music is hushed.
- The music is bland.
- The music is almost sickening.

- Some people are very sick.
- The sickness is obvious.
- They cough a lot.

- The people around them turn away.
- The people hold their breath.
- They are afraid of becoming infected.

- Time passes.
- It passes slowly.
- All the people count.
- They count the number of people ahead of them.
- The counting is careful.

- Suddenly the moment comes.
- The moment has been long awaited.
- The moment is for each patient.

- The receptionist smiles.
- The receptionist looks at the patient.
- The receptionist says the magic words.
- "The doctor will see you now."

7 Dracula's Revenge

- Mickey Raines had a dislike.
- The dislike was of horror movies.
- His friends were different.
- They loved to see such movies.

- They would always invite Mickey to go with them.
- He would always refuse.

- He thought horror films were stupid.
- The actors were covered with fake blood.
- They were pretending to writhe in agony.

- Mickey thought their behavior was disgusting.
- He did not think their behavior was frightening.

- Once his friends persuaded him to come with them.
- They went to see a movie.
- The movie was called *Halloween 14—The Horror Continues.*

- Mickey found it ridiculous.
- He laughed aloud through parts of the movie.
- They were the scariest parts.

- His friends were embarrassed.
- They were so embarrassed they moved.
- They moved away from him.
- They moved to another part of the theater.

- Then one night Mickey was alone.
- He was alone in his house.
- His mother was out for the evening.
- He turned on the televison.

- A movie was playing.
- It was called *Nosferatu.*

- It was the original film version of the Dracula story.
- The film version was silent.
- It was made in Germany.
- It was made in 1922.

- The movie was not gory at all.
- There were no teenage girls in it getting chased.
- There were no teenage girls in it getting murdered.

- The villain was a vampire.
- He was hideous.
- He was shriveled.
- He was terrifying.

- His victims did not die.
- His victims grew weaker.
- They grew weaker after every attack.

- The vampire reminded Mickey of a parasite.
- The parasite was terrible.
- It was a dead thing.
- It was feeding off the living.

- Mickey trembled.
- He was trembling at the thought of such a creature.
- It could be lurking just out of sight.
- It could be lurking in the darkness.

- Then he heard a scraping noise.
- The noise was at the front door.
- He almost cried out in terror.

- The door opened quickly.
- Cold air rushed in.
- His mother appeared.
- She was back from her date.

- Mickey was relieved to see her.
- His relief was enormous.
- He rushed up to greet her.

- The spell of the movie was broken.
- Mickey closed the door onto the night.

8 Star Trek

- *Star Trek* was a television series.
- *Star Trek* went off the air in 1969.
- It was an experiment.
- The experiment was in science fiction.
- The science fiction was for adults.

- It was a production.
- The production had a low budget.
- The production had few special effects.

- There was no money to show the landing of a spaceship.
- The landing would be on a planet.
- The planet would be alien.

- The show's writers thought up the idea of "beaming."
- They "beamed" the characters down.
- They "beamed" them down anywhere they wished to visit.

- One character was the most striking.
- He was Mr. Spock.
- He was an alien.
- He had pointy ears.
- He bled green blood.

- He worked well with another character.
- This character was Captain Kirk.
- Captain Kirk was commander of the starship.
- The starship was named the *Enterprise*.

- Spock was a symbol of the reason in human nature.
- Kirk was a symbol of the emotion in human nature.

- Spock and Kirk worked well together.
- Together they represented a tension.
- The tension is basic.
- The tension is between reason and emotion.
- The tension is in all of us.

- *Star Trek* was on the air for three seasons.
- Ratings declined.
- Soon the show was canceled.

- Then a miracle happened.
- The show refused to die.
- The refusal was stubborn.

- Reruns became popular.
- Some fans watched every episode.
- They called themselves Trekkies.
- They watched the episodes many times.
- They began to hold conventions.
- Some of these conventions attracted as many as twenty thousand people.

- Soon *Star Trek* was made into a movie.
- This movie was feature-length.
- It was successful.

- More movies have followed.
- There is no end in sight.

- The characters are one reason for the success of *Star Trek*.
- But another reason is the attitude of Trekkies.
- The Trekkies feel superior.
- They feel superior to their fellow humans.

- Some of them have bumper stickers.
- They have them on their cars.
- The stickers read as follows.
- "Beam me up, Scotty."
- "There's no intelligent life down here!"

9 Robins' Behavior

- Robins are so common.
- Most people pay little attention to them.

- Robins' behavor can be observed.
- Robins' behavior can be interpreted.
- The observation and interpretation must be careful.

- Robins communicate with each other.
- Their communication is frequent.
- It is done in a fascinating way.

- One robin faces another.
- The robin lowers its head.
- The robin raises its tail.
- The robin is delivering a message.
- The message is, "Get out of my territory."

- One pair of robins feeds in a territory.
- The territory may take up the space of several backyards.

- The pair of robins builds its nest in the territory.
- The pair of robins spends most of its time in the territory.

- A muddy line has a meaning.
- The line is across a robin's breast feathers.
- The line means that the robin has been forming its nest.

- It does so by pressing against the muddy nest materials.
- It presses with its breast.

- The flicking of a tail has a meaning.
- The flicking is when someone approaches.
- The flicking warns the robin's mate.
- The warning is of possible danger.

- The tail flicks are also a sign to passersby.
- The flicks tell them that the robin has a mate.
- The flicks tell them that a nest is nearby.

- Another robin message is increased singing.
- The singing is early and late in the day.
- It means the young are about to hatch.

- Yet another sign is as follows.
- Robins sometimes fly with food in their beaks.
- They are carrying it to their nestlings.

- Bird-watchers will not be surprised a few days later.
- They will see speckled young.
- The young will be running after their parents.
- The young will be begging for food.

◎ 10 Word Processing

- Lucille had been hinting steadily for a computer.
- She had been hinting for a printer.

- She opened the big boxes containing them.
- She opened them on her birthday.
- She had trouble pretending to be surprised.

- What did surprise her was the challenge.
- The challege was substantial.
- The challenge was in learning to do her own word processing.
- The word processing was on the computer.

- Somehow she had expected the word processor to do more.
- She had expected it almost to write her college papers.

- She had been gloating about good grades.
- They were the grades she expected to get.

- Following the step-by-step instructions was easy enough.
- The instructions were for turning on the computer.
- Understanding how to use all the keys seemed beyond her.
- The keys were on the keyboard.

- The instruction manual gave advice.
- It gave advice on how to create a file.
- It gave advice on how to move the cursor.
- It gave advice on how to save material.

- None of this made sense to Lucille.
- This was at first.
- This was until she studied the manual.
- This was until she experimented with commands.

- Gradually she learned to add letters.
- She learned to delete letters.
- Each small success encouraged her.

- A week later she had learned more.
- She had learned how to rearrange sentences.
- She had learned how to rearrange paragraphs.
- She had learned how to add details.
- She had learned how to delete unneeded words.
- She had learned how to delete unneeded phrases.

- She then wrote a paper.
- The paper was on the computer.
- She printed the paper.

- Lucille corrected all the errors on the printout.
- Then she made the changes on the computer.
- She printed off a second copy of the paper.
- The copy was error-free.

- Her friend Alvin said something.
- He said it when their papers were returned in class.
- It was, "I see you got an A."
- "The computer probably did the work for you."

- Lucille replied.
- "*I* wrote the paper."
- "*I* did the work."
- "But the computer made it easier to revise."

PART FOUR

WRITING ASSIGNMENTS

INTRODUCTION

Part Four provides a series of writing assignments so that you can apply the sentence skills practiced in the earlier parts of the book. Applying these skills *in actual writing situations* is the surest way to achieve mastery of grammar, mechanics, punctuation, and usage rules. The first few assignments will develop your ability to provide specific details—a vital skill in writing. You will then practice writing paragraphs in which you support a topic sentence and essays in which you support a thesis statement. Some assignments involve personal writing in which you draw upon your own experience; others involve persuasive writing in which you apply your reasoning abilities. Basic information about the composing process has been included with some of the assignments. However, such information has been kept to a minimum because the primary concern in Part Four, as in the whole book, is with the mastery of sentence skills.

Note: Make a special effort to apply the sentence skills you have already learned to each writing assignment. To help you achieve such a transfer, your instructor may ask you to rewrite a paper as many times as necessary for you to correct sentence-skills mistakes. A writing progress chart on pages 478–479 (in Appendix C) will help track your performance.

Twenty Writing Assignments

1 Freewriting

Freewriting means that you write for ten minutes or more without stopping. You don't worry about spelling, punctuation, erasing mistakes, or finding exact words. Instead, you work on keeping your pen moving. If you get stuck for words, write "I am looking for something to say" or repeat words until something comes. Don't feel inhibited; mistakes do not count, and you will not have to hand in your paper.

Freewriting will limber up your writing muscles and make you familiar with the act of writing. It is a way to break through mental blocks about writing and the fear of making errors. Since you don't have to worry about making mistakes, you can concentrate on discovering what you want to say about a subject. Your initial ideas and impressions will often become clearer after you have gotten them down on paper. Through continued practice in freewriting, you will develop the habit of thinking as you write. And you will learn a technique that is a helpful way to get started on almost any paper that you write.

Freewriting Subjects: Here is a series of subjects for twelve separate freewriting activities. Remember that the only requirement is that you write for ten minutes without stopping. Once you are given a subject, you should be able to write on it for ten minutes if you get into details of the subject. If you run out of words, then write about anything—just don't stop writing.

1. People you live with
2. Money
3. Teachers
4. Next weekend
5. Your neighborhood
6. Relaxing
7. Children
8. Stresses in your life
9. Health
10. Marriage
11. What motivates you
12. Your future

2 A Typical Morning

What is getting-up time in the morning like for you? Is it leisurely or hectic? Are you alert or zombie-like? Do you stumble around until you have coffee? Do you feel like you are in a race against the clock?

Write in detail about this early morning time in your life—what you do, how you react, how you feel, and so on. To prepare for this paper, try to be especially observant on a given morning. Notice details and write them down in a notebook. Refer to your notebook when working on your paper, and strive to provide honest, specific details that will make your writing interesting to others.

Use time order in presenting your details. *Time order* simply means that details are listed as they take place in time: *first* this happened; *next* this; *then* this; *after* that, this; and so on.

3 A Letter of Advice

Giving advice is tricky, and giving it in writing, as is done in the newspaper advice columns, is even trickier. The writer must give carefully thought out advice in a limited space and a helpful tone of voice. Try your hand at it by writing a paragraph of advice to the author of one of the following letters.

Dear Advice Columnist:

I am caught between my parents and my boyfriend, and I don't know what to do. Recently my mother discovered birth control pills in my purse. She said she was looking for a pen, but I'm not so sure. Anyway, she was not pleased. My father was pretty angry, too, when he found out.

I am almost fifteen years old, which I think is old enough to make a decision about my own body. But, of course, my parents don't agree. In fact, they have forbidden me to see my boyfriend and are threatening to call his parents if we do see each other. But Bob and I do love each other, and we can't bear not to be together just because my mother was nosing around in my purse. I also love my parents, but I don't want them to run my life. How can I make them understand I'm old enough to make my own decisions?

Signed, Juliet

Dear Advice Columnist:

I am not a snoopy mother, so it is quite by accident that while putting away some laundry I discovered a bag of marijuana in my son's bureau. Though I was very surprised—and disappointed—I felt that this was the final piece in a puzzle that had been disturbing my husband and me for some time. Our son, who is in his second semester at a local community college, has been acting strangely for the last several months. His grades have gone down, and he has been spending time with new friends whom we consider a bad influence. In addition, he has become much more interested in money and has added many hours to his work schedule. I believe he has even taken some money from my purse at times. We recently confronted him with our discovery, and he accused us of snooping and not trusting him. He said that he smokes pot only on weekends and that the reason he's working more is to buy a new stereo. We don't know what to do next, if anything. What do you suggest?

Signed, Worried and Confused

Dear Advice Columnist:

The only time my parents pay any attention to me is when they boss me around. They've been having marital problems for years, and a lot of their time is spent fighting with each other or being depressed or trying to make up. Both of them party too much and drink too much. They don't care what I do in school as long as I don't get into trouble. They prefer that I watch TV in my own room so I don't get in their way in the house. I plan on getting a job and getting out of this house as soon as I can. Or is there some way to make them realize that I am a person with feelings and that they should give me a little attention and respect?

Signed, On the Verge of Running

4   Collaborative Story Writing

Choose one of the story openings that follow and develop it for about ten minutes. Your instructor then will ask you to exchange your story with someone else. You will read what the person wrote and then continue writing his or her story for another ten minutes or so. Finally, you will exchange with a third person and spend another ten minutes completing the story that has been given to you. Remember to write clearly and legibly enough so that your coauthors can read what you write; also, don't kill off your main characters before the final act. Have fun while you do this activity.

Afterward, exchange papers with a fourth person and proofread the completed story for fragments, run-on sentences, and mistakes with quotation marks.

Beginnings for Collaborative Short Stories

1. We should have known better than to have a party on a night when the moon was full.
2. All the newspaper said was that an animal had escaped from the zoo.
3. The inventor had a strange look in his eyes as he entered his laboratory.
4. Our adventure began when we innocently stepped into a new magic shop to look around.
5. My fingers were trembling as I opened the telegram.
6. It all began when my neighbor knocked frantically on my door.
7. You may not believe this, but I really did go back in time.
8. When Stella stared at the lamp and it began to float, we knew we were in for a strange evening.
9. Let me tell you about the time my car got stuck on a lonely road in the middle of a storm.
10. As we were getting ready to go to sleep in our tents, we heard a noise in the woods.

5   Self-Knowledge

A person may be very talented at math but terrible at public speaking or be wonderful at art but inept at athletics. Everyone has strong and weak points, and knowing what you are good at can be useful. What are your strong points? Write a paragraph in which you describe three of your best qualities or talents.

Your opening sentence might be something like the following: "Three qualities that have helped me in the past and that I would like to develop further are my good salesmanship, my organizational skills, and my ability to understand others." Be sure to provide specific examples that help prove to the reader that you really possess each of the qualities you mention.

6 Describing an Object

Write a description of a common object. Imagine that you are from Mars and do not know what the object is used for; you only know what it looks and feels like. Be very detailed in your description, including such aspects of the object as size, shape, color, and texture. But, of course, do not include the name or function of the object.

To help you write this description, first make up a list of all the characteristics of the object involved. For example, if you were writing about a pencil, you would include such features as the following:

- A thin, yellow, sticklike object about six inches long
- Pointed at one end
- Point made up of a soft, black material
- Spongy, round object at the other end
- Object attached by a grooved, shiny casing

Also, use words like *next to, above, across,* and *on top* to help the reader picture the object in his or her mind.

After you have finished, give your paper to another student, who should be able to guess what object you have written about.

7 A Helpful Experience

Write an account of an experience you have had that taught you something important. It might involve a mistake you made or an event that gave you insight into yourself or others. Perhaps you have had problems with school that taught you to be a more effective student, or you have had a conflict with someone that you now understand could have been avoided. Whatever experience you choose to write about, be sure to tell how it has changed your way of thinking.

8 Supporting a Topic Sentence

The two basic steps in effective writing involve (1) making a point of some kind and (2) providing specific evidence to support that point. In a *paragraph,* a short paper of about eight to twelve sentences, the point is called a *topic sentence.* The topic sentence is generally the first sentence of the paragraph. All the sentences that follow support or develop the point expressed in the topic sentence.

Listed below are three points, followed by specific examples that support the points. On separate paper, invent two additional examples to support each point. Try to make your examples as specific and as realistic as the ones shown.

Point 1: My friend (or sister or brother) and I have totally different life-styles.
Support: (1) For one thing, I am very messy and he (she) is compulsively neat. (2) . . . (3) . . .

Point 2: Working has been very useful to me.
Support: (1) First of all, my worst jobs have taught me what I do not like to do, which includes sitting at a desk all day. (2) . . . (3) . . .

Point 3: My neighbor (or roommate or some other person) is a very inconsiderate person.
Support: (1) For one thing, when cleaning his sidewalk or backyard, he often sweeps debris onto my property. (2) . . . (3) . . .

Suggestions on How to Proceed

1 Supply a title (for example, "Different Life-Styles" or "The Benefits of Working" or "An Inconsiderate Neighbor").

2 Copy the point and the first supporting example.

3 Add your own two supporting examples, which you should rewrite and expand on separate paper until they are fully developed in complete, error-free sentences.

4 Introduce your examples with word signals such as *Another way our life-styles differ is . . .; In addition, work has benefited me by . . .; A second example of his lack of consideration . . . ; Finally, ...*

9   Looking Ahead

Most people's activities include those which are done for today and those which are done for the near future. Usually, however, we do not think much about the far future—what we want our lives to be like in, say, ten years. Write a paper about where you would like to find yourself and how you expect to be living in ten years. Describe a realistic situation, one that you feel is possible on the basis of the plans and goals you have now. If you prefer, base your paper on where you want to be in five years rather than ten years.

10   Students and Jobs

Increasingly, educators are concerned about the time that many students spend working in part-time jobs each week, as opposed to time spent studying or involved in extracurricular activities. Examine the issue yourself by writing a paragraph that begins with and supports this point: "Full-time students should not work more than fifteen hours a week."

Before you begin, consider various aspects of this issue. How much time do students need to make the most of school? What can be the problems that result from working, say, thirty hours a week? What do most students do with their earnings? Jot down a series of notes as you think about this issue, and decide upon three separate reasons why students should not work more than fifteen hours a week. As you go on to write the first draft of your paragraph, introduce each of your reasons with word signals such as *first of all, another danger of working too many hours,* and *last of all.*

11   Your Position in the Family

Psychologists have concluded that there are significant differences in being an only, oldest, middle, or youngest child. Which of these are you, and how did it influence the way you were brought up? Did you have more responsibilities than your brothers and sisters? If you were an only child, did you spend a lot of time with adults? Were you a spoiled youngest child? Jot down the advantages and disadvantages that come to mind.

Use the most important ideas in your list to develop a paragraph on how you think your position in your family affected you. One student's beginning for this paragraph was, "As the second of three children, I received less attention, was given more independence, and was pushed less to achieve than my brother and sister." Remember to use specific examples to illustrate your ideas.

12   Three Paragraph Topics: Personal

Draw on your personal experience to write a paragraph on any one of the following topics:

1. A quality you most (or least) prefer in a friend
2. A problem that you are trying to deal with
3. A person who has had an important impact on your life

Begin with a topic sentence that states what your paragraph will be about. Then provide plenty of details to develop and support that topic sentence. Use the checklist on the inside back cover when proofreading your paper for sentence-skills mistakes.

13   Three Paragraph Topics: Persuasive

Apply your reasoning abilities and general experience to write a paragraph on one of the following topics:

1. Why many women are having children at a later age
2. Why more people than ever before are exercising
3. Why Americans are obsessed with diet

Begin with a topic sentence that states what your paragraph will be about. Then provide at least three reasons that support your topic sentence. Use word signals such as *first of all, second,* and *finally* to introduce each reason. Refer to the checklist on the inside back cover when proofreading your paper for sentence-skills mistakes.

14   Supporting a Thesis Statement

You will probably be asked in college to write papers of several paragraphs that support a single point. The central idea or point developed in a several-paragraph essay is called a *thesis statement,* rather than, as in a paragraph, a *topic sentence.* The thesis statement appears in the introductory paragraph, and specific support for the thesis statement appears in the paragraphs that follow.

Read through the clearly organized student essay that follows, and then look at the comments on page 434.

SAVING FOR A HOUSE

Introductory paragraph

It is harder than ever now for a couple to buy that first house. This is a frustrating fact of life that my husband and I learned after we were married. In order to make our dream of being homeowners come true, we decided to take certain steps. By moving in temporarily with my parents, severely limiting our leisure expenses, and working extra jobs, we hope to have enough money for a down payment on a modest house within two years.

First supporting paragraph

As the first part of our strategy, we moved in with my parents instead of renting our own apartment. Luckily, they have a house with a finished basement, and they were willing to have us live with them. Tom and I set up a bedroom and a living room for ourselves in the basement, and we eat our meals with my parents. We pay $200 a month for room and board, which is a considerable savings over the $400 that we would have to pay in rent alone for an apartment in this area. We do not have total privacy, and we sometimes feel more like kids than married adults because we live at home, but we are willing to make the sacrifice in order to afford a house.

Second supporting paragraph

In addition, we are saving money by agreeing to limit our expenses for recreation. We watch television instead of going to the movies. We have a radio, but we have to put off buying stereo equipment. We don't eat out, except for a rare $7 meal at Pizza Hut. Tom has given up the pro basketball games he used to attend several times a season. I have dropped out of my exercise classes at a health club and now do my workouts on a mat at home. When we feel deprived, as we sometimes do, we add up how much money we are putting away for our house by giving up costly leisure activities. Often, the total is $100 or more a month.

(Continues on next page)

*Third
supporting
paragraph*

> The most important part of our plan is working extra jobs. In addition to his job as a TV cable installer, Tom works at night in the appliance department of a Sears store. I type in a title company office five days a week; on weekends I am a hostess in a local restaurant. The hours are long for both of us, and we miss spending time together. Often we are tired and cranky when we get home. But the two extra jobs allow us to save an added $5,500 a year. Once we save the $12,000 we estimate we will need to buy a house, I will probably quit my extra job. Until then, we are willing to work doubly hard for these two years.

*Concluding
paragraph*

> Tom and I always assumed that we would live in our own house someday. Once we were married, though, we learned how expensive houses are in today's market. But we decided that, instead of giving up or getting angry, we would make sacrifices now to reach our goal in the future.

Comments: The essay begins with an *introductory paragraph* that attracts the reader's interest. It also presents the thesis statement: "In order to make our dream of being homeowners come true, we decided to take certain steps." The last sentence of this paragraph outlines a plan of development, a preview of the major points that will support the thesis: "By moving in temporarily with my parents, severely limiting our leisure expenses, and working extra jobs, we hope to have enough money for a down payment on a modest house within two years."

The *second paragraph* presents the first supporting point, or topic sentence ("As the first part of our strategy, we moved in with my parents instead of renting our own apartment"), and specific evidence for that point.

The *third paragraph* presents the second supporting point ("In addition, we are saving money by agreeing to limit our expenses for recreation") and specific evidence for the second point.

The *fourth paragraph* presents the third supporting point ("The most important part of our plan is working extra jobs") and specific evidence for the third point.

The brief *concluding paragraph* restates the main point of the paper and makes a closing comment or two.

Assignment: Listed below are three thesis statements, any one of which you might develop into an essay. Choose one of the statements and fill in three reasons you can use to support it. Then write your paper, taking it through the three or four drafts that may be necessary to complete it satisfactorily.

Thesis 1: Over the next year, I plan to accomplish three important goals.

1. _____

2. _____

3. _____

Thesis 2: While much has been written about the negative aspects of television, I believe it offers certain important benefits.

1. _____

2. _____

3. _____

Thesis 3: There are several advantages to attending college besides what is learned in classes.

1. _____

2. _____

3. _____

15 Leaving Home

Sooner or later most young people leave the home they have grown up in to begin life on their own. While the feeling of independence may be thrilling, flying the coop also involves numerous problems. Write about three problems that many people are likely to meet when they live away from home for the first time. Your thesis statement should be similar to this one: "When young adults move out on their own for the first time, they are likely to experience problems

with _____, _____, and _____."

Suggestions on How to Proceed

1   First make a list of five to ten problems that young people on their own for the first time are likely to experience.

2   Next, take the three most promising items on your list and develop each of them with specific details. For instance, one student's thesis was, "Young people are likely to experience problems with finances, household and personal chores, and loneliness." He then began to develop the point that financial problems arise by writing, "The first time my car broke down, I discovered I had no extra money to pay for repairs. Luckily, my parents lent me the money that time. After that, I began to build up a reserve in a savings account for future emergencies."

3   After you have fully developed and supported the three items you selected, arrange them in an order that makes sense to you. In each case, save what you feel is the most important item for last, for readers always remember best the final thing that they have read.

4   Use the five-part structure of an introduction, three supporting paragraphs (each devoted to one problem), and a conclusion. Refer to the checklist on the inside back cover when proofreading your paper for sentence-skills mistakes.

16   Taking a Position: I

Sometimes we use our abilities to observe and reason in order to understand a situation. We may, for example, observe that fast-food restaurants are more popular than ever. And we can use experience and reason to analyze why that might be. But sometimes we want to go a step or two further and decide whether a situation is good or bad and, perhaps, what should be done about it. Then we are taking a position on an issue.

Write an essay in which you argue *for* or *against* any *one* of the following positions. Support your argument by using your reasoning ability and general experience.

Option 1

Parents frequently consider education to be the school's problem. That is unfortunate, as there is much parents can and should do to contribute to their children's education.

Option 2

Classroom exams are meant to provide useful feedback to teachers and students. However, because of the way some tests are designed and the pressures they create for students, exams often do more harm than good.

Option 3

People in favor of capital punishment often point to the deterrent, or "scare," effect of execution as the primary reason for their support of such a harsh penalty. Therefore, to assure that the death penalty serves as the most effective deterrent possible, executions should be broadcast on public television.

Suggestions on How to Proceed

1   Take your time in selecting the position you want to write about. Be sure to choose one for which you will have three supporting points that can be solidly developed with details.

2   Begin an outline by writing down your thesis statement—the central point of your essay. It should clearly state the position you are taking.

3   Under your thesis statement, write the three points that support it. Now you have a brief outline for your essay.

4   To further guide you as you write your essay, expand your outline by writing in the details you will use to develop the supporting points. Here is a sample thesis statement with one supporting point and the details that will be used to develop that supporting point.

Thesis statement: There are several advantages to attending college besides what is learned in class.

Point 1: First of all, the extracurricular activities at school have much to offer. (a) Some are fun—for example, the dances and choir. (b) Student committees provide organizational experience. (c) Some offer training that could be included in a job résumé—for example, taking photos for the school newspaper.

5   After you have prepared a thorough outline and soundly thought out your paper, you are ready to begin writing.

○ 17 Taking a Position: II

Follow the same directions as those given for the preceding assignment.

Option 1

Our country no longer teaches basic values to the young. As a result, young people today are concerned only with success in terms of having money and possessions. But there are more important kinds of success and satisfaction than money and material things.

Option 2

Professional baseball, football, and basketball have declared war on drugs. Yet the biggest sponsors of sports telecasts are the large breweries. Their beer ads promote the consumption of alcohol, America's biggest drug. To avoid the charge of hypocrisy, the commissioners of each sport should ban beer advertising from appearing on sports telecasts.

Option 3

Rock music has a great influence on young people. Since many rock music lyrics promote themes of sex and violence, as well as encourage other antifamily values, rock songs should be subject to government rating and censorship.

○ 18 Changing the World

Though we would all like to see improvements in the world, most of us are unable to make really big changes on our own. But we all can contribute at least in small ways to the progress we would like to see. Write an essay in which you describe three ways anyone can have a positive impact on problems in everyday life.

One student who wrote such a paper used as his thesis the following statement: "Over the past year, I have helped people I care about by paying my parents some rent money, driving my grandmother to her doctor, and baby-sitting with my nephew." Another student's paper began: "There are several ways the average person can make the world better in small ways."

Use the five-part structure of an introduction, three supporting paragraphs, and a conclusion. Refer to the checklist on the inside back cover when proofreading your paper for sentence-skills mistakes.

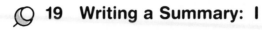

19 Writing a Summary: I

Making a summary is an excellent way to improve your writing and reading skills. To summarize a selection, you must first read it carefully. Only after you understand fully and clearly what is being said can you reduce a selection to a few sentences. For this assignment, you will be asked to read a selection titled "Students in Shock" (on pages 440–442) and condense it to no less than 125 and no more than 150 words. Below are reading and writing steps you should take to do an effective summary.

Steps to Follow in Summarizing

1   Take a few minutes to preview the work. You can preview an article by taking a quick look at the following:

   a   *Title:* The title often summarizes what the article is about. Think about the title and how it may condense the meaning of an article.

   b   *Subtitle:* A subtitle or caption, if given, consists of words in special print appearing under or next to the title. Such words often summarize the article or provide a quick insight into its meaning.

   c   *First and last paragraphs:* In the first paragraph, the author may introduce you to the subject and state the purpose of the article. In the last paragraph, the author may present conclusions or a summary. These previews or summaries can give you a quick overview of what the entire article is about.

2   Read the article for all you can understand the first time through. Don't slow down or turn back. Look for general statements and for details or examples that support those statements. Mark off what appear to be the main points and key supporting details.

3   Go back and reread more carefully the areas you have identified as most important. Also, focus on other key points you may have missed in your first reading.

4   Take notes on the material. After you have formulated what you think is the main idea of the selection, ask yourself the question, "Does all or most of the material in the article support the idea in this statement?" If it does, you have probably identified the main idea. Write it out in a sentence. Then write down the main supporting details for that idea.

5 Keep the following points in mind when working on the drafts of your summary:

a Express the main idea and supporting ideas in your own words. Do not imitate or stay too close to the style of the original work.

b Don't write an overly detailed summary. Your goal is a single paragraph not less than 125 words and not more than 150 words in length.

c Preserve the balance and proportion of the original work. If the original devoted 70 percent of its space to one idea and only 30 percent to another, your summary should reflect that emphasis.

d Use the checklist on the inside back cover to proofread your summary for sentence-skills mistakes, including spelling.

STUDENTS IN SHOCK

If you feel overwhelmed by your college experiences, you are not alone—many of today's college students are suffering from a form of shock. Going to college has always had its ups and downs, but today the "downs" of the college experience are more numerous and difficult, a fact that the schools are responding to with increased support services.

Lisa is a good example of student shock. She is an attractive, intelligent twenty-year-old college junior at a state university. Having been a straight-A student in high school and a member of the basketball and softball teams there, she remembers her high school days with fondness. Lisa was popular then and had a steady boyfriend for the last two years of school.

Now, only three years later, Lisa is miserable. She has changed her major four times already and is forced to hold down two part-time jobs in order to pay her tuition. She suffers from sleeping and eating disorders and believes she has no close friends. Sometimes she breaks out crying for no apparent reason. On more than one occasion, she has considered taking her own life.

Dan, too, suffers from student shock. He is nineteen and a freshman at a local community college. He began college as an accounting major but hated that field. So he switched to computer programming because he heard the job prospects were excellent in that area. Unfortunately, he discovered that he has little aptitude for programming and changed majors again, this time to psychology. He likes psychology but has heard horror stories about the difficulty of finding a job in that field without a graduate degree. Now he's considering switching majors again. To help pay for school, Dan works nights and weekends as a sales clerk at K Mart. He doesn't get along with his boss, but since he needs the money, Dan feels he has no choice except to stay on the job. A few months ago, his girlfriend of a year and a half broke up with him.

Not surprisingly, Dan has started to suffer from depression and migraine headaches. He believes that despite all his hard work, he just isn't getting anywhere. He can't remember ever being this unhappy before. A few times he considered talking to somebody in the college psychological counseling center. He rejected that idea, though, as he doesn't want people to think there's something wrong with him.

What is happening to Lisa and Dan happens to millions of college students each year. As a result, roughly one-quarter of the student population at any time will suffer from symptoms of depression. Of that group, almost half will experience depression intense enough to warrant professional help. At schools across the country, psychological counselors are booked up months in advance. Stress-related problems such as anxiety, migraine headaches, insomnia, anorexia, and bulimia are epidemic on college campuses.

Suicide rates and self-inflicted injuries among college students are higher now than at any time in history. The suicide rate among college youth is 50 percent higher than among nonstudents of the same age. It is estimated that more than five hundred college students take their own lives each year.

College health officials believe that these reported problems represent only the tip of the iceberg. They fear that most students, like Lisa and Dan, suffer in silence.

Why are today's college students suffering more than those in earlier generations? Unfortunately, there are several reasons. First is a weakening family support structure. The transition from high school to college has always been difficult, but in the past there was more family support to help get through it. Today, with divorce rates at a historical high and many parents experiencing their own psychological difficulties, the traditional family structure is not always available for guidance and support. When students do not find stability at home when they are bombarded with numerous new and stressful experiences, the results can be devastating.

Another problem college students face is financial pressure. In the last decade tuition costs have skyrocketed—about 66 percent up at public colleges and 90 percent at private schools. For students living away from home, costs range from six thousand dollars to as much as fifteen thousand dollars a year and more. And at the same time that tuition costs have been rising dramatically, there has been a cutback in federal aid to students. College loans are now much harder to obtain and are available only at near-market interest rates. Consequently, it is necessary for most college students to work at least part-time. For some students, the effort to do well in school while holding down a job is too much to handle.

A third cause of student shock is the large selection of majors available. Because of the magnitude and difficulty of choosing a major, college can prove a time of great indecision. Many students switch majors, some a number of times. As a result, it is becoming commonplace to take five or six years to get a degree. It can be depressing to students not only to have taken courses that don't count toward a degree but to be faced with the added tuition costs, which are prohibitive in some cases.

A final and perhaps the most difficult problem that today's college students experience is the bad luck of being born at the tail end of the "baby boom," the highest number of births in the history of the United States. Simply because there are so many of them, baby boomers must contend with heavy competition in every facet of their lives. Thus, today's students face severe competition for good schools, high grades, and satisfying jobs. Perhaps most distressing of all is that for the first time in American history, young people may have to accept "downward mobility." Because of the tremendous competition they face, many baby boomers will be worse off financially than their parents.

While there is no magic cure-all for student shock, colleges have begun to recognize the problem and are trying in a number of ways to help students cope with the pressures they face. First of all, many colleges are upgrading their psychological counseling centers to handle the greater demand for services. Additional staff is being hired, and experts are doing research to learn more about the psychological problems of college students. Some schools even advertise these services in student newspapers and on campus radio stations. Also, juniors and seniors are being trained as peer counselors. It is hoped these peer counselors can act as a first line of defense in the battle for students' well-being by spotting and helping to solve problems before they become too big for students to handle.

In addition, stress-management workshops have become common on college campuses. At these workshops, instructors teach students various techniques for dealing with stress, including biofeedback, meditation, and exercise.

Finally, many schools are improving their vocational counseling services. By giving students more relevant information about possible majors and career choices, colleges can lessen the anxiety and indecision often associated with choosing a major.

If you ever feel that you're "in shock," remember that your experience is not unique. Try to put things in perspective. It is true that the end of a romance and failing on an exam, for example, are not events to look forward to. But realize that rejection and failure happen to everyone sooner or later. And don't be reluctant to talk to somebody about your problems. The useful services available on campus won't help you if you don't take advantage of them.

20 Writing a Summary: II

One of the oldest and most popular television shows is *Sixty Minutes*. This show covers both topics of importance and less serious subjects of general interest. Watch this show the next time it is on and take detailed notes on one or two of the segments that interest you. Then write a summary of one of the segments, using the guidelines given in the previous assignment. A summary of one *Sixty Minutes* episode appears as an editing passage on page 371.

Appendixes

INTRODUCTION

Three appendixes follow. Appendix A consists of diagnostic and achievement tests that measure many of the skills in this book. Appendix B supplies answers to the introductory projects and the practice exercises in Part One. The answers, which should be referred to only after you have worked carefully through each exercise, give you responsibility for testing yourself. (To ensure that the answer key is used as a learning tool only, answers are *not* given for the review tests in Part One or for the reinforcement tests in Part Two. These answers appear only in the Instructor's Manual, where they can be copied and handed out at the discretion of your teacher.) Finally, Appendix C contains a series of handy progress charts that you can use to track your performance on all the tests in the book and the writing assignments as well.

Appendix A

Diagnostic and Achievement Tests

SENTENCE-SKILLS DIAGNOSTIC TEST

Part 1

This test will help check your knowledge of a number of sentence skills. In each item below, certain words are underlined. Place an *X* in the answer space if you think a mistake appears at the underlined part. Place a *C* in the answer space if you think the underlined part is correct.

A series of headings ("Sentence Fragments," "Run-Ons," and so on) will give you clues to the mistakes to look for. However, you do not have to understand the heading to find a mistake. What you are checking is your own sense of effective written English.

Sentence Fragments

_____ 1. After Christine listened to the radio for half an hour. She realized that class would not be canceled. Then she went outside to scrape the ice and snow off her car.

_____ 2. My friends and I love to eat pizza, especially pizza with unusual toppings. We plan to visit a different pizza place every week this month.

_____ 3. Clifford went to seven jewelry stores. Trying to find the perfect ring for Hilde. Finally he asked her to help him choose the ring.

_____ 4. Jesse was looking forward to spring vacation. She wanted to spend time with her family. And sleep late every day.

Run-Ons

_____ 5. Adam is always losing <u>things, he</u> misplaces his house keys at least once a week.

_____ 6. A stray cat wants to move in with <u>us she</u> is often on our step pawing at the front door.

_____ 7. Sara bought a new <u>swimsuit, so</u> she wants to go swimming next week.

_____ 8. I rarely eat regular breakfast <u>foods, I</u> prefer food like hamburgers for breakfast.

Standard English Verbs

_____ 9. The new television game show <u>interests</u> my whole family.

_____ 10. When the news ended, Frank <u>turn</u> off the television set.

_____ 11. After the concert, we <u>was</u> all very tired.

_____ 12. Linda <u>have</u> to study harder than her twin sister.

Irregular Verbs

_____ 13. I know I <u>seen</u> my flashlight somewhere in the basement.

_____ 14. Jack <u>had taken</u> the bus to Piney Hollow.

_____ 15. After the pond <u>freezed</u>, all the neighborhood children went ice skating.

_____ 16. The water pipes <u>burst</u> while the storm sewer was being repaired.

Subject-Verb Agreement

_____ 17. A large box of tissues <u>lasts</u> more than twice as long as a small one.

_____ 18. There <u>was</u> two fire exits in the auditorium.

_____ 19. Cindy and Ted <u>take</u> their children to the beach every summer.

_____ 20. Each of the supervisors <u>has</u> special duties.

Consistent Verb Tense

_____ 21. After Joyce studied the recipe, she bought the ingredients and <u>prepared</u> the lasagna.

_____ 22. Before the temperature dropped any further, Rita tried to start her car and then <u>calls</u> her father.

Misplaced Modifiers

_____ 23. The book that impressed me the most is about an army doctor.

_____ 24. We sent the present to my sister that was wrapped.

Dangling Modifiers

_____ 25. After being on my feet all day, the chair in front of the television set was a welcome sight.

_____ 26. Suddenly remembering the combination, I snapped the lock open.

Faulty Parallelism

_____ 27. To become a licensed driver, Vicki had to study her instruction manual, pass a written test, and a driving test was required.

_____ 28. Good managers are friendly, understanding, and show confidence.

Pronoun Reference, Agreement, and Point of View

_____ 29. All part-time workers should check their time cards.

_____ 30. Lisa wants to study law because she thinks they do interesting work.

_____ 31. A student can do well in this class if you work hard.

Pronoun Types

_____ 32. I practice more often, but Bruce types faster on our word processor than me.

_____ 33. My father and I attend the same school.

Adjectives and Adverbs

_____ 34. The men worked so quick that before we knew it, the logs were neatly stacked outside the house.

_____ 35. William writes correctly, but he is not very creative.

_____ 36. The living room is the most sunniest room in the house.

_____ 37. Traveling by train is more interesting to Tiffany than driving.

Capital Letters

_____ 38. I have been eating <u>Kellogg's</u> cereals since I was four years old.

_____ 39. My <u>mother</u> does not feel awake in the morning until she has had a cup of coffee.

_____ 40. In the <u>winter</u> my grandparents' walking club does its walking in a shopping mall.

_____ 41. Regina said, "<u>you</u> left your gloves on your desk."

Numbers and Abbreviations

_____ 42. Denver is one of my <u>3</u> favorite cities.

_____ 43. An explanation of static electricity is given on page <u>323</u>.

_____ 44. Savita is less than five <u>ft</u>. tall, but her sister is much taller.

End Marks

_____ 45. Gerald wondered whether he should study with the radio on<u>.</u>

_____ 46. Do you make a point of getting some vitamin C every day<u>?</u>

Apostrophe

_____ 47. <u>Sals</u> car has a dented fender.

_____ 48. I <u>didnt</u> know that thin people could be out of shape.

_____ 49. <u>Dan's</u> most recent accomplishment was winning a motorcycle race.

_____ 50. Both my <u>brother's</u> moved to Chicago.

Quotation Marks

_____ 51. <u>Someone once said, "The more one has, the more one desires."</u>

_____ 52. <u>"When I decided to study engineering, I did not even know what engineers did, Dan admitted."</u>

_____ 53. <u>"Groundwater is out of sight," the scientist said, "so people too often ignore the threat of toxic waste to their water supply."</u>

_____ 54. <u>"I'd like a brownie with chocolate ice cream, Lisa said to the waiter, and put chocolate syrup on top."</u>

Comma

55. My favorite belongings are <u>my compact disk player my photograph album and my</u> old teddy bear.

56. My <u>brother, who has much more energy than I do, likes</u> to help his friends move.

57. When Orrin had eaten the last piece of <u>bread he</u> realized that Francine had not yet had lunch.

58. Marion is usually the first person to arrive at a <u>party, and</u> she is always the last person to leave.

Spelling

59. <u>Beginning</u> a sewing project is easy for me, but I often put off finishing a garment.

60. Demetrios has lived in four different <u>countrys</u>.

61. My grandmother looks <u>alright,</u> but I know she gets tired very easily.

62. All of Amy's baby <u>picture</u> are adorable.

Omitted Words and Letters

63. <u>Maya's spoon collection is displayed in the dining room.</u>

64. <u>The first snow-making machine looked like lawn sprinkler</u> on a sled.

65. <u>All the cars I have owned have given me problem.</u>

Commonly Confused Words

66. Alice thinks she is <u>to</u> busy to work out regularly.

67. Will and Jonathan keep <u>their</u> hubcap collection in the storage shed.

68. The dog wagged <u>it's</u> tail whenever someone stood up.

69. If <u>your</u> planning to have a flu shot, get it before flu season begins.

Effective Word Choice

70. Yolanda must be <u>losing it;</u> she always seems confused.

71. Mountain streams are <u>usually clearer</u> than other streams.

72. Nick is <u>on top of the world</u> since he got the job he wanted.

73. At the <u>present point in time,</u> Elyse and I are best friends.

74. When my mother was a child, she <u>resided</u> in Iowa.

75. My cousin takes medication for his depression <u>due to the fact that</u> therapy did not help.

Part 2 (Optional)

Do the following at your instructor's request. This second part of the test will provide more detailed information about skills you need to know. On separate paper, number and correct all the items you have marked with an *X*. For example, suppose you had marked the word groups below with an *X*. (Note that these examples are not taken from the actual test.)

4. When I picked up the tire. Something in my back snapped. I could not stand up straight as a result.

7. The phone started ringing, then the doorbell sounded as well.

15. Marks goal is to save enough money to get married next year.

29. Without checking the rearview mirror the driver pulled out into the passing lane.

Here is how you should write your corrections on a separate sheet of paper:

4. When I picked up the tire, something in my back snapped.

7. The phone started ringing, and then the doorbell sounded as well.

15. Mark's

29. mirror, the driver

There are over forty corrections to make in all.

SENTENCE-SKILLS ACHIEVEMENT TEST

Part 1

This test will help check your knowledge of a number of sentence skills. In each item below, certain words are underlined. Place an *X* in the answer space if you think a mistake appears at the underlined part. Place a *C* in the answer space if you think the underlined part is correct.

A series of headings ("Sentence Fragments," "Run-Ons," and so on) will give you clues to the mistakes to look for. However, you do not have to understand the heading to find a mistake. What you are checking is your own sense of effective written English.

Sentence Fragments

_____ 1. After I sharpened five pencils. I cleaned off my desk. Then it was too late to start my homework.

_____ 2. My uncle is an expert on cars, especially older ones. He helped me find a good used car.

_____ 3. Marie read the instruction booklet carefully. Trying to understand how to put her new barbecue together. Finally, she decided to ignore the instructions.

_____ 4. Dave makes stained-glass ornaments. He designs them himself. And never makes any two alike.

Run-Ons

_____ 5. The supervisor makes a new work schedule each Friday, she also distributes the paychecks.

_____ 6. The cash machine outside my bank is rarely busy most people prefer to do their banking inside.

_____ 7. The little girl next door is exactly the same age as Jerry, but she has a much larger vocabulary.

_____ 8. I like weekends better than any other time, I never work on weekends.

Standard English Verbs

_____ 9. Bernita's husband eats whatever she cooks.

_____ 10. When the restaurant closed, Ken lock all the doors.

_____ 11. Because the heater did not work, we was wearing our coats indoors.

_____ 12. On Fridays, Susan have her women friends drop in for a visit.

Irregular Verbs

_____ 13. Bev <u>seen</u> her sister at the shopping mall.

_____ 14. Before the movie <u>had begun</u>, every seat was taken.

_____ 15. Either I gained weight or all my clothes <u>shrinked</u>.

_____ 16. The boots Robert bought last year <u>cost</u> half as much as the same style does now.

Subject-Verb Agreement

_____ 17. The commuters on the express train <u>arrive</u> promptly every morning.

_____ 18. There <u>was</u> only seven students in the class.

_____ 19. The president and the vice president <u>plan</u> the staff meetings each month.

_____ 20. Each of the boys <u>believe</u> a different version of the story.

Consistent Verb Tense

_____ 21. Before Tricia bought a television set, she <u>asked</u> her friends for advice.

_____ 22. When Ben found a new job, he said good-bye to his friends and <u>thanks</u> his supervisor for her help.

Misplaced Modifiers

_____ 23. The workers <u>who come in early</u> usually stock shelves and sweep the floors.

_____ 24. The people expect something for nothing <u>who fall for frauds</u>.

Dangling Modifiers

_____ 25. <u>While studying for my English test</u>, the telephone rang.

_____ 26. <u>Walking through the park</u>, Helene noticed the spring flowers blooming.

Faulty Parallelism

_____ 27. Porter likes to fish, to camp, and <u>hiking in a wildlife refuge</u>.

_____ 28. To keep fit, people need exercise, good diets, and <u>getting regular checkups</u>.

Pronoun Reference, Agreement, and Point of View

_____ 29. All students should carry their identification cards.

_____ 30. Carlos ran for the student senate because they select the musical groups that perform at the college.

_____ 31. I like watching daytime dramas on television because you can identify with the characters.

Pronoun Types

_____ 32. My sister writes letters more often than me.

_____ 33. My boss and I often go bowling together.

Adjectives and Adverbs

_____ 34. Doug paints so slow that it took him all day to finish one small room.

_____ 35. The class listened carefully to the instructor's explanation.

_____ 36. If we work more harder, we may finish early.

_____ 37. The most difficult thing I ever did was quit smoking.

Capital Letters

_____ 38. With the money we are saving, we hope to join the swim club this summer.

_____ 39. Lorraine's favorite treat is a cadbury's chocolate bar with raisins and nuts.

_____ 40. Every Thursday night my brother and I argue about which television shows to watch.

_____ 41. Toni asked, "have you ever eaten better chili?"

Numbers and Abbreviations

_____ 42. The 110-story World Trade Center is a New York City landmark.

_____ 43. By 7:10 A.M. Tracy should be leaving for work.

_____ 44. Gina hopes to have her degree in four yrs.

End Marks

_____ 45. I want to know how the dog learned to open the back door<u>.</u>

_____ 46. Are you worried about the rising cost of health car<u>e?</u>

Apostrophe

_____ 47. <u>Jeffs</u> favorite snack is popcorn with plenty of butter and salt.

_____ 48. We <u>couldn't</u> believe that our aunt had once been a carhop.

_____ 49. The <u>artist's</u> best paintings were displayed in a one-woman show.

_____ 50. The most uncomfortable <u>chair's</u> at the college are in the student lounge.

Quotation Marks

_____ 51. <u>Pamela always says, ''Wasting time isn't a waste of time.''</u>

_____ 52. <u>''Please draw a sketch of yourself, the psychologist said.''</u>

_____ 53. <u>''One small change in our environment,'' the scientist warned, ''can have an impact on all our lives.''</u>

_____ 54. <u>I would like to go to Florida,'' Steven said, if I can save enough money.''</u>

Comma

_____ 55. In our neighborhood we recycle <u>old newspapers glass bottles and aluminum cans.</u>

_____ 56. My <u>sister, who sips soft drinks all day long, cannot</u> understand why she is not losing weight.

_____ 57. When Luis wants to be <u>alone he</u> walks to Point Pleasant Park.

_____ 58. Brian reads the advice column letters to <u>Sandy, and</u> tries to guess the advice that Dear Abby has given.

Spelling

_____ 59. I <u>droped</u> my psychology class last semester.

_____ 60. Evelyn always <u>studys</u> early in the morning.

_____ 61. My current job is <u>alright</u>, but I would prefer a job that pays better.

_____ 62. Some <u>advertisement</u> are so silly that they are impossible to forget.

Omitted Words and Letters

_____ 63. People have trouble believing that gray is my favorite color.

_____ 64. A fever helps body fight infection.

_____ 65. Several container of soup are kept in the freezer for last-minute meals.

Commonly Confused Words

_____ 66. Diane and Todd scheduled their wedding for the day after Christmas.

_____ 67. A dinosaur had left it's footprints in the soft mud.

_____ 68. The conference room is to small for your presentation.

_____ 69. When your finished in the shower, please hang up the towel.

Effective Word Choice

_____ 70. Subsequent to our wedding, we took a honeymoon trip to Jamaica.

_____ 71. Cecil is really into his job at the bank.

_____ 72. To help prepare for a party, I make most of the food the day before.

_____ 73. They parked their vehicle in the driveway and walked into the house.

_____ 74. Although Lynn is saving money, what she has so far is only a drop in the bucket.

_____ 75. My own personal opinion is that the camera takes mediocre pictures.

Part 2 (Optional)

Do the following at your instructor's request. This second part of the test will provide more detailed information about skills you need to know. On separate paper, number and correct all the items you have marked with an X. For example, suppose you had marked the word groups below with an X. (Note that these examples were not taken from the actual test.)

4. When I picked up the tire. Something in my back snapped. I could not stand up straight as a result.

7. The phone started ringing, then the doorbell sounded as well.

15. Marks goal is to save enough money to get married next year.

29. Without checking the rearview mirror the driver pulled out into the passing lane.

Here is how you should write your corrections on a separate sheet of paper:

4. When I picked up the tire, something in my back snapped.
7. The phone started ringing, and then the doorbell sounded as well.
15. Mark's
29. mirror, the driver

There are over forty corrections to make in all.

Answers to Introductory Projects and Practice Exercises

This answer key can help you teach yourself. Use it to find out why you got some answers wrong—you want to uncover any weak spot in your understanding of a given skill. By using the answer key in an honest and thoughtful way, you will master each skill and prepare yourself for the many tests in this book that have no answer key.

SUBJECTS AND VERBS

Introductory Project (page 9)

Answers will vary.

Practice 1 (11)

1. Carl spilled
2. ladybug landed
3. Gary eats
4. waitress brought
5. I found
6. Diane stapled
7. audience applauded
8. boss has
9. I tasted
10. paperboy threw

Practice 2 (12)

1. I am
2. parents were engaged
3. Tri Lee was
4. dog becomes
5. Estelle seems
6. hot dog looks
7. people appear
8. students felt
9. cheeseburger has
10. telephone seemed

Practice 3 (12)

1. rabbits ate
2. father prefers
3. restaurant donated
4. Stanley looks
5. couple relaxed
6. Lightning brightened
7. council voted
8. throat kept
9. sister decided
10. I chose

Practice (13)

1. By accident, Fran dropped her folder in the mailbox.
2. Before the test, I glanced over my notes.
3. My car stalled on the bridge at rush hour.
4. I hung a photo of Whitney Houston above my bed.
5. On weekends, we visit my grandmother at a nursing home.
6. During the movie, some teenagers giggled at the love scenes.
7. A pedestrian tunnel runs beneath the street to the train station.
8. The parents hid the Christmas gifts for their daughter in the garage.
9. All the teachers, except Mr. Blake, wear ties to school.
10. The strawberry jam in my brother's sandwich dripped onto his lap.

Practice (15)

1. Ellen has chosen
2. You should plan
3. Felix has been waiting
4. We should have invited
5. I would have preferred
6. Classes were interrupted
7. Sam can touch
8. I have been encouraging
9. Tony has agreed
10. students have been giving

Practice (16)

1. Boards and bricks make
2. We bought and finished
3. fly and bee hung
4. twins look, think, act, and dress
5. salmon and tuna contain
6. I waited and slipped
7. girl waved and smiled
8. bird dived and reappeared
9. Singers, dancers, and actors performed
10. magician and assistant bowed and disappeared

SENTENCE FRAGMENTS

Introductory Project (18)

1. verb
2. subject
3. subject . . . verb
4. express a complete thought

Practice 2 (23)

Note: The underlined part shows the fragment (or that part of the original fragment not changed during correction).

1. When the waitress coughed in his food, Frank lost his appetite. He didn't even take home a doggy bag.
2. My little brother had chicken pox this summer. He was very upset because he didn't get to miss any school.
3. Tony doesn't like going to the ballpark. If he misses an exciting play, there's no instant replay.

4. After the mail carrier comes, I run to our mailbox. I love to get mail even if it is only junk mail.
5. Even though she can't read, my little daughter likes to go to the library. She chooses books with pretty covers while I look at the latest magazines.

Practice 1 (25)

1. Vince sat nervously in the dentist's chair, waiting for his x-rays to be developed.
2. Looking through the movie ads for twenty minutes, Lew and Marian tried to find a film they both wanted to see.
3. As a result, it tipped over on its side.

Practice 2 (26)

1. Some workers dug up the street near our house, causing frequent vibrations inside.
2. I therefore walked slowly into the darkened living room, preparing to look shocked.
   Or: I was preparing to look shocked.
3. Jen's stomach grumbled all morning because she skipped breakfast to get to the bus on time.
   Or: The reason was that she skipped breakfast to get to the bus on time.
4. Wanting to finish the dream, I pushed the snooze button.
5. To get back my term paper, I went to see my English teacher from last semester.

Practice 1 (28)

1. For example, he took a bus home from work on a day he drove his car there.
2. My eleventh-grade English teacher picked on everybody except the athletes.
3. For example, he bought an air conditioner in December.

Practice 2 (28–29)

1. I find all sorts of things in my little boy's pockets, including crayons, stones, and melted chocolate.
2. There are certain chores I hate to do, especially cleaning windows.
3. Also, he was weak as a kitten.
4. Some people on television, for example, game show hosts, really annoy me.
5. By midnight, the party looked like the scene of an accident, with popcorn and crumpled napkins all over and people stretched out on the floor.

Practice (30)

1. Artie tripped on his shoelace <u>and then looked around to see if anyone had noticed</u>.
   Or: <u>Then</u> he <u>looked around to see if anyone had noticed</u>.
2. I started the car <u>and quickly turned down the blaring radio</u>.
   Or: <u>And I quickly turned down the blaring radio</u>.
3. She does toe touches while sitting at her desk <u>and also does deep-knee bends when she files</u>.
   Or: She <u>also does deep-knee bends when she files</u>.
4. An obnoxious driver tailgated me for five blocks <u>and then passed me on the right</u>.
   Or: <u>Then</u> he <u>passed me on the right</u>.
5. She places herself in front of a seated young man <u>and stands on his feet until he gets up</u>.
   Or: <u>And</u> she <u>stands on his feet until he gets up</u>.

RUN-ONS

Introductory Project (36)

1. period
2. *but*
3. semicolon
4. *Although*

Practice 1 (39)

1. month. Its
2. door. I
3. make. It
4. do. He
5. gray. A
6. B.C. The
7. cheaply. She
8. desk. She
9. fireplace. The
10. traffic. Its

Practice 2 (40)

1. man. He
2. mailbox. Then
3. common. The
4. tiny. A
5. grayhound. It
6. gold. Some
7. one. The
8. lovely. It
9. drink. One
10. times. For

Practice 1 (42)

1. , but
2. , and
3. , and
4. , so
5. , but
6. , so
7. , and
8. , but
9. , for
10. , for

Practice (44)

1. obvious; I
2. ate; the
3. screen; it
4. out; brown
5. queens; birth

Practice (45)

1. drive; however, the
2. art; otherwise, it
3. gasoline; as a result, spectators (*or* thus *or* consequently *or* therefore)
4. time; however, all
5. feelers; consequently, they (*or* as a result *or* thus *or* therefore)

STANDARD ENGLISH VERBS

Introductory Project (49)

played . . . plays
hoped . . . hopes
juggled . . . juggles

1. past time . . . . -*ed* or -*d*
2. present time . . . . -*s*

Practice 1 (51)

1. drives
2. gets
3. announces
4. makes
5. brushes
6. falls
7. *C*
8. comes
9. watches
10. wraps

Practice 2 (52)

My little sister wants to be a country singer when she grows up. She constantly hums and sings around the house. Sometimes she makes quite a racket. When she listens to music on the radio, for example, she sings very loudly in order to hear herself over the radio. And when she takes a shower, her voice rings through the whole house because she thinks nobody can hear her from there.

Practice 1 (53)

1.	thumped	6.	C
2.	jailed	7.	insisted
3.	burned	8.	constructed
4.	tied	9.	leveled
5.	measured	10.	realized

Practice 2 (53)

My cousin Joel completed a course in home repairs and offered one day to fix several things in my house. He repaired a screen door that squeaked, a dining room chair that wobbled a bit, and a faulty electrical outlet. That night when I opened the screen door, it loosened from its hinges. When I seated myself in the chair Joel had fixed, one of its legs cracked off. Remembering that Joel had also fooled around with the electrical outlet, I quickly called an electrician and asked him to stop by the next day. Then I prayed the house would not burn down before he arrived.

Practice 1 (55)

1.	is	6.	do . . . have
2.	has	7.	is
3.	is	8.	does
4.	do	9.	has
5.	does	10.	were

Practice 2 (56)

1.	~~does~~ do	6.	~~have~~ had
2.	~~be~~ is	7.	~~was~~ were
3.	~~be~~ are	8.	~~done~~ did
4.	~~has~~ have	9.	~~do~~ does
5.	~~were~~ was	10.	~~have~~ has

Practice 3 (56)

My cousin Rita has decided to lose thirty pounds, so she has put herself on a rigid diet that does not allow her to eat anything that she enjoys. Last weekend, while the family was at Aunt Jenny's house for dinner, all Rita had to eat was a can of Diet Delight peaches. We were convinced that Rita meant business when she joined an exercise club whose members have to work out on enormous machines and do twenty sit-ups just to get started. If Rita does reach her goal, we are all going to be very proud of her. But I would not be surprised if she does not succeed, because this is her fourth diet this year.

IRREGULAR VERBS

Introductory Project (58)

1.	screamed . . . screamed	6.	chose . . . chosen
2.	wrote . . . written	7.	rode . . . ridden
3.	stole . . . stolen	8.	chewed . . . chewed
4.	asked . . . asked	9.	thought . . . thought
5.	kissed . . . kissed	10.	danced . . . danced

Practice 1 (62)

1.	came	6.	fallen
2.	stood	7.	broken
3.	built	8.	blew
4.	swum	9.	written
5.	did	10.	knew

Practice 2 (62–64)

1.	(a) sleeps (b) slept (c) slept	6.	(a) shrink (b) shrank (c) shrunk
2.	(a) rings (b) rang (c) rung	7.	(a) eats (b) ate (c) eaten
3.	(a) write (b) wrote (c) written	8.	(a) choose (b) chose (c) chosen
4.	(a) stands (b) stood (c) stood	9.	(a) freezes (b) froze (c) frozen
5.	(a) swims (b) swam (c) swum	10.	(a) meets (b) met (c) met

Practice (65)

1. lie
2. lying
3. laid
4. lain
5. lay

Practice (66)

1. sitting
2. set
3. sat
4. Set
5. setting

Practice (67)

1. rises
2. raised
3. rose
4. risen
5. raise

SUBJECT-VERB AGREEMENT

Introductory Project (69)

Correct: There were many applicants for the position.
Correct: The pictures in that magazine are very controversial.
Correct: Everybody usually watches the lighted numbers while riding in the elevator.

1. applicants . . . pictures
2. singular . . . singular

Practice (71)

1. trail ~~of bloodstains~~ leads
2. clothes ~~in the hall closet~~ take
3. basket ~~of fancy fruits and nuts~~ was
4. logs ~~in the river from the recent storm~~ pose
5. air ~~from the registers in the bedroom~~ dries
6. Workers ~~at that automobile plant~~ begin
7. date ~~on any of the cemetery gravestones~~ appears
8. line ~~of supermarket carts~~ seems
9. instructions ~~for assembling the bicycle~~ were
10. bags ~~with the new synthetic insulation materials~~ protect

Practice (72)

1. is noise
2. are berries
3. were cans
4. sits cabin
5. were students
6. stands cutout
7. was shape
8. were sneakers
9. are magazines
10. was row

Practice (73)

1. keeps
2. brags
3. pays
4. have
5. slips
6. leans
7. expects
8. was
9. stops
10. has

Practice (74)

1. sadden
2. belong
3. have
4. continue
5. tears

Practice (74–75)

1. has
2. goes
3. become
4. look
5. are

CONSISTENT VERB TENSE

Introductory Project (77)

Mistakes in verb tense: Alex discovers . . . calls . . . present . . . past

Practice (78–79)

1. shrieked
2. jumped
3. purchased
4. crashed
5. snatched
6. covered
7. lifted
8. argues
9. swallowed
10. glowed

ADDITIONAL INFORMATION ABOUT VERBS

Practice (Tense; 84)

1.	had dried	6.	had opened
2.	had planned (*or* were planning)	7.	is caring
3.	is growing	8.	has watched
4.	had thrown	9.	had cracked
5.	was carving (*or* had carved)	10.	were trying

Practice (Verbals; 85)

1.	*P*	6.	*I*
2.	*G*	7.	*G*
3.	*I*	8.	*I*
4.	*G*	9.	*P*
5.	*P*	10.	*P*

Practice (Active and Passive Verbs; 86–87)

1. A man with a live parrot on his shoulder boarded the bus.
2. A large falling branch broke the stained-glass window.
3. The entire team autographed baseballs for hospitalized children.
4. A fire that started with a cigarette destroyed the hotel.
5. Doctors must face the pressures of dealing with life and death.
6. A sophisticated laser system directed the missile to its target.
7. A thick layer of yellowish grease covered the kitchen shelves.
8. The compulsively neat child stuffed all the wrapping paper into the wastebasket.
9. The state police captured most of the escaped convicts within a mile of the jail.
10. Judges awarded prizes in the hog-calling and stone-skipping categories.

MISPLACED MODIFIERS

Introductory Project (88)

1. Intended: The farmers were wearing masks.
   Unintended: The apple trees were wearing masks.
2. Intended: The woman had a terminal disease.
   Unintended: The faith healer had a terminal disease.

Practice 1 (89–90)

Note: In each of the corrections below, the underlined part shows what was the misplaced modifier.

1. At the back of his cage, the tiger growled at a passerby.
2. Arthur spilled a full bottle of soda on the table.
3. Standing on our front porch, we watched the fireworks.
4. Jason has almost two hundred baseball cards.
5. With a smile, the sales clerk exchanged the blue sweater for a yellow one.
6. Jenny kept staring at the man with curly hair in the front row.
7. I love the cookies with the chocolate frosting from the bakery.
8. During their last meeting, the faculty decided to strike.
9. Larry looked on with disbelief as his car burned.
10. My cousin sent me instructions in a letter on how to get to her house.

Practice 2 (91)

1. I was thrilled to read in a telegram that my first niece was born.
2. My father agreed over the phone to pay for the car repairs.
   Or: Over the phone, my father agreed to pay for the car repairs.
3. I found a note from Jeff on the kitchen bulletin board.
4. The children ate almost the whole bag of cookies.
5. During class, Jon read about how the American Revolution began.
   Or: Jon read during class about how the American Revolution began.

DANGLING MODIFIERS

Introductory Project (93)

1. Intended: The giraffe was munching leaves from a tall tree.
   Unintended: The children were munching leaves.
2. Intended: Michael was arriving home after ten months in the service.
   Unintended: The neighbors were arriving home after ten months in the service.

Practice 1 (95–96)

1. Since the milk had turned sour, I would not drink it.
2. When I was five, my mother bought me a chemistry set.
3. *C*
4. Because my car needed the brakes fixed, I drove it slowly.
5. While I was talking on the phone, my hot tea turned cold.
6. Pete hated to look at the kitchen sink, which was piled high with dirty dishes.
7. Having locked my keys in the car, I had to have the police open it for me.
   Or: Because I locked my keys in the car, the police had to open it for me.
8. Because the plants were drooping, the children watered them.
9. After I sat through a long lecture, my foot was asleep.
10. Since we were late, stopping for coffee was out of the question.

FAULTY PARALLELISM

Introductory Project (99)

Correct sentences:

I use my TV remote control to change channels, to adjust the volume, and to turn the set on and off.

One option the employees had was to take a cut in pay; the other was to work longer hours.

The refrigerator has a cracked vegetable drawer, a missing shelf, and a strange freezer smell.

Practice 1 (101)

1. waited
2. cramming
3. illness
4. mumbles
5. late buses
6. to suffocate
7. interrupted
8. financial security
9. the birds chirping
10. breathed fire

PRONOUN REFERENCE, AGREEMENT, AND POINT OF VIEW

Introductory Project (105)

1. b
2. b
3. b

Practice (107–108)

Note: The practice sentences could be rewritten to have meanings other than the ones indicated below.

1. The defendant told the judge, "I am mentally ill."
2. Fran removed the blanket from the sofa bed and folded the blanket up.
3. Before the demonstration, the demonstration leaders passed out signs for us to carry.
4. Renni had to keep reminding her aunt that her aunt had a dentist appointment at three o'clock.
   Or: Renni had to keep telling her aunt, "You have a dentist appointment at three o'clock."
5. Because I didn't rinse last night's dishes, the kitchen smells like a garbage can.
6. A film on environmental pollution really depressed the students.
   Or: Watching a film on environmental pollution really depressed the students.
7. The veterinarian said that if I find a tick on my dog I should get rid of the tick immediately.
8. My sister removed the curtains from the window so that she could wash the curtains.
   Or: So that she could wash the curtains, my sister removed them from the window.
9. Richard said his chiropractor could help my sprained shoulder, but I don't believe in chiropractic.
10. I discovered when I went to sell my old textbooks that publishers have put out new editions, and nobody wants to buy my textbooks.
    Or: I discovered when I went to sell my old textbooks that nobody wants to buy them because publishers have put out new editions.

Practice (109)

1. they   3. it   5. their
2. their   4. them

Practice (111)

1. his   6. his or her
2. his   7. her
3. its   8. he
4. her   9. her
5. them   10. his or her

Practice (112–113)

1. my blood
2. they don't go
3. he can't prevent
4. they should receive
5. know me
6. we find
7. he can worry . . . his own
8. we don't even know
9. she can still have . . . her day
10. our rights

PRONOUN TYPES

Introductory Project (116)

Correct sentences:

Andy and I enrolled in a computer course.

The police officer pointed to my sister and me.

Lola prefers men who take pride in their bodies.

The players are confident that the league championship is theirs.

Those concert tickets are too expensive.

Our parents should spend some money on themselves for a change.

Practice 1 (119)

2. She (S)   7. they (S)
3. me (O)   8. me (O)
4. her and me (O)   9. We (S)
5. he (S)   10. I (S)
6. I (am is understood) (S)

Practice 2 (120)

2. me *or* him
3. they
4. I *or* we
5. us
6. I *or* he *or* she *or* they *or* we
7. they *or* he *or* she
8. I *or* he *or* she *or* they *or* we
9. I *or* he *or* she *or* they *or* we
10. us

Practice 1 (122)

1. which
2. that
3. who
4. which
5. who

Practice (123)

1. yours
2. his
3. theirs
4. your
5. mine

Practice 1 (124)

1. This town
2. those seats
3. That dress
4. those candies
5. those potholes

Practice (126)

1. themselves
2. herself
3. himself
4. ourselves
5. themselves

ADJECTIVES AND ADVERBS

Introductory Project (129)

Answers will vary for 1–4.
adjective . . . adverb . . . ly . . . er . . . est

Practice 1 (131)

tougher	toughest
more practical	most practical
quieter	quietest
more aggressive	most aggressive
clearer	clearest

Practice 2 (132)

1. best . . . better	6. less
2. dirtier	7. more sincere
3. more considerate	8. sillier
4. worse	9. softest
5. surest	10. most fattening

Practice (133)

1. badly	6. peacefully
2. harshly	7. bright
3. steep	8. loudly
4. frequently	9. carefully
5. colorful	10. bitterly

Practice (134)

1. well
2. good
3. well
4. good
5. well

PAPER FORMAT

Introductory Project (136)

In "A," the title is capitalized and centered and has no quotation marks around it; there is a blank line between the title and the body of the paper; there are left and right margins around the body of the paper; no words are incorrectly hyphenated.

Practice 1 (138)

2. No quotation marks around the title.
3. Capitalize the major words in the title ("Being a Younger Sister").
4. Skip a line between the title and first line of the paper.
5. Indent the first line of the paper.
6. Keep margins on either side of the paper.

Practice 2 (138–139)

1. Benefits of Pets
2. Learning How to Budget
3. The Value of a Study Group
4. A Special Relationship *or* Grandparents and Grandchildren
5. A Wise Decision

Practice 3 (139–140)

1. The best children's television shows educate while they entertain, and they don't preach violence.
2. Women have made many gains in the workplace in the last decade.
3. The generation gap results from differing experiences of various age groups.
4. Correct.
5. One of my important accomplishments was to finish high school despite the divorce of my parents.

CAPITAL LETTERS

Introductory Project (141)

1–13: Answers will vary, but all should be capitalized.
1– 3: On . . . "Let's . . . I

Practice (144)

1. I . . . Boy Scouts
2. Smokenders . . . July . . . Marlboro
3. Hanes Ceramics . . . If
4. New England . . . Republicans . . . Democrats
5. State Farm . . . Nationwide . . . Prudential Building
6. California . . . *National Geographic*
7. Valentine's Day . . . Mother's Day
8. Cokes . . . Fritos . . Clue
9. Ford Taurus . . . Saturday
10. Broadway . . . *My Fair Lady*

Practice (147)

1. Hundred Years' War
2. Aunt Sophie . . . Polish
3. President Kennedy's . . . Arlington Cemetery
4. World History . . . Middle Ages
5. Cuban . . . Spanish-language . . . Hispanic

Practice (148)

1. uncle . . . college education
2. high school . . . basketball coach
3. shop . . . musical video
4. parents' groups . . . ads . . . maniac
5. piano teacher . . . week

NUMBERS AND ABBREVIATIONS

Introductory Project (150)

Correct choices:

First sentence: 8:55 . . . 65 percent
Second sentence: Nine . . . forty-five

Second sentence: brothers . . . mountain
Second sentence: hours . . . English

Practice (152)

1. 6:15
2. nine o'clock
3. January 28, 1986
4. six
5. 1700 Pennsylvania Avenue
6. Forty-three
7. $930.20
8. 60 . . . 64
9. 27 . . . 52
10. 50 percent

Practice (153)

1. floor . . . months
2. bushels . . . market . . . Route
3. Monday . . . September
4. psychology . . . England
5. January . . . company . . . year
6. ounce . . . tablespoon
7. chemistry . . . Sunday . . . hours
8. television . . . time
9. license . . . medical
10. veteran . . . business . . . college

END MARKS

Introductory Project (155)

1. depressed.
2. paper?
3. parked.
4. control!

Practice (157)

1. drown?
2. redhead.
3. me.
4. it!''
5. ''videoits.''
6. accurate.
7. life?
8. truck!''
9. forward?''
10. myself.''

APOSTROPHE

Introductory Project (158)

1. The apostrophes indicate omitted letters: *You are, he is, does not.*
2. In each case, the apostrophe indicates possession or ownership.
3. In the first sentence in each pair, the *s* in *books* and *cars* indicates plural number; in the second sentence in each pair, the *'s* indicates possession.

Apostrophe in Contractions

Practice 1 (159)

she's	we're	couldn't
you've	you'll	they'll
haven't	we'd	doesn't
he's		

Practice 2 (160)

1. didn't . . . wasn't
2. We're . . . doesn't
3. You're . . . can't
4. isn't . . . you've
5. We'd . . . don't

Practice (161)

1. It's . . . you're
2. whose . . . who's
3. You're . . . your
4. There . . . their
5. It's . . . their

Apostrophe to Show
Ownership or Possession

Practice 1 (162–163)

1. chef's demonstration
2. Phil's car
3. Murphy's law
4. computer's memory
5. my wife's mother
6. yesterday's meat loaf
7. My sister's promotion
8. Maria's bratty little brother
9. the referee's call
10. the tanker's hull

Practice 2 (163)

1. horse's
2. brother's
3. son's
4. comedian's
5. landlord's
6. Ted's
7. teller's
8. people's
9. studio's
10. girl's

Practice 3 (164)

Sentences will vary.
2. teacher's
3. insect's
4. husband's
5. salesperson's

Practice (165)

1. *Plural:* vents
   Possessive: parlor's
2. *Plurals:* bones . . . shivers
   Possessive: rabbit's
3. *Plural:* plants . . . stakes
   Possessive: Karen's
4. *Plurals:* officials
   Possessive: lake's
5. *Plural:* positions
   Possessive: exterminator's

6. *Plural:* plates . . . goblets
   Possessive: candlelight's
7. *Plurals:* Crackers . . . slices . . . snacks
   Possessive: father's
8. *Plurals:* statements . . . drivers
   Possessive: officer's
9. *Plurals:* seabirds . . . surfers
   Possessive: ocean's
10. *Plurals:* prayers . . . batteries
    Possessives: mother's . . . daughter's

Practice (166)

1. rhinoceros' temper
2. sisters' feet
3. Charles' leg
4. Tylers' new television set
5. parents' wedding pictures

QUOTATION MARKS

Introductory Project (168)

1. Quotation marks set off the exact words of a speaker.
2. Commas and periods following quotations go inside quotation marks.

Practice 1 (170)

1. The chilling bumper sticker read, "You can't hug children with nuclear arms."
2. "One day we'll look back on this argument, and it will seem funny," Bruce assured Rosa.
3. "Hey, lady, this is an express line!" shouted the cashier to the woman with a full basket.
4. My grandfather was fond of saying, "Happiness is found along the way, not at the end of the road."
5. "When will I be old enough to pay the adult price at the movie?" the child asked.
6. "The trouble with Easy Street is that it's a blind alley," said our minister.
7. The sign on the classroom wall read, "When you come to the end of your rope, make a knot and hold on."
8. "I'm not afraid to die," said Woody Allen. "I just don't want to be there when it happens."
9. My son once told me, "Sometimes I wish I were little again. Then I wouldn't have to make so many decisions."
10. "I don't feel like cooking tonight," Eve said to Adam. "Let's just have fruit."

Practice 2 (170–171)

1. Simon said, "Take three giant steps forward."
2. "Please don't hang up before leaving a message," stated the telephone recording.
3. Clark Kent stopped a man on the street and asked, "Can you direct me to the nearest phone booth?"
4. "You'll be deaf before you're twenty if you play that music any louder," my father shouted.
5. "Nothing can be done for your broken little toe," the doctor said. "You just have to wait for it to heal."

Practice 1 (172)

2. I said, "It's hard to believe since Herb is a do-nothing."
3. Agnes replied, "Even so, he's gone up in the world."
4. I told her, "You must be kidding."
5. Agnes laughed and said, "Herb was moved from the first to the fourth floor today."

Practice 2 (173)

1. My doctor said that I need to lose weight.
2. Lola asked Tony if he ever washes his car.
3. The operator asked if I had tried to look up the number myself.
4. Janie whispered that Harold's so boring he lights up a room when he leaves it.
5. The teacher said that movies are actually a series of still pictures.

Practice (174–175)

1. My sister just bought a videocassette recorder so she won't have to miss any more episodes of General Hospital.
2. Rita grabbed the National Enquirer and eagerly began to read the article "I Had a Space Alien's Baby."
3. Our exam will cover two chapters, "The Study of Heredity" and "The Origin of Diversity," in our biology textbook, Life.
4. The last song on the bluegrass program was called "I Ain't Broke but I'm Badly Bent."
5. A three-page short story like Shirley Jackson's "The Lottery" is more exciting to me than a full-length action film like The Delta Force.
6. At last night's performance of Annie Get Your Gun, the audience joined the cast in singing "There's No Business Like Show Business."

7. A typical article in Cosmopolitan will have a title like "How to Hook a Man without Letting Him Know You're Fishing."
8. One way Joanne deals with depression is to get out her Man of La Mancha album and play the song "The Impossible Dream."
9. I read the article "How Good Is Your Breakfast?" in Consumer Reports while munching a doughnut this morning.
10. According to a Psychology Today article titled "Home on the Street," there are 36,000 people living on New York City's sidewalks.

COMMA

Introductory Project (178)

1. a. news, a movie, a *Honeymooners* rerun,
   b. check, write your account number on the back, (commas between items in a series)
2. a. indoors,
   b. car, (commas after introductory words)
3. a. opossum, an animal much like the kangaroo,
   b. Derek, who was recently arrested, (commas around interrupters)
4. a. pre-registration, but
   b. intersection, and (commas between complete thoughts)
5. a. said, "Why
   b. interview," said David, "I (commas with direct quotations)
6. a. 1,500,000
   b. Highway, Jersey City, New Jersey, January 26, 1990, (commas with everyday material)

Practice (180)

1. work, food, or a place to live
2. Ice cream, crushed candy, Pepsi, and popcorn
3. dribbled twice, spun to his left, and lofted
4. gum wrappers, pennies, and a sock
5. eight hours, four hundred miles, and three rest stops

Practice (180)

1. done,
2. tape,
3. time,
4. aisle, . . . wedding,
5. presents, . . . that,

Practice (182)

1. dancer, aided by members of the chorus,
2. Anderson, who were married on the Fourth of July,
3. trees, even the most gigantic,
4. repairman, unaware of the grease on his shoes,
5. Jefferson, the second and third presidents of the United States,

Practice (183–184)

1. opened, but
2. canceled, so
3. C
4. space, for
5. C
6. businessman, but
7. C
8. college, but
9. schoolwork, but
10. C

Practice (184)

1. said, ''Your
2. temptation,'' Oscar Wilde advised, ''is
3. read, ''If
4. down,'' stated
5. think,'' the judge asked the defendant, ''you

Practice (186)

1. me, madam,
2. 6,000 . . . 15,000
3. March 8, 1985, . . . Boston, Massachusetts,
4. Teresa, . . . Love,
5. Washington, D.C., . . . 50,000 . . . 6,500 . . . 114,000

Practice (186–187)

1. We grew a pumpkin last year that weighed over one hundred pounds.
2. Anyone with a failing grade must report to the principal.
3. The witness said she had seen the face of the robber only for an instant.
4. After watching my form on the high diving board, Mr. Riley, my instructor, asked me if I had insurance.
5. Rosa flew first to Los Angeles, and then she went to visit her parents in Mexico City.
6. The tall, thin man who bought the red socks is a nightclub comedian.

7. Onions, radishes, and potatoes seem to grow better in cooler climates.
8. Whenever Larry is in Las Vegas, you can find him at the blackjack table or the roulette wheel.
9. While I watched in disbelief, my car rolled down the hill and through the front window of a Chinese restaurant.
10. The question, sir, is not whether you committed the crime but when you committed the crime.

OTHER PUNCTUATION MARKS

Introductory Project (190)

1. Artist:
2. life-size
3. (1856–1939)
4. track;
5. breathing—but alive

Practice (191)

1. diet:
2. summer:
3. columns:

Practice (192)

1. night; consequently,
2. raining; all
3. beard; Robert . . . best-groomed; Matt . . . whitest; and

Practice (193)

1. sea—shivering
2. —her first since the operation—
3. time—eight

Practice (194)

1. slow-moving . . . no-passing
2. sugar-free . . . double-cheese
3. hard-hearted . . . teary-eyed

Practice (194)

1. Americans (31 percent) can
2. hours (3 to 4 P.M.) are
3. often (1) make lists and then (2) check off items I have done.

DICTIONARY USE

Introductory Project (196)

1. fortutious (fortuitous)
2. hi/er/o/glyph/ics
3. be
4. oct/to/ge/nar'/i/an
5. (1) an identifying mark on the ear of a domestic animal
   (2) an identifying feature or characteristic

Answers to the practice activities are in your dictionary. Check with your instructor if you have any problems.

SPELLING IMPROVEMENT

Introductory Project (205)

Misspellings:

akward . . . exercize . . . buisness . . . worryed . . . shamful . . . begining . . . partys . . . sandwichs . . . heros

Practice (208)

1. hurried
2. admiring
3. denies
4. jabbing
5. magnified
6. committed
7. diving
8. hastily
9. propelling
10. nudges

Practice (210)

1. buses
2. groceries
3. potatoes
4. taxis
5. themselves
6. theories
7. passersby
8. alumni
9. sandwiches
10. mice

OMITTED WORDS AND LETTERS

Introductory Project (213)

bottles . . . in the supermarket . . . like a wind-up toy his arms . . . an alert shopper . . . with the crying

Practice (214–215)

1. I grabbed a metal bar on the roof of the subway car as the train lurched into the station.
2. For most of our country's history, gold was the basis of the monetary system.
3. Maggie made about a quart of French-toast batter— enough to soak a few dozen slices.
4. Several pairs of sneakers tumbled around in the dryer and banged against the glass door.
5. To err is human and to forgive is divine, but to never make a mistake in the first place takes a lot of luck.
6. Raccoons like to wash their food in a stream with their nimble, glovelike hands before eating.
7. When I got to the grocery store, I realized I had left my shopping list in the glove compartment of my car.
8. Game shows are an inexpensive way for networks to make a high profit.
9. Soap operas, on the other hand, are very expensive to produce because of the high salaries of many cast members.
10. One memorable Friday the thirteenth, a friend of mine bought a black cat, broke a mirror, and walked under a ladder. He had a wonderful day!

Practice 1 (215–216)

1. sightseers . . . ghouls
2. sets . . . names
3. Dozens . . . beetles
4. dentists . . . restaurants . . . lines
5. workers . . . departments
6. lights . . . games . . . cars . . . persons
7. games . . . balls
8. shoes . . . jeans . . . months
9. stamps . . . pens
10. Workers . . . logs . . . chunks . . . chips

COMMONLY CONFUSED WORDS

Introductory Project (218)

1. Incorrect: your	Correct: you're
2. Incorrect: who's	Correct: whose
3. Incorrect: there	Correct: their
4. Incorrect: to	Correct: too
5. Incorrect: Its	Correct: It's

Homonyms (219–227)

all ready . . . already	plain . . . plane
brake . . . break	principal . . . principle
course . . . coarse	right . . . write
here . . . hear	then . . . than
whole . . . hole	there . . . their . . . they're
its . . . it's	through . . . threw
new . . . knew	two . . . too . . . to
know . . . no	where . . . wear
pair . . . pear	weather . . . whether
passed . . . past	who's . . . whose
peace . . . piece	you're . . . your

Other Words Frequently Confused (227–233)

an . . . a	desert . . . dessert
except . . . accept	dose . . . does
advice . . . advise	fewer . . . less
affect . . . effect	former . . . latter
Among . . . between	learn . . . teach
beside . . . besides	loose . . . lose
can . . . may	quite . . . quiet
cloths . . . clothes	though . . . thought

Incorrect Word Forms (233–235)

being that (233)

1. Since (*or* Because) our stove doesn't work
2. since (*or* because) they don't speak to each other
3. since (*or* because) it's my birthday

can't hardly/couldn't hardly (234)

1. I can hardly
2. James could hardly
3. You could hardly

could of (234)

1. you could have
2. you could have
3. I could have

irregardless (234)

1. Regardless of your feelings
2. regardless of the weather
3. regardless of age

must of/should of/would of (235)

1. I must have
2. he would have
3. You should have

EFFECTIVE WORD CHOICE

Introductory Project (238)

Correct sentences:

1. After the softball game, we ate hamburgers and drank beer.
2. Someone told me you're getting married next month.
3. Psychological tests will be given on Wednesday.
4. I think the referee made the right decision.

1 . . . 2 . . . 3 . . . 4

Practice (240)

1. If you keep overeating like that, you're going to be fat.
2. My parents always refuse when I ask them for some money to buy new tapes.
3. First the home team was defeated by a wide margin, and then the visiting fans damaged the field.
4. If Ellen would get less serious and stop talking about her troubles, a date with her wouldn't be so depressing.
5. I'm going to have to anxiously bide my time for the next couple of days, hoping the boss doesn't discover the mistake I made.

Practice 1 (241–242)

1. Subsitute In brief for To make a long story short.
2. Substitute Very quickly for As quick as a wink.
3. Substitute is ignored for goes in one ear and out the other.
4. Substitute was delighted for felt like a million dollars.
5. Substitute rare for few and far between.

Practice (243)

1. Please ask one of our salespeople.
2. The weather is terrible today.
3. My parents prefer that I get a college degree.
4. Do not put your arm out of the car, or an accident might happen.
5. Many fires are caused by the careless use of portable heaters.

Practice (245)

1. There is no cure for the common cold.
2. My paper's main point is that our state should legalize gambling.
3. Because Rafael's car wouldn't start, he took a bus to work.
4. Even when I was a boy, my goal was to be a stockbroker.
5. Susan's daily exercises energize her.

Note: The above answers are examples of how the clichés could be corrected. Other answers are possible.

Appendix C

Progress Charts

PROGRESS CHART FOR MASTERY TESTS

Enter Your Score for Each Test in the Space Provided

Individual Tests	1 Mastery	2 Mastery	3 Mastery	4 Mastery	5 Ditto	6 Ditto	7 I's M	8 I's M
Subjects and Verbs								
Sentence Fragments								
Run-Ons								
Standard English Verbs								
Irregular Verbs								
Subject-Verb Agreement								
Consistent Verb Tense								
Added Information about Verbs								
Misplaced Modifiers								
Dangling Modifiers								
Faulty Parallelism								
Pronoun Reference, Agreement, and Point of View								
Pronoun Types								
Adjectives and Adverbs								

(Continues on next page)

Note to Instructors: Mastery tests are on perforated pages in this book. Ditto master tests, ready to run, are available free with *Sentence Skills*. Tests in the Instructor's Manual are full-sized and can be reproduced on a copying machine.

PROGRESS CHART FOR MASTERY TESTS (CONTINUED)

Individual Tests (continued)	1 Mastery	2 Mastery	3 Mastery	4 Mastery	5 Ditto	6 Ditto	7 I's M	8 I's M
Capital Letters								
Numbers and Abbreviations								
End Marks								
Apostrophe								
Quotation Marks								
Comma								
Other Punctuation Marks								
Dictionary Use								
Spelling Improvement								
Omitted Words and Letters								
Commonly Confused Words								
Effective Word Choice								

Combined Tests	1 Mastery	2 Mastery	3 Mastery	4 Mastery	5 Ditto	6 Ditto	7 I's M	8 I's M
Sentence Fragments and Run-Ons								
Verbs								
Faulty Modifiers and Parallelism								
Pronouns								
Capital Letters and Punctuation								
Word Use								

PROGRESS CHART FOR
EDITING AND PROOFREADING TESTS

Date	Step	Comments	To Do Next	Instructor's Initials
9/27	1a	Missed -ing frag; 3 copying mistakes	1b	JL
9/27	1b	No mistakes—Good job!	2a	JL

(Continues on next page)

PROGRESS CHART FOR
EDITING AND PROOFREADING TESTS
(CONTINUED)

Date	Step	Comments	To Do Next	Instructor's Initials

PROGRESS CHART FOR COMBINED EDITING TESTS

Enter Your Score for Each Test in the Space Provided

Editing Test 1		Editing Test 6	
Editing Test 2		Editing Test 7	
Editing Test 3		Editing Test 8	
Editing Test 4		Editing Test 9	
Editing Test 5		Editing Test 10	

PROGRESS CHART FOR
WRITING ASSIGNMENTS

Date	Paper	Comments	To Do Next
10/15	Worst job	Promising but needs more support. Also, 2 frags and 2 run-ons.	Rewrite

Date	Paper	Comments	To Do Next

Index